To Hugo,
Buy low & hold.

Gene Walde

TABLE OF CONTENTS

INTRODUCTION

Much has been made over the past decade of corporate America's inability to compete effectively in the world market. There are those who say that American industry has become complacent, that American ingenuity is not what it once was, that the world market has changed and American corporations have failed to adapt.

But the fact is, there is a strong core of American corporations that have continued to increase sales, increase profits, increase dividends, increase world market share year in and year out despite fierce competition from the Japanese, despite the dollar's wide gyrations and the staggering U.S. trade deficit, and despite claims that corporate America has lost its edge.

This book features 100 of America's best publicly traded companies. All the companies on this list have flourished during the past decade as a result of strong, creative management and a penchant for being the best at what they do. Not every firm on the list is a household name. In fact, many of the blue-chip firms you might have expected to make the list didn't. IBM, General Motors, GTE, Apple, Sears and Eastman Kodak are among the more prominent no-shows. Instead you'll be surprised to find some less familiar names—like Automatic Data Processing, Abbott Laboratories, Standard Products, Giant Foods, Torchmark and VF Corporation—that go about their business without glamour, without fanfare, steadily adding to their profits and dividends year after year.

In a sense, these 100 companies and their products provide a revealing mirror-image of America—and the tastes of the American people over the past ten years. While the top 100 companies span virtually every sector of American business, just a handful of segments dominate the top rankings: beer, drugs, tobacco and the four basic food groups—frozen food, fast food, instant food and snack food.

It would appear that the much-heralded health and fitness trend has had little impact on corporate America's bottom line—unless you consider light beer and reduced-tar cigarettes healthful. Anheuser-Busch, brewer of Budweiser, Busch and Michelob beers, is by this book's evaluation, the number one ranked publicly traded corporation in America—the best stock overall for individual investors over the past ten years. Also among the leaders are food producers Kellogg, Quaker Oats, ConAgra, Hershey, Heinz and Ralston Purina, tobacco giants Philip Morris, Loews and UST, and drug and medical products makers Abbott Labs, Merck, Marion and Bristol-Myers.

Acquisitions have played a key role in the success of many of the companies on the "Best 100" list. Buy-outs, of course, have been big news lately. We've all heard about the mega-deals: Chrysler buys out American Motors;

Philip Morris swallows Kraft. Kohlberg Kravis Roberts & Company wrests control of RJR-Nabisco. But behind the headlines, deep in the trenches of corporate warfare, an unprecedented wave of smaller takeovers—primarily friendly ones—have turned acquisitions into everyday business. Borden, the dairy giant, has been acquiring companies at a rate of almost 20 per year. National Services Industries made 14 acquisitions in 1987. Banc One has acquired 20 other banking organizations in the past three years.

There's no guarantee that the coming decade will be as kind to the 100 companies listed here as the past decade has been. Certainly they will face new wrinkles in the marketplace and new challenges from the competition in the years ahead. A few will stumble. Others will merge or be acquired by other companies. But many will rely on the adaptability that contributed to their past success to continue their stellar performance in the years ahead.

THE CASE FOR STOCKS

While an individual's first investment priority should be money in the bank—everyone needs a cash cushion to fall back on—stocks should be a key component of any well-balanced portfolio.

Why buy stocks rather than collecting that safe, consistent flow of interest earnings a bank account would offer? Here are some numbers to reflect on:

- Stocks of the S&P 500 yielded an average annual rate of return of about 16 percent over the past ten-year period (through the spring of 1988).
- In spite of the turbulence in the market over the past ten years, in spite of the whopping crash in October of 1987, a $10,000 investment in the broad stock market in 1978 was worth $45,000 in 1988. That represents total earnings of $35,000 over and above the initial $10,000 investment.
- By contrast, that safe 6 percent interest you might have earned in a bank money market fund would have returned about $8,000 after ten years.
- That's $35,000 stocks, $8,000 bank; you make the choice.

Certainly there's no guarantee that stocks will continue to perform at that level. Stock performance varies greatly from one ten-year period to another. An investor in the market from 1949 to 1958 would have reaped a 20 percent average annual return, whereas an investor entering the market in 1965 would have experienced an agonizing 1.2 percent average annual return over the next ten years. On average, over the 63 years for which records are available—which includes both the crash of '29 and the crash of '87—stocks have paid an average annual return of 9.9 percent, roughly double the return of bonds and three times the return of money funds. Over the past ten-year period (through late 1988) stocks paid a higher return than any other commonly traded form of investment, including corporate bonds, T-bills, stamps, coins, oil, housing and precious metals.

STOCKS OR MUTUAL FUNDS

The other issue for many investors is whether they should invest in individual stocks or stock mutual funds. The fact is, mutual funds probably should be the investment of choice for many investors—particularly those individuals who haven't the time, the expertise or the resources to invest in a well-diversified selection of stocks. But if you have an interest in the market, the time to research it and the money to diversify your portfolio, individual stocks can offer several advantages that mutual funds can't.

First of all, buying stocks can be challenging, stimulating and, at times, fulfilling. You pit your wits against the market, and against the millions of other unseen investors who are also scouring the market for a bargain. It is a test of your insight, your shrewdness. At times it can also be a test of your endurance, or—during downturns in the market—a test of your courage as you hold fast to your position in anticipation of that next market rally.

When you pick a winner, the results can be exhilarating. You watch the price move up, you see the stock split two-for-one. Your investment grows to a multiple of your initial outlay. You've won at the age-old game of picking stocks. And the victory is a boon not only to your pocketbook, but to your ego as well. It's that psychic reward of picking a winner that motivates so many investors to set aside mutual funds and test their hands in the stock market.

There's also another important—though less publicized—reason to choose stocks over mutual funds. "Money," it has been said, "is power." But it's only power if you use it as power. That means controlling it yourself and deciding exactly where each dollar is put to work.

With individual stocks (and bonds) you have that option. With mutual funds you don't. By investing in mutual funds, you're putting the ultimate fate of your investment dollars into the hands of someone else. If you have strong personal concerns about defense companies, tobacco and liquor manufacturers, nuclear power companies or chemical producers, you should be aware that most stock mutual funds invest freely in those types of companies.

There are, of course, mutual funds that avoid investing in companies with questionable ethical connections. The problem is, when you invest in those funds you're still letting someone else decide the fate of your money. After all, you may not necessarily agree with all the fund's ideals. You might, for instance, enjoy a beer on a hot afternoon and see no reason to avoid investing in alcoholic beverage manufacturers. You may prefer not to invest in a weapons manufacturing company, but you may think nuclear power is the best thing since windmills. You may oppose the racist tactics of the South African regime but still believe American businesses can have a positive influence there. So a mutual fund that invests according to all the popular ethical issues of our time may not be exactly right for you.

Stocks give you the freedom to make those choices for yourself.

That's one area in which this book can help you. In addition to the statistical information on earnings, revenues, dividends and stock price growth included in each of the 100 company profiles, the book also provides a basic overview of each company's operations. By reading through the profile of a given company, you can decide whether it is the type of business in which you would feel comfortable investing your money, based on your own values, principles and prejudices.

PICKING WINNERS

There is no infallible system for predicting tomorrow's market winners— only ratios and theories and computer-generated formulas that seem foolproof but aren't. For investors who trade actively in stocks, the key to beating the market is not so much which stocks to buy, but when to buy them and when to sell them. And that's about as easy to predict as next month's weather.

Even Wall Street's finest can't consistently outfox the market. Stock mutual funds offer an interesting example. Despite being actively managed by some of the sharpest, most well-supported analysts in the investment industry, the average rate of return of stock mutual funds over the past ten years has actually trailed the market average (as gauged by the Standard and Poor's (S&P) 500 index, which is a weighted, composite index of 500 widely traded common stocks.) In other words, you could have done better just buying and holding a representative sample of stocks for the past ten years— without ever making a single trade—than most mutual fund managers did during the same period with their wealth of investment research, their finely honed trading strategies and all of their very carefully calculated market maneuvers.

Nor have investment newsletters, on average, fared any better than the mutual fund managers at timing their trade recommendations, according to Mark Hulbert, publisher of the *Hulbert Financial Digest.* "Most newsletters have not kept up with the S&P 500 over the past eight years," says Hulbert. In fact, in tracking the seven-year performance of a sampling of investment newsletters, Hulbert found that the ones that recommended the greatest number of buys and sells (switches) did the worst.

"We've also conducted some studies that show that in the case of most newsletters, if you had bought and held the stocks they recommended at the first of the year, you would have done better than if you had followed all of their trading recommendations for these same stocks throughout the year."

The moral? For sustained, long-term growth, it's hard to beat a buy and hold strategy. Buy good companies with the intention of holding onto them for many years.

THE THEORY OF BENIGN NEGLECT

Most of us know someone who bought a few shares of a stock many years ago, stashed the certificates in a drawer and then discovered years later that the stocks had grown to a multiple of the original cost. Benign neglect is often the smartest policy for stock market investors.

Besides avoiding the difficulties of making timely buying and selling decisions, the buy and hold approach offers some other excellent advantages:

No commission costs. Let's assume that you turn over your stock portfolio just once a year. You sell out all the stocks you own and buy new stocks that you think have greater short-term potential. Typically, you would incur about a 2 percent commission to sell the old stocks and a 2 percent commission to buy new ones—a total of a 4 percent in round-trip commissions. That means, for instance, that a respectable 12 percent gain on your investments would suddenly shrink to 8 percent after you've paid off your broker. That commission may not seem like much at the time, but over the long term, it can add up to a significant amount. (See chart I-1).

Tax-sheltered earnings. A buy and hold strategy is one of the best tax-advantaged investments available today. You pay no taxes on the price appreciation of your stocks until you sell them—no matter how long you keep them. (You are taxed, however, on any dividend income you receive from your stocks—even if you use those dividends to purchase additional shares.)

However, every time you sell a stock, the federal government taxes up to 28 percent on your gains (for most working professionals). And state taxes would very likely nibble away an additional amount. That means each year federal and state taxes can bite off about a third of your investment profits. So you're looking at losing 33 percent of your gains, plus the brokerage house commission, every time you sell a stock at a profit. How does that translate into real dollars?

Assume that (1) you start with an investment of $10,000; (2) each of the stocks in your portfolio appreciates at a rate of 12 percent per year, and (3) you sell each of your stocks, take the profit and buy new stocks once a year. The following chart compares your performance with that of a buy and hold investor with an identical 12 percent compounded average annual appreciation rate:

I-1 **The Hidden Costs of a Buy and Sell Approach**			
$10,000 investment @ 12% annual growth	Buy and hold (No commission & no taxes)	Buy and sell results*1 With commission*2	And with taxes*3
After 1 year	$11,200	$10,800	$10,540
After 5 years	17,600	14,700	13,000
After 10 years	31,000	21,600	17,000
After 20 years	96,000	47,000	28,000
Total 20-yr. **profit:** (minus initial $10,000)	$86,000	$37,000	$18,000

1. assumes investor sells all stocks in portfolio one time per year (and reinvests in new stocks).
2. assumes commission of 2% to buy and 2% to sell (an annual total of 4% of total portfolio price).
3. assumes federal and state taxes totaling 33% of the profits each year.

As you can see, over a 20-year period, the buy and hold portfolio could earn more than four times the profit of a buy-and-sell approach—even though both portfolios earn an average annual return of 12 percent.

Of course, if you do decide to sell your buy and hold portfolio after 20 years, your taxes would be substantial. Based on taxes of 33 percent, your total portfolio would drop from $96,000 to $68,000 after taxes.

On the other hand, if you wait until retirement before you begin selling off your shares, you might qualify for the 15 percent federal tax bracket (plus state taxes, which—for the sake of our example—we will estimate at 4 percent). Under those circumstances, your after-tax cash value would be about $80,000.

Less emotional wear and tear. By adhering to a buy and hold strategy you avoid the high anxiety of trying to buy and sell stocks actively—of watching the financial pages each day to see how your stocks have fared, and of the inevitable disappointment of watching them rise and fall, then rise and fall again. Every stock goes through many ups and downs. There are no exceptions. The market ebbs and flows like the tide of the ocean, and every time it moves it carries with it the broad market of individual stocks. About 70 percent of the movement of a stock is attributable to the stock market itself. If the broad market is moving up, almost any stock you pick will also rise, but if the market is in a tailspin, almost any stock you pick—even those with record earnings—will fall with it. The remaining 30 percent of the movement of a stock is attributable to its industry group and to the performance of the company that issued the stock.

You skirt much of the emotional pressure that the market inflicts if you invest with a buy and hold approach. You don't have to concern yourself with the inevitable daily—or even yearly—ups and downs of the market. If you've bought stocks of solid, growing companies, over the long term the value of your portfolio will eventually reflect the strong performance of those companies. That's why it's crucial to select your stocks carefully. Because these are "one-decision stocks," that one decision takes on much greater importance.

The 100 stocks featured in this book are, by and large, the type of stocks that one might consider buying to hold for the long term.*

---

* The information contained in this book was believed accurate as of January 1, 1989. By the time you read this book, however, the status of some of the firms listed here may have changed. Some firms may have merged with or been acquired by other companies. Others may have acquired new subsidiaries, or sold off existing subsidiaries. We hope this book will serve as a tool to help you assess the long-term past performance of the companies listed here, recognizing, however, that superior past performance in no way guarantees superior future performance.

RATING THE COMPANIES

In selecting the 100 stocks featured in this book, I restricted my inquiry to the handful of basic facts that paint the truest picture—from an individual investor's perspective—of a corporation's stock performance. Is it total return? Is it stock price growth? Is it dividend yield? Is it sales and earnings growth? What criteria should concern you most if you are interested in investing in a particular company? To do this I looked at several factors. Has the company had consistent earnings growth and consistent stock growth for the past ten years (or longer)? Does it pay a good dividend? Does the dividend increase regularly? Is the company a leader in its market sector? How does the company treat its individual shareholders? Does it offer a dividend reinvestment plan or other perks designed to involve the shareholder in the company? In addition, I limited my search to companies that had at least $300 million in sales and that had track records as publicly traded companies for the past 10 to 15 years. The companies featured here have passed the test. They are the 100 major U.S. corporations that have fared the best over the past decade and given their shareholders the most.

GETTING TECHNICAL

There are five scoring categories, each worth up to five points. I have divided the scoring among earnings, stock growth, dividend yield, dividend growth and perks, and I've tried to bridge the long-term performance with the short-term performance. Earnings and stock growth are judged on the most recent ten-year performance record. (Year-to-year stock performance records are based on the yearly stock price highs.) Dividend growth is rated based on the most recent four-year period, and the dividend yield is averaged out over the past three years. That gives the rating system a blend of the long term and the short term. As noted in the profiles, stock price growth is measured through the fall of 1988, earnings growth is measured to the latest fiscal year end (through the fall of 1988 at the latest and December 31, 1987 at the earliest, depending on the company's fiscal year-end date.) Dividend growth goes from 1983 to 1987 (or fiscal 1984 to fiscal 1988). Dividend yield is an average of a stock's yield from 1985 to 1987 (or fiscal 1986–88).

Accompanying each company profile you will see a ratings chart similar to this showing the exact breakdown in scoring.

ABCDE CORPORATION

EARNINGS GROWTH	★ ★ ★ ★ ★
STOCK GROWTH	★ ★ ★ ★
DIVIDEND YIELD	★
DIVIDEND GROWTH	★ ★
SHAREHOLDER PERKS	★ ★
NYSE—ABE	**14 points**

Each star represents one rating point. This company scored the maximum (five points) for stock growth and somewhat less for the other categories. The lower right gives the total score, and the lower left gives the exchange the stock is traded on (NYSE = New York Stock Exchange; OTC = over-the-counter exchange; ASE = American Stock Exchange) and the symbol (ABE in this case) that the stock is traded under.

There are a total of five categories with a maximum of 25 points.

Earnings.   Is the company growing and becoming more profitable every year? Is its growth consistent, or does it grow in spurts? My rating system rewards consistency and penalizes erratic growth. A company with superior earnings that has had seven or fewer years of increased earnings over the past ten years would be penalized a point for its inconsistency. A company with ten consecutive years of earnings growth may receive extra credit for that consistency.

Stock price.   Does the stock continue to rise year after year, or is it up one year and down the next? If you hope to buy stocks to hold for the long term, you don't want to lose sleep over stocks that bounce around a lot. You want ones that increase steadily year after year. Again, my system rewards consistency and penalizes erratic growth.

"STOCK GROWTH" and "EARNINGS GROWTH"
(The same scale applies to both categories)

10-year Growth Rate	Average Annual Rate	CONSISTENCY — Number of years in which earnings (or stock price) increased		
		7 of past 10 years or less	8 or 9 of past 10 years	10 consecutive years
under 150%	9.%	★ (1 point)	★	★
150% – 199%	9.5% – 11%	★★ (150%–299%)	★★ (150%–249%)	★★
200% – 249%	11% – 13%			★★★ (200%–299%)
250% – 299%			★★★ (250%–349%)	
300% – 349%		★★★ (300%–399%)		★★★★ (300%–399%)
350% – 399%			★★★★ (350%–449%)	
400% – 449%		★★★★ (400% & over)		★★★★★ (400% & over)
450% – and over			★★★★★ (450% & over)	

Dividend yield.   How much cash back are you getting for your investment? You want a dividend with a competitive rate. A high yield can make a significant impact in the total return of a stock. A couple of "Best 100" companies offer a good example. Consolidated Edison, the New York utility, has had moderate stock growth of about 13 percent per year over the past ten years (through late 1988) but has paid an outstanding dividend. McDonald's Corporation has had a better stock price appreciation (16 percent per year) but traditionally pays a meager dividend yield. Comparing an investment of $10,000 in each company ten years ago, Con Edison, despite its lower stock price growth, would have earned its shareholders $25,000 more over the ten-year period than McDonald's because of the difference in their dividend yields. (Assumes all dividends were reinvested in additional stocks.)

DIVIDEND YIELD

(Based on dividend yield average over past three years)

0.1 to 0.9%	★
1.0 to 1.9%	★ ★
2.0 to 3.4%	★ ★ ★
3.5 to 4.9%	★ ★ ★ ★
5.0% and above	★ ★ ★ ★ ★

Dividend growth.   In one sense, dividend growth may be even more important than the dividend yield. As the dividend grows, the current return on your original investment grows with it. A stock yielding 2 percent when you bought it ten years ago at $10 a share may still be yielding a current return of only 2 percent, but if the stock has appreciated in value to $100 a share, then that 2 percent yield has now grown from its original 20 cents a share on a $10 stock to $2 per share on the $100 stock—the equivalent of a very generous 20 percent yield on your original $10 investment.

DIVIDEND GROWTH

(Based on dividend increase over the past four years)

10 to 24%	★
25 to 49%	★ ★
50 to 99%	★ ★ ★
100 to 149%	★ ★ ★ ★
150% and above	★ ★ ★ ★ ★

Shareholder perks. This is a subjective category, although there are some basic guidelines. A company with a dividend reinvestment and voluntary cash purchase plan would always score two points for perks. Other factors that could add points are free sample packets or coupons sent to shareholders of record, Christmas gift purchase plans, free meals or sample packets for shareholders who attend the annual meeting, and discounts on services or accommodations for shareholders.

The perks program of 3M Corporation would receive a perfect score (except that 3M didn't make the top 100 because of slow stock and earnings growth; it is an honorable mention selection). 3M offers several perks: a dividend reinvestment plan (two points), a gift packet of samples it mails out to new shareholders (one point), a free package of samples at its annual meeting, plus a free lunch and a chance to shop through a specially discounted company store at the meeting (one point), and a holiday gift option in which shareholders may order gift packs of 3M products to be sent to friends and relatives for about $9 a package (one point). That would give 3M a perfect score. The grading is generally very tough in this category. Very few companies earned a perfect score, and many scored no points at all.

Size and strength. No points are awarded for this category, but it was instrumental in paring down the list to the final 100. There were about 70 companies in contention for the final 15 to 20 spots on the top 100 list, all with excellent stock and earnings growth. To make the final selections, I looked at a number of factors: Has the company's growth been consistent? Is it a leader in its market segment? Is it still on the rise or has its growth flattened out in recent years? The stocks chosen for the *Best 100* list strike a pretty fair balance between old, established firms like ConAgra, Exxon, Westinghouse, Bristol-Myers and Anheuser-Busch that have been piling up average annual returns of more than 20 percent over the past ten years, and new emerging companies such as Fuqua Industries (29 percent annual return), Standard Products (30 percent annual return), Phillips Industries (31 percent annual return) and Marion Labs (38 percent annual return).

Breaking Ties

The 100 companies are listed in order by points, from the company with the most points, ranked first (Anheuser-Busch with 22 points), through to the company with the fewest points (Hewlett-Packard with 11). To break a tie, the company with the higher total return on shareholder investment gets the higher ranking. If two companies tie on both total points and return on shareholder investment, the company with the higher total revenue gets the higher ranking.

FUTURE PROSPECTS

While there is no assurance that any of these companies will outperform the market in the years to come, they do have a couple of strong points in their favor. For one, each company featured here has proven its ability to compete as a market leader in one or more areas. Their concepts are working. Their products or services have made an impact in the marketplace and have been highly profitable over the past 10 to 15 years. The companies also have management teams that have proven capable of turning a profit on a consistent basis. They've ridden the ups and downs of the economy over the past decade, survived the rash of mergers and acquisitions (and probably made a few of their own), weathered the crash of 1987 and have still come away with outstanding records of earnings and stock price growth. Presumably some of their past successes will continue into the next decade.

For example, it's certainly possible that companies like McDonald's (more than 22 consecutive years of record quarterly earnings), Automatic Data Processing, (27 consecutive years of double-digit quarterly growth in both earnings and revenues), Torchmark (36 consecutive years of record earnings), RPM (41 consecutive years of record sales and earnings), Kellogg (43 consecutive years of increased sales) and Deluxe Corporation (49 consecutive years of record sales) could slip into a sudden free-fall. But after decades of uninterrupted growth, the odds would seem to indicate otherwise.

HOW TO USE THIS BOOK

Think of this book as a Sears catalog of stocks. If you're looking for new stocks to add to your portfolio, you'll find a wealth of excellent choices by thumbing through the book and reading through the profiles.

Let's assume that you have $20,000 to invest in stocks. Here is the process I would recommend you use to select the best stocks for you based on the entries in this book:

1. Read through the list—both the top 100 and the honorable mention—and narrow your choices to ten to twelve stocks. I would select those stocks by looking at a number of simple criteria:

   • Are they companies that you like, that are involved in business activities that you think have a strong future?

   • Are they located in your part of the country? This is not essential, but it is easier to follow companies based close to home, because the local press tends to give those companies better coverage so that you can stay better informed on your investment.

   • Do they represent a diverse cross-section of industries? I wouldn't choose more than two or three companies from the same industrial segment. I would spread my choices around. You might select a food company, a medical products firm, a heavy manufacturer, perhaps a publisher, a retailer, an entertainment firm, a computer or data processing company or any of several other types of companies. By making a broad selection, you can minimize your losses if one sector goes sour.

2. Once you've chosen your ten to twelve favorites, try to condense that list to four to six companies that you will ultimately invest in.

If you wish to use a stock broker or financial advisor, call him or her, read your list of choices and ask if the broker's company has any current research on your choices. If so, find out which ones the broker recommends, and buy the stocks through the broker. If you are interested in enrolling in the dividend reinvestment plan or in receiving the special perks your chosen companies might offer, instruct your broker to put the stocks in your name rather than holding them at the brokerage office in *street name*. Most dividend reinvestment plans and perks programs are available only to shareholders of record.

GOING IT ALONE

If you have no broker, or wish to go it alone through a discount broker, these are the steps I would recommend to narrow down your list to the four or five companies you will ultimately end up investing in:

- Write or call those ten to twelve companies to request their annual reports, then skim through the reports.
- Go to the library, look up the most recent articles in periodicals on those stocks and request any other information the library may have on your selections. Make sure the company hasn't become involved in any major scandals or business problems. The library may have two or three investment research books. *ValueLine Investment Surveys* and *The Standard & Poors Report* both offer up-to-date information and recommendations on hundreds of companies.
- Keep an eye on the stock prices of the companies you are interested in. Find out what range each stock has been trading in over the past few months. Then select the four or five stocks that appear at present to be the best values. Timing can be very important in your overall success. All stocks fluctuate in price, tugged along by the current of the general market. But some stocks fluctuate more than others. For instance, you could have bought Walt Disney stock in 1973 for $27 a share (split-adjusted), and sold it for a mere $4 a share a year later. You could have reinvested in the stock in 1976 at $15 a share and sold out in disgust in 1984 at $11.50 a share. Or, on the other hand, you might have bought the stock for that same $11.50 a share in 1984 and sold out with a smile for $80 a share in 1987. So even with stocks like Disney that qualified as a *Best 100* entry, timing can make a significant difference.

WHEN TO BUY

Volumes have been written on this topic. But the best advice on when to buy could be summarized in four words: *as often as possible.*

The investors who do the best over the long term are those who are the most persistent. They continue to contribute to their investment programs year-in and year-out.

One of the easiest and most effective investment strategies is called "dollar cost-averaging" and it's as simple as this: Pick a number, any number—100 for instance—and invest that amount in dollars every month (or every quarter or every year) in the same stock. Period. It's that simple.

Elementary as it is, however, the dollar cost-averaging method is also a very effective technique for beating the market. The reason? By sticking to a set sum each time you invest, you automatically buy fewer shares when the stock price is high and more shares when the price is low.

The following table illustrates the advantages of dollar cost-averaging. The table assumes that the stock price fluctuates somewhat each month (and lists the monthly price of the stock). The table compares the number of shares purchased through a dollar cost-averaging strategy with the number of shares purchased through a method in which the investor buys a set number of shares each month.

As the table indicates, the investor using the dollar cost-averaging method would have purchased 3.3 more shares than the investor who bought a set amount of shares each month, even though both spent a total of $1,200 during the year.

It should be emphasized that the dollar cost-averaging method is effective only when you can make your purchases at no commission (or minimal commissions) through a company's dividend reinvestment and voluntary stock purchase plan. Such plans are ideal for dollar cost-averaging because they enable the investor to buy fractional shares and to make regular contributions (some companies offer stock purchase options once per month, others once per quarter). However, if the company you're interested in has no stock purchase plan, the brokerage commissions you would have to pay to make regular investments in the company's stock would greatly diminish the advantages of a dollar cost-averaging plan. Most of the companies listed in this book offer a dividend reinvestment and voluntary stock purchase plan.

WHEN NOT TO BUY

Assuming that you've selected ten to twelve prospective stocks, that you've researched the companies and you're ready to buy, what financial factors should you look at to decide which four or five of those ten to twelve stocks represent the best value at the time?

The easiest way to select your finalists might be through the process of elimination: weed out the stocks that appear to be overvalued, and invest in the others.

To assist you with your elimination process, I'll offer you perhaps the two most common "don'ts."

Don't buy when a stock is at an all-time high. Stocks constantly rise and fall. There's an adage in the securities industry that goes like this: "The market always gives you a second chance." In almost every case, when a stock reaches an all-time high, it will eventually drop back in price, bounce back up, then drop back again. Nothing goes in a straight line. If you see that a stock is at its all-time high, it's probably not a very good value at that time. Prior to the October 1987 crash, most stocks were at or near their all-time highs, which is one reason why many investment experts claimed—correctly—that there were few good values in the market.

DOLLAR COST AVERAGING
(Investing a set dollar amount each month
– versus –
buying a set number of shares each month)

Month	Jan.	Feb.	Mar.	Apr.	May	June	July	Aug.	Sept.	Oct.	Nov.	Dec.	Totals
Stock Price*	$10	9	12	13	9	10	8	7	9	12	10	11	
Dollar Cost-Averaging** ($100/month) Investment	$100	100	100	100	100	100	100	100	100	100	100	100	$1,200
Shares	10	11.1	8.3	7.7	11	10	12.5	14.3	11	8.3	10	9.1	123.3 shares
Set quantity (10 shares per month)+ Investment	$100	90	120	130	90	100	80	70	90	120	100	110	$1,200
Shares	10	10	10	10	10	10	10	10	10	10	10	10	120 shares

*Indicates price of the stock each month.
**Assumes investor invests $100 a month in the stock.
+Assumes investor buys 10 shares of the stock per month.

Don't buy when the price-earnings ratio is unusually high. It sounds complicated, but the price-earnings ratio is actually a very simple formula that offers yet another barometer of a stock's relative value. And best of all, the price-earnings ratio (or P/E ratio as the pros call it) is listed along with the company's stock price in the financial section of most newspapers, so you don't ever have to calculate it yourself.

Specifically, the price-earnings ratio is the current price of the stock divided by the company's earnings per share:

Example:
ABC Corporation's stock price is $30
Its earnings per share for the trailing four quarters is $3.

stock price $30.00 ÷ *earnings per share* $3.00 = *P/E ratio* 10.0

P/E ratios are like golf scores—the lower the better. Generally speaking, the P/Es of most established companies are in the 10 to 20 range (although, a handful of the stocks listed in this book have P/Es over 20, and a few have P/Es under 10). The real key, however, is not how the P/E of one company compares to the P/E of another, but how a company's current P/E compares to its P/E ratios of the past.

In this book, at the end of each company profile, you will see a financial summary that lists the company's annual revenues, earnings, recent stock price, dividends, ten-year average annual return and its trailing P/E ratio.* You might use that P/E ratio loosely as a guidepost to provide a relative point of comparison.

One more way to save Once you've decided which stocks to buy, you may be able get more for your money by taking one more step:

* Call around to several discount brokerage firms to find out which firm has the lowest minimum, then buy your stocks through the discounter with the lowest minimum. Have the broker put the stocks in your name (rather than street name), and mail you the certificates. If you feel the stock is at a particularly good price or the company has no dividend reinvestment plan, you might decide to go a little above the minimum in your initial order. Otherwise, buy a few shares—whatever you feel comfortable with, enroll in the company's dividend reinvestment and stock purchase plan, and make your subsequent stock purchases through the company. You may never have to pay commissions again.

*The P/E ratios in this book were calculated based on the earnings of the company's most recent four quarters (just as they are in the daily newspaper).

WHEN—IF EVER—TO SELL

Having already pointed out the futility of trying to outguess the market, it's a little difficult to provide any concrete advice on when, if ever, to sell out your position. The safest advice for those who want to play the market is to put your new money in new stocks and keep your old money in your old stocks. (Of course, if you *really* enjoy playing the market—as sport, more or less—you might want to allocate 10 to 20 percent of the money you've set aside for stocks just to play the market. It can be an exhilarating roller coaster experience. Consider yourself a success if your play money keeps up with your buy and hold money.)

Probably the most common mistake investors make in selling their stocks is that they tend to sell their winners to take a (fully taxable) profit, and hold onto their losers in hopes that those stocks will someday rebound. That's an excellent way to assemble a portfolio full of losers. Prevailing wisdom in the investment business calls for the opposite approach: "Cut your losses and let your profits run."

With that in mind, there are a couple of basic strategies for selling stocks that you might consider:

When news is grim.   If a company you own stock in comes under legal siege or becomes involved in some type of disaster or health controversy (a la Union Carbide, A.H. Robbins, Manville Corporation), take your lumps and get out as fast as you can.

Sell when it drops relative to the market.   Barring disaster, however, you might also want to set up some other type of safety valve for your stocks. For instance, if the stock drops 15 to 20 percent while the market in general is moving up, it might be time to move on to something more promising. Some investors use a ten percent/ten percent rule in which they sell a stock when it drops 10 percent from its recent high and drops 10 percent relative to the market. For example, if your stock drops 10 percent from $100 to $90, it meets the first criterion. But if the market has also gone down with it, then the stock still hasn't met the second criterion. If, on the other hand, the broad market has stayed the same or moved up while your stock dropped 10 percent, then it's time to sell based on the 10 percent/10 percent rule.

I would lean toward a modified version of this: call it the 20 percent/20 percent rule. If your stock drops 20 percent, and drops 20 percent relative to the market, then sell it and move on to something more promising.

Sell when it gets acquired.   If you make your stock selections based on the information in this book, another good time to sell is if one of your stock picks is taken over by another company. Naturally every case is different, but for lack of a better system, my inclination would be: If the takeover company is listed in this book (as either a top 100 or an honorable mention selection), hold; if not, let the corporate suitor bid up the price, then take the money and run.

Mark Hulbert addresses the sell timing issue this way: "You need to approach those decisions realizing that more than half the time you're inclined to sell you would be better off holding than selling. Look at the crash of 1987. A lot of people sold right after the crash, and missed out on a 23 percent gain in the market in the following months. So you better make sure there's a preponderance of evidence in your favor before you sell."

You won't find much of that on the pages that follow. But, if I've done my homework, you will find some very good reasons to buy. Happy shopping.

ANHEUSER-BUSCH COMPANIES, INC.

One Busch Place
St. Louis, MO 63118
(314) 577-2000
Chairman, CEO and President: August A. Busch III

EARNINGS GROWTH	★ ★ ★ ★ ★
STOCK GROWTH	★ ★ ★ ★ ★
DIVIDEND YIELD	★ ★ ★
DIVIDEND GROWTH	★ ★ ★ ★
SHAREHOLDER PERKS	★ ★ ★ ★ ★
NYSE—BUD	**22 points**

Even if you can't tell a malt from an ale, a stout from a draft or a light from a lager, if you can read a balance sheet, then you can cultivate a taste for Anheuser-Busch. The St. Louis-based brewer has concocted a robust record of sales, earnings and stock price growth that confirms what its commercials have been telling us for years: Bud truly is "the king of beers."

Anheuser-Busch, maker of Budweiser, Michelob, Bud Light and half a dozen other brews, is the world's largest beer producer. It brews nearly 80 million barrels of beer a year. Over the past 15 years the company has enjoyed the kind of sustained success that could drive its competitors to drink. Its earnings have increased every year since 1976, and it has raised its market share to an extraordinary 40 percent of the nation's lucrative suds business.

Anheuser-Busch, however, has not been content to put all its kegs in one basket. The company has built a diversified operation with such subsidiaries as Campbell Taggart (the nation's second largest producer of bakery goods), Eagle Snacks, Busch Gardens and the St. Louis Cardinals baseball team.

Anheuser-Busch traces its roots to a small St. Louis brewery started in 1852. After a few years of lackluster results, the original owner, George Schneider, sold out the struggling operation to an investment group headed by St. Louis soap tycoon Eberhard Anheuser. Anheuser ultimately turned the business over to his son-in-law, a portly, gregarious man by the name of Adolphus Busch. Mr. Busch, who converted the small brewery into a national force, is generally recognized as the founder of Anheuser-Busch.

Budweiser, which Mr. Busch helped develop in 1876, was one of the first beers to achieve widespread distribution. Michelob, the company's *premium* beer, was first brought to market in 1896. When Adolphus Busch died in 1913, his son August A. Busch, assumed control of the business. The reins have since been passed through two more generations of the Busch family. August A. Busch III, 51, now directs the company as its president and chairman of the board.

In addition to Bud, Bud Light and Michelob, the company makes Busch, Natural Light, LA, King Cobra, Michelob Light and Michelob Classic Dark. It also imports two European-brewed beers, Calsberg and Elephant Malt Liquor. Beer sales account for about 77 percent of the company's $8.3 billion a year in total revenue.

When discussing the reasons behind Bud's unparalleled commercial success, Busch officials like to talk about *kraeusening* and *beechwood aging* and the *Old World brewing process.* And, most of all, they key on the word *quality.* "Quality is what got us where we are, and it's what will keep us here," asserts August Busch III. The reality, however, is that Bud maintains its throne as the king of beers through relentless marketing muscle. The company spends hundreds of millions of dollars each year on advertising and promotional campaigns. (In 1987, the company reported expenditures of $1.8 billion for marketing, research and administration.) In addition to its many TV and radio advertising campaigns ("This Bud's for you," "Gimmie a Light—ZAPPP—I wanted a Bud Light," Spuds McKenzie, "The night belongs to Michelob," "the Original Bud Man" and "Head for the Mountains of Busch"), the company sponsors golf, bowling, horse racing, auto racing, soccer, pool, track and field and other sports competitions.

The company's success is aided also by its efficient operation. Its brewing business is fully integrated. It operates 12 breweries in the U.S., owns a beverage can manufacturer, a barley processing plant, a label printing operation and a refrigerated rail car transportation subsidiary.

The company's other segments include:

- Food Products (20 percent of revenues). Campbell Taggart, the country's second largest bakery, has 70 plants in the U.S., Spain and France. It markets its baked goods primarily under the Colonial Rainbo or Kilpatrick's label. The company also supplies sandwich buns to commercial customers such as Burger King, McDonald's, Rax, Arby's and General Mills.

    Eagle Snacks produces peanuts, pretzels, potato chips and other snack food products.
- Diversified operations (3 percent of revenues). Busch Entertainment operates a number of theme parks throughout the U.S. including The Dark Continent (Busch Gardens) and Adventure Island in Tampa, Florida, The Old Country in Williamsburg, Virginia, Sesame Place in Lang-

horne, Pennsylvania and Kingsmill on the James, a 2,900-acre resort and residential development.

Anheuser-Busch also owns the St. Louis Cardinals National League baseball team, which has been one of the most successful franchises in sports history.

EARNINGS GROWTH

Anheuser-Busch has had 11 consecutive years of increased earnings. Its earnings per share have jumped 500 percent (20 percent per year) over the past decade.

The company has 42,000 employees and 65,000 shareholders.

The brewing industry may face some obstacles to growth in the future. Congress has considered requiring health warning labels on all alcoholic beverages. (Studies have shown that drinking may cause as many as 100,000 deaths a year in the U.S.) Anheuser-Busch, not surprisingly, opposes such legislation, pointing out that moderate consumption of beer may actually have some health benefits. Legislation has also been proposed that would ban beer and wine advertising from radio and television. Such legislation, if enacted, could have an adverse effect on the company's sales and earnings.

STOCK GROWTH

The company has enjoyed excellent stock price appreciation over the past decade, with one 2-for-1 stock split and one 3-for-1 split since 1985. Over the past ten years, the stocks has increased 753 percent (24 percent per year) from its median of $3.75 in 1978 to its late 1988 price of $32 a share.

Including reinvested dividends, a $10,000 investment in Anheuser-Busch stock at its median price in 1978 would have grown to about $110,000 ten years later. Average annual compounded rate of return (including stock growth and reinvested dividends): about 27 percent.

DIVIDEND YIELD

The company generally pays a fairly low yield, which has averaged just under 3 percent per year over the past ten years. During the three-year rating period from 1985 to 1987, the stock paid an average annual current return of 2 percent.

DIVIDEND GROWTH

Anheuser-Busch traditionally raises its dividend every year. The dividend increased 100 percent over the four-year rating period from 1983 to 1987, from 27 cents to 54 cents.

SHAREHOLDER PERKS

Anheuser-Busch knows how to treat its shareholders. New shareholders of record are sent a letter of welcome, a fact book on the company and a pamphlet on its dividend reinvestent plan.

The company makes a point of moving its annual meetings around the country. In recent years, meetings have been staged in Tampa, Florida; Williamsburg, Virginia; and Ft. Collins, Colorado. Those who attend get a chance to sample all of the company's brews, including Bud, Busch, Bud Light, Michelob, Michelob Light, Michelob Classic Dark, LA and Natural Light. (Who said there was no such thing as a free lunch?)

Shareholders are also entitled to a discount on admission to all of the company's amusement parks.

The company's dividend reinvestment plan allows investors to have all or part of their dividends reinvested in Anheuser-Busch stock. Shareholders also may contribute $25 to $5,000 per quarter to the company's voluntary stock purchase plan—all without fees or commissions.

So, to Anheuser-Busch, America's number one ranked company to invest in: For all you do, this Bud's for you.

SUMMARY

Total revenues: $8.3 billion, 1987. Earnings per share: $2.04, 1987; $0.34, 1977; 500% increase. Stock price: $32, 11/9/88; $3.75 (median), 1978; 753% increase (24% per year); price rose 8 of 10 years, 1977–87. Dividend: $0.54, 1987; $0.27, 1983; 4-year increase: 100%. Dividend yield: 2% average, 1985–87. P/E ratio: 13, 1/3/89. Average annual total return to investors, 1978–88: about 27%.

2

THE STANDARD PRODUCTS CO.

2130 West 110th St.
Cleveland, OH 44102
(216) 281-8300
Chairman and President: James S. Reid, Jr.

EARNINGS GROWTH	★ ★ ★ ★ ★
STOCK GROWTH	★ ★ ★ ★ ★
DIVIDEND YIELD	★ ★ ★
DIVIDEND GROWTH	★ ★ ★ ★ ★
SHAREHOLDER PERKS	★ ★
NYSE—SPD	**20 points**

Standard Products has made the most of a very limited window of opportunity in the automotive industry. Standard's lead product is the automobile "glass run channel"—that's the assembly inside a car door that holds the window in place. The company also makes the rubber sealing lips that shut out wind noise around the windows. More than half the cars manufactured in the U.S. are equipped with Standard's window channels. The company deals with all three major U.S. automakers. If your Ford Thunderbird, Chevy Celebrity or Chrysler LeBaron cruises the highways in tranquil silence, then Standard Products probably deserves some of the credit.

While the U.S. automotive industry has faced a rocky road the past few years, Cleveland-based Standard Products has continued to roll up impressive gains—earnings increases of 25 percent per year and total return to investors of 30 percent per year (on average) for the past 10 years.

Standard, which was founded in 1927, is basically a one-segment manufacturer. Its product line consists entirely of plastic and rubber products, most of which are geared to the automotive industry.

In addition to its window assembly products, Standard makes rubber seals for car doors, hoods and trunks. It also manufactures molded rubber engine mounts and body cushions and exterior and interior vinyl trim.

About 70 percent of the company's $508 million in annual revenue comes from sales to General Motors, Ford and Chrysler. Through a joint venture with Nishikawa Rubber Company of Japan, Standard has also begun manufacturing door and trunk seals for Mazdas and Hondas manufactured in the U.S.

Standard does stray somewhat from the automotive field. It makes neoprene glazing gaskets for building windows as well as rubber and plastic trim and seals for the construction and marine industries. It also makes rubberized track for tanks and other military vehicles.

The company's subsidiary, Oliver Rubber, makes pre-cure and mold-cure truck tire rubber, bonding gum, repair materials and equipment for the tire retreading industry. Oliver accounts for about 14 percent of Standard's total annual revenue.

"The company anticipates strong continued growth," says Joseph A. Robinson, Standard's vice president of finance. "I'm not sure whether we can continue to grow at the rate we have been—that's been pretty spectacular—but we should continue to have pretty strong growth."

EARNINGS GROWTH

Standard Products has had impressive earnings gains over the past ten years, with a total increase in earnings per share during that period of 824 percent. Earnings increased nine of the past ten years (from fiscal 1978 to 1988).

The company reported annual revenues of $508 million in fiscal 1988. Standard Products has 6,000 employees and about 1,000 shareholders of record. Insiders control about 30 percent of common stock.

STOCK GROWTH

The company's stock price growth has been every bit as impressive as its earnings growth. Since 1983, the stock has had two 3-for-2 splits, one 3-for-1 split and one 5-for-4 split. Over the past ten years the stock price has increased 918 percent (26 percent per year), from its median of $2.75 in 1978 to its late 1988 price of $28 a share.

Including reinvested dividends, a $10,000 investment in Standard Products stock at its median price in 1978 would have grown to about $140,000 ten years later. Average annual compounded rate of return (including stock growth and reinvested dividends): about 30 percent.

DIVIDEND YIELD

The company generally pays a fairly good yield, which has averaged just under 4 percent over the past ten years. During the three-year rating period from 1985 to 1987, the stock paid an average annual current return of 2.5 percent.

DIVIDEND GROWTH

Standard's dividend growth has been somewhat erratic over the past 10 years, although the dividend has been increasing dramatically over the past four years, jumping 443 percent from 14 cents in fiscal 1984 to 76 cents in 1988.

SHAREHOLDER PERKS

The company provides a good dividend reinvestment and voluntary stock purchase plan for its shareholders of record. There are no fees or commissions, and shareholders may purchase $50 to $3,000 per quarter in additional shares through the voluntary stock purchase plan.

SUMMARY

Total revenues: $508 million, fiscal 1988 (ended 6/30/88). Earnings per share: $3.14, 1988; $0.34, 1978; 824% increase. Stock price: $28, 11/3/88; $2.75 (median), 1978; 918% increase (26% per year); price rose 8 of 10 years, 1977–87. Dividend: $0.76, 1988; $0.14, 1984; 4-year increase: 443%. Dividend yield: 2.5% average, 1986–88. P/E ratio: 9, 1/4/89. Average annual total return to investors, 1978–88: about 30%.

3

PHILIP MORRIS COMPANIES INC.

120 Park Avenue
New York, NY 10017
(212) 880-5000
Chairman and CEO: Hamish Maxwell.
President: John A. Murphy.

EARNINGS GROWTH	★ ★ ★ ★ ★
STOCK GROWTH	★ ★ ★ ★ ★
DIVIDEND YIELD	★ ★ ★ ★
DIVIDEND GROWTH	★ ★ ★ ★
SHAREHOLDER PERKS	★ ★
NYSE—MO	**20 points**

It's becoming a lonely lot for America's 51 million smokers. Banned from many offices, clubs, restaurants, airlines and other public places, and besieged with new evidence of the ills their vice creates, smokers are justifiably feeling a little paranoid, a little persecuted and more than a little bit unloved.

But weep not for the Marlboro man. Despite an antismoking movement that's been spreading like a cancer across America, Marlboro and its manufacturer, Philip Morris, continue to increase sales, increase earnings and increase market share year after year. With its acquisition of Kraft in 1988, Philip Morris became the world's largest consumer products company with nearly $40 billion a year in total sales.

Americans light up 1.5 billion times a day—that's 80 million packs a day and 570 billion cigarettes each year. Philip Morris is the nation's (and the world's) leading cigarette manufacturer with a 38 percent share of the U.S. market. The company, which is now based far from its Virginia roots on Park Avenue in New York, sells about 216 billion cigarettes a year in the U.S. Marlboro, the company's—and the country's—leading brand, accounts for about 60 percent of Philip Morris' U.S. sales—135 billion cigarettes a year.

The past two decades have not been easy for the U.S. tobacco industry. Cigarette ads on television and radio were banned in 1971. Explicit health warning labels have been required for all cigarette packs. New studies underscoring the dangers of smoking have spurred a rash of bans on cigarettes in public places. And the U.S. cigarette market has been shrinking at a rate of about 2 percent per year. Yet in the face of all that adversity, cigarettes remain an immensely profitable commodity.

To get a whiff of their enormous profitability, one needs only to compare Marlboro's sales with sales from Philip Morris' other subsidiaries, including Kraft, General Foods and Miller Brewing. Total combined operating profit from all of the company's food products—Miller beer, Oscar Mayer meats, Maxwell House and Sanka coffees, Post cereals, Jell-O, Kool-Aid, Birds Eye frozen foods, Parkay margarine, Kraft mayonnaise, Miracle Whip, Cheez Whiz, Velveeta, Seven Seas and Sealtest, Light n' Lively and Breyers dairy products—comes to about $1.8 billion a year— about the same as Marlboro earns each year. And, when you add in Philip Morris' other brands—Virginia Slims, Benson & Hedges, Merits, Parliament, Lark, L&M and Cambridge—cigarettes account for about two-thirds of the company's approximately $5 billion a year in operating profit. Philip Morris makes more profit each year selling cigarettes than Mobil makes selling oil or Chrysler makes selling automobiles.

How does Philip Morris (and the rest of the tobacco industry) continue to wring out increasing profits in a market environment that seems to grow more hostile each year?

Simple. They have a nearly perfect product—a marketer's dream. Cigarettes foster intense loyalty among merchants because they require a minimum of floor space yet generate enormous income. And, more importantly, they engender intense loyalty among smokers because, as U.S. Surgeon General C. Everett Koop claims, cigarettes are highly addictive. Koop contends that cigarettes are "as addictive as heroin or cocaine," and cites surveys showing that 75 to 85 percent of U.S. smokers say they would like to quit but can't. Now that's a classic captive market!

If there's a downside for tobacco companies, it's that they lose many of their most faithful customers prematurely. An estimated 300,000 Americans die each year of smoking-related lung ailments and heart disease. But those losses—even coupled with the 40 million Americans who have quit smoking—seem to have had little impact on Philip Morris' bottom line. By increasing profit margins on the cigarettes it sells, Philip Morris has managed to keep earnings per share growing at nearly 20 percent per year for the past 10 to 15 years.

Philip Morris is also turning increasingly to the world market, where volume sales potential is astronomical, although sales margins fall well below the estimated 25 percent margins of the domestic market. At present, Philip Morris holds only about a 7 percent share of the world tobacco market, which the company estimates at 4.5 trillion cigarettes per year (the equivalent of 616 million packs per day). The company exported 63.5 billion cigarettes in 1987 (an increase of 38 percent over 1986) and has manufacturing plants in 34 countries outside the U.S. In total, the company sold 315 billion cigarettes outside the U.S. in 1987 in about 170 countries.

Marlboro is the world's most popular cigarette. Packs of Marlboros are swapped like currency on Russia's black market; they are a symbol of prestige in the People's Republic of China; and in Japan, where tobacco advertising is virtually unrestricted, the Marlboro man has become one of the most familiar faces on television. Philip Morris is also mounting some major marketing campaigns in several other Asian countries, including Taiwan and Korea, aided by diplomatic pressure from the U.S. government.

EARNINGS GROWTH

(The following information is based on Philip Morris' financial position prior to the Kraft acquisition, unless otherwise noted).

With revenues of $27.7 billion a year, Philip Morris is the world's leading tobacco company. (With Kraft, the total would be nearly $40 billion.) The company has about 113,000 employees and 40,000 shareholders of record. (Kraft has an additional 50,000 employees.)

Philip Morris has had more than 15 consecutive years of increased earnings per share. Earnings have increased 460 percent over the past ten years (19 percent per year).

STOCK GROWTH

The company's stock price has also been climbing steadily, with increases every year from 1975 through 1987. Over the past ten years the stock price has increased 485 percent (19.5 percent per year) from its median of $6.75 in 1978 to its recent 1988 price of $98 a share.

Including reinvested dividends, a $10,000 investment in Philip Morris stock at its median price in 1978 would have grown to about $82,000 ten years later. Average annual compounded rate of return (including stock growth and reinvested dividends): about 23.5 percent.

DIVIDEND YIELD

Philip Morris tends to pay a fairly good dividend yield, which averaged about 4 percent over the past ten years (and 4 percent during the three-year rating period from 1985 through 1987.)

DIVIDEND GROWTH

The company traditionally raises its dividend each year, and has increased it 23 times in the last 20 years. Over the four-year rating period from 1983 to 1987, the company raised its dividend 117 percent.

SHAREHOLDER PERKS

The company offers an excellent dividend reinvestment and voluntary stock purchase plan. There are no fees or commissions, and shareholders of record may buy $10 to $60,000 per year in additional shares through the voluntary payment plan.

SUMMARY

(The following information is based on Philip Morris' financial position prior to its acquisition of Kraft.) Total revenues: $27.7 billion, 1987 (with Kraft, the total would be nearly $40 billion). Earnings per share: $7.84, 1987; $1.40, 1977; 460% increase. Stock price: $98, 10/24/88; $6.75 (median), 1978 (485% total increase; 19.5% annual increase); price rose every year from 1977–87. Dividend: $3.15, 1987; 4-year increase: 117%. Dividend yield: 4%, 1985–1987. Average annual total return to investor, 1978–88: about 23.5%.

4

ABBOTT LABORATORIES

Abbott Park, IL 60064
(312) 937-6100
Chairman and CEO: Robert A. Schoellhorn.
President: Jack W. Schuler.

EARNINGS GROWTH	★ ★ ★ ★ ★
STOCK GROWTH	★ ★ ★ ★ ★
DIVIDEND YIELD	★ ★ ★
DIVIDEND GROWTH	★ ★ ★ ★
SHAREHOLDER PERKS	★ ★ ★
NYSE—ABT	**20 points**

Over the past century, Abbott Laboratories has turned disease and debilitation into a $5 billion a year business. Since 1888, when Dr. Wallace C. Abbott began a sideline venture in his small Chicago apartment making pills from the alkaloids of plants, Abbott Labs has come up with products to detect, cure and ease the symptoms of dozens of ailments, from hepatitis to hypertension.

Abbott Labs has experienced remarkably consistent growth during its 101-year history—particularly in recent years. The company has posted record sales, earnings and dividends every year since 1971.

One of Abbott's latest growth areas is AIDS testing. Abbott was the first company to introduce an AIDS antibody test, and it continues to be a world leader, controlling an estimated 10 to 12 percent of the AIDS testing market. "One of the keys to Abbott's success is that it not only makes the tests, it also makes the instrumentation systems that the tests can run on," explains David Lothson, an analyst with PaineWebber.

The company is also a major manufacturer of urine sample drug testing systems for corporations and other organizations. Abbott's AD_x drug testing system, available for just under $10,000, is a fast, efficient system for on-site testing. Ultimately, the commercial success of Abbott's drug testing systems may rest with the courts. In a highly controversial proposal, former President Reagan endorsed broad testing as a step toward a "drug-free work place." But Ira Glasser, executive director of the American Civil Liberties

12

Union, is among many outspoken opponents to drug tests, calling them "humiliating and intrusive." Several challenges to drug testing are now pending in the courts. But if drug testing continues to proliferate, Abbott stands to be among the industry leaders. "No one product is going to have what you would call a significant impact on Abbott's bottom line—this is a $5 billion a year company—but it [drug testing] could be a nice, profitable area for them," says Lothson.

Abbott is also a world leader in the manufacture of diagnostic products, including thyroid tests, therapeutic drug and cancer monitoring tests and diagnostic tests for hepititis.

The company's hospital and laboratory products segment accounts for 47 percent of its annual revenue.

While most of Abbott's products are specialized for the medical profession, the company produces a handful of consumer products such as Murine eye drops, Selsun Blue dandruff shampoo, Tronolane hemorrhoid medication and the nutritional infant formulas Isomil and Similac.

Pharmaceutical and nutritional products account for about 53 percent of the company's $4.4 billion a year in total revenue. Abbott makes drugs for the treatment of anxiety, epilepsy and hypertension. It is a leading producer of antibiotics, and it manufactures a broad line of cardiovascular products, cough and cold formulas and vitamins.

Abbott manufactures diagnostic systems for blood banks and hospitals, and is a major manufacturer of intravenous fluid delivery systems. It manufactures a line of critical-care systems that monitor patient's vital functions.

The company also does a good business in agricultural-related products such as plant growth regulators and herbicides, and is the world's leading supplier of biological pesticides.

The Chicago-based manufacturer boasts a strong international business, which accounts for about 34 percent of its total revenue. The company claims to have operations in more than 130 countries "including every major health care market in the free world" (and one that's not so free, South Africa, where the company's wholly owned subsidiary, Abbott Laboratories South Africa, Ltd., manufactures and markets $9.5 million annually in health care products).

One of Abbott's great strengths is its significant commitment to research and development. In 1987, the company spent $361 million for research and development.

EARNINGS GROWTH

Abbott has had 17 consecutive years of record sales and earnings. Earnings per share climbed 456 percent over the past ten years.

The company has 38,000 employees and 46,000 shareholders of record.

STOCK GROWTH

The company's stock price has climbed quickly through the past decade, with two 2-for-1 stock splits since 1981. Over the past ten years the stock has increased 470 percent (19 percent per year) from its median of $8.25 in 1978 to its late 1988 price of $47 a share.

  Including reinvested dividends, a $10,000 investment in Abbott stock at its median price in 1978 would have grown to about $70,000 ten years later. Average annual compounded rate of return (including stock growth and reinvested dividends): about 21.5 percent.

DIVIDEND YIELD

The company tends to pay a fairly low yield, which has averaged about 2.5 percent over the past ten years. During the three-year rating period from 1985 to 1987, the stock paid an average annual current return of 2.1 percent. ·

DIVIDEND GROWTH

Abbott Labs has raised its dividend 15 consecutive years. The dividend increased 100 percent over the four-year rating period from 1983 to 1987.

SHAREHOLDER PERKS

Shareholders who attend the annual meetings are invited to have lunch courtesy of the company, and are offered a sampling of Abbott's consumer products such as Selsun Blue, Murine and Similac baby formula.

  The company also provides a dividend reinvestment and voluntary stock purchase plan for its shareholders of record. There are no fees or commissions, and participants may purchase $10 to $1,000 per quarter in additional shares through the voluntary stock purchase plan.

SUMMARY

Total revenues: $4.4 billion, 1987. Earnings per share: $2.78, 1987; $0.50, 1977; 456% increase. Stock price: $47, 11/6/88; $8.25 (median), 1978; 470% increase (19% per year); price rose 9 of 10 years, 1977–87. Dividend: $1, 1987; $0.50, 1983; 4-year increase: 100%. Dividend yield: 2.1% average, 1985–87. P/E ratio: 15, 1/5/89. Average annual total return to investors, 1978–88: 21.5%.

GIANT FOOD, INC.

6300 Sheriff Road
Landover, MD 20785
(301) 341-4100
Chairman, President and CEO: Israel Cohen.

EARNINGS GROWTH	★ ★ ★ ★ ★
STOCK GROWTH	★ ★ ★ ★ ★
DIVIDEND YIELD	★ ★ ★
DIVIDEND GROWTH	★ ★ ★ ★
SHAREHOLDER PERKS	★ ★
ASE—GFSA	**19 points**

Giant Food has buttered the bread of more than a few congressmen. Nothing underhanded, you understand. It's just that Giant is where Washington, D.C., gets its groceries. With 150 stores in and around the nation's capital, Giant is the Goliath of the district's grocery market.

The company has posted outstanding sales, earnings and stock price gains over the past ten years. A $10,000 investment in Giant in 1978 would have been worth about $300,000 a decade later—an average total return to shareholders of 40 percent per year, over the past ten years.

Giant's stores, as the name implies, are spacious emporiums of foods and other consumer goods. Its largest new stores cover 65,000 square feet—an acre and a half—and carry everything from basic grocery products to fresh seafood, floral arrangements, prescriptions and Gourmet-to-Go. Giant, which was founded in 1935, has grown to become the 12th largest grocery store chain in the U.S.

The company has grown in other ways as well. Giant owns its own 173,000-square-foot bakery, its own dairy, its own soft drink bottling plant, its own ice cube plant, its own ice cream plant, a tobacco wholesaler and a flower warehouse. It also owns a construction subsidiary that builds its stores and often wins the contracts to build the shopping centers where its stores are located. In nine of the company's store locations, Giant not only owns its store buildings, it also owns the shopping centers in which they are located.

Of the company's 150 stores, about 100 are located in the Washington, D.C., metropolitan area, about 40 are in the Baltimore area, and the others are scattered through Virginia and Maryland.

Giant has built its empire through steady, controlled growth. It added five new stores in fiscal 1988. It is scheduled to add four more in 1989 and to begin construction on four others. About a dozen of its stores underwent substantial remodeling in 1988.

Of the company's $2.7 billion in total sales, about 25 percent comes from meat, delicatessen, dairy and seafood; 66 percent from grocery and non-food items and 9 percent from fresh produce.

EARNINGS GROWTH

Giant has had excellent earnings growth over the past decade, with earnings gains eight of the past ten years and an increase in earnings per share of 660 percent during that period.

The company has 23,000 employees and 7,000 shareholders of record. Insiders control about 30 percent of common stock and 100 percent of the voting stock.

STOCK GROWTH

Giant has had exceptional stock price growth, with two 2-for-1 splits and 3-for-1 split since 1983. The company's stock price increased nine of ten years from 1977 to 1987 and increased 1,900 percent (35 percent per year) from its median of $1.25 in 1978 to its recent 1988 price of $25 a share.

Including reinvested dividends, a $10,000 investment in Giant Foods stock at its median price in 1978 would have grown to about $290,000 ten years later. Average annual compounded rate of return (including stock growth and reinvested dividends): about 40 percent.

DIVIDEND YIELD

Giant normally pays a fairly good dividend yield—averaging nearly 5 percent over the past ten years. During the most recent three-year period, the stock paid an average annual current return of 2.1 percent.

DIVIDEND GROWTH

Giant has increased its dividend each year for more than a dozen consecutive years. Its dividend jumped 120 percent during the four-year rating period from 1983 to 1987.

SHAREHOLDER PERKS

The company offers a good dividend reinvestment and voluntary stock purchase plan. There are no fees or commissions, and shareholders of record may buy $10 to $1,000 per month in additional shares.

SUMMARY

Total revenues: $2.7 billion, 1987. Earnings per share: $1.26, 1987; $0.17, 1977; 660% increase. Stock price: $25, 10/24/88; $1.25 (median), 1978 (1,900% total increase; 35% annual increase); price rose 9 of 10 years, 1977–87. Dividend: $0.33, 1988; $0.15, 1984; 4-year increase: 120%. Dividend yield: 2.1%, 1985–1987. P/E ratio: 18, 1/3/89. Average annual total return to investors, 1978–88: about 40%.

6

MARION LABORATORIES

9300 Ward Parkway
Kansas City, MO 64114
(816) 966-4000
Chairman: Ewing M. Kauffman.
President and CEO: Fred W. Lyons, Jr.

EARNINGS GROWTH	★ ★ ★ ★ ★
STOCK GROWTH	★ ★ ★ ★ ★
DIVIDEND YIELD	★ ★
DIVIDEND GROWTH	★ ★ ★ ★ ★
SHAREHOLDER PERKS	★ ★
NYSE—MKC	**19 points**

Marion Laboratories is a mender of broken hearts and troubled gastrointestinal tracts. The Kansas City-based drug and medical products company has tapped a lucrative vein in the cardiovascular treatment field and has come up with its own way to spell relief for those troubled by intestinal distress.

Marion's most successful drug is Cardizem, used in the treatment of angina pectoris and other heart-related illnesses. The company touts Cardizem as the number-one cardiovascular product in the United States. Marion has ridden Cardizem's success to extraordinary growth the past few years. The company has reported annual earnings growth in excess of 50 percent each of the past six years.

Cardizem accounts for more than half of Marion's total income. To grasp the impact Cardizem has had on Marion's bottom line, you need only look back to Marion's pre-Cardizem days. In 1980 total sales for all of Marion's products came to about $100 million. By 1988, sales from Cardizem alone reached nearly $500 million—five times the company's total revenue of a few years earlier.

While Cardizem is known primarily for its success in treating angina, Marion Labs has also applied to the Food and Drug Administration to use Cardizem for the treatment of hypertension (high blood pressure). The company believes that with the FDA's approval, Cardizem could become a leading drug in the treatment of hypertension—a market that takes in 60 million

Americans, compared with the five million-patient angina market. The company is also examining Cardizem's use for the treatment of diastolic dysfunction and other heart-related ailments.

Marion Labs' other major product is Carafate, an anti-ulcer medication that has quickly grown to sales of more than $100 million a year. The drug is used primarily for duodenal, or upper intestinal ulcers. It uses an ulcer-adherent complex that covers the ulcer site and protects it against further assault by acid, pepsin and bile salt. The company is also looking into other uses for Carafate, including the treatment of stress ulcers and mouth sores.

Marion Labs also manufactures Os-Cal, an over-the-counter calcium supplement, Gaviscon, an over-the-counter antacid drug, Nitro-Bid, an anti-angina drug, Ditropan, a urological agent, and Silvadene, a burn treatment medication used to control wound infection. In all, Marion manufactures more than 50 different products (or product variations).

EARNINGS GROWTH

Marion Laboratories has enjoyed rocketing growth through the 1980s and now boasts total annual revenues of $750 million.

Marion's earnings per share have soared 966 percent, from 9 cents a share in 1978 to 96 cents per share in fiscal 1988.

Like other emerging medical and pharmaceutical companies, however, Marion Labs' success remains precarious. The patent protection for Carafate ended in 1986, and generic imposter medications could soon begin to eat away at its market share. Cardizem, which accounts for more than 50 percent of the company's revenue, lost its patent protection in February 1988, but the company expects to maintain *significant regulatory exclusivity* for Cardizem through November 1992. After that, Cardizem could be in for some stiff competition from the lower-priced generic brands. By then, however, the company hopes to have some new winners on the market and some additional applications for Cardizem and Carafate that could lead to increased profitability.

The company has about 3,000 employees and 17,000 shareholders.

STOCK GROWTH

The company's stock price has exploded over the past decade, climbing 1,900 percent (35 percent per year) from its median of $1 a share in 1978 to its late 1988 price of $20 a share. The company has had four 2-for-1 stock splits since 1983.

Including reinvested dividends, a $10,000 investment in Marion Labs stock at its median price in 1978 would have grown to about $250,000 ten years later. Average annual compounded rate of return (including stock growth and reinvested dividends): about 38 percent.

DIVIDEND YIELD

In the past, Marion paid a fairly good dividend yield (around 4 percent in the early 1980s), but with its rapidly rising stock price, the yield has dropped off considerably. During the three-year rating period from 1986 to 1988, the stock paid an average annual current return of 1 percent.

DIVIDEND GROWTH

Marion raised its dividend five consecutive years. The company increased the dividend 420 percent over the four-year rating period from 1984 to 1988, from 5 cents per share to 26 cents.

SHAREHOLDER PERKS

Marion offers a good dividend reinvestment and voluntary stock purchase plan for shareholders. Shareholders may contribute up to $3,000 per quarter to the plan, free of fees or commissions. The company will also sell shares for shareholders at no commission.

SUMMARY

Total revenues: $752 million, 1988. Earnings per share: $0.96, 1988; $0.09, 1978; 966% increase. Stock price: $20, 11/9/88; $1.00 (median), 1978 (1900% total increase; 35% annual increase); price rose 9 of 10 years, 1977–87. Dividend: $0.26, 1988; $0.05, 1984; 4-year increase: 420%. Dividend yield: 1.0%, 1986–1988. P/E ratio: 19, 1/3/89. Average annual total return to investor, 1978–88: 38%.

BRUNSWICK CORPORATION

One Brunswick Plaza
Skokie, IL 60077
(312) 470-4700
Chairman, President and CEO: Jack F. Reichert.

EARNINGS GROWTH	★ ★ ★ ★ ★
STOCK GROWTH	★ ★ ★ ★ ★
DIVIDEND YIELD	★ ★ ★
DIVIDEND GROWTH	★ ★ ★ ★
SHAREHOLDER PERKS	★ ★
NYSE—BC	**19 points**

If you've ever been bowling, you've probably slammed a Brunswick ball down a Brunswick lane, flattened some Brunswick pins, and had your ball beamed back by a Brunswick ball return, while the automatic Brunswick pinsetter picked up your pins and summed up your score.

Brunswick is the world's leading manufacturer of bowling equipment. The company also operates more than 100 bowling centers throughout the U.S. and several foreign countries. In Seoul, South Korea, where bowling was introduced as an exhibition sport in the 1988 Summer Olympics, the official Olympic bowling alley was fully-equipped with Brunswick gear.

But Brunswick's bowling division makes up only about 10 percent of the total revenues of this conglomerate, based in Skokie, Illinois. Brunswick owns Mercury Marine, the largest and most profitable boat engine company in the world; it owns Sea Ray and Bayliner, the two largest pleasure boat manufacturers in the world; and it owns Zebco fishing gear, the world's leading producer of fishing reels.

Brunswick's corporate interests, however, are not entirely devoted to good, clean family fun. Brunswick is involved in the chemical warfare business (it makes chemical agent detectors) and it acquired Honeywell's chemical defense center in 1987. The company also makes launch tubes for the Army's multiple launch rocket systems, rocket motor castings, tactical aircraft decoy systems, radar and infrared-hiding camouflage, honeycomb transportable shelters and other defense and aerospace equipment.

Brunswick's industrial products division manufactures door-operating systems, climate control, heating and air-conditioning systems, pumps, valves, filters and electronic control systems.

Brunswick's recreational operations account for just over 80 percent of its $3 billion a year in total revenues, with the marine division by far the largest recreational segment (72 percent of total revenue). Defense and industrial products each account for less than 10 percent of total revenues.

Founded in 1845, Brunswick is one of the country's oldest manufacturing corporations.

EARNINGS GROWTH

Brunswick has enjoyed exceptional earnings growth over the past decade, with a total increase of 757 percent in its earnings per share.

The company has annual revenues $3.1 billion. It has nearly 30,000 employees and a like number of shareholders of record.

STOCK GROWTH

Like its earnings growth, the company's stock price has surged during the past ten years, increasing 800 percent (24.5 percent per year) from its median of $2 a share in 1978 to its recent 1988 price of $18. The company has had three 2-for-1 stock splits since 1983.

Including reinvested dividends, a $10,000 investment in Brunswick stock at its median price in 1978 would have grown to about $128,000 ten years later. Average annual compounded rate of return (including stock growth and reinvested dividends): about 29 percent.

DIVIDEND YIELD

The company generally pays a fairly good yield, which has averaged just under 4 percent over the past ten years. During the three-year rating period from 1985 to 1987, the stock paid an average annual current return of 2 percent.

DIVIDEND GROWTH

Brunswick has had more than 15 consecutive years of dividend increases. The dividend jumped 129 percent over the four-year rating period from 1983 to 1987.

SHAREHOLDER PERKS

Brunswick offers a dividend reinvestment and voluntary stock purchase plan that is free to shareholders of record. Shareholders may contribute $10 to $1,000 per month to the voluntary stock purchase plan.

SUMMARY

Total revenues: $3.1 billion, 1987. Earnings per share: $1.97, 1987; $0.23, 1977; 757% increase. Stock price: $18, 11/7/88; $2.00 (median), 1978; 800% increase (24.5% per year); price rose 9 of 10 years, 1977–87. Dividend: $0.32, 1987; $0.14, 1983; 4-year increase: 129%. Dividend yield: 2.0%, 1985–87. P/E ratio: 7, 1/3/89. Average annual total return to investors, 1978–88: about 29%.

WM. WRIGLEY JR. COMPANY

410 North Michigan Ave.
Chicago, IL 60611
(312) 644-2121
President and CEO: William Wrigley.

EARNINGS GROWTH	★ ★
STOCK GROWTH	★ ★ ★ ★ ★
DIVIDEND YIELD	★ ★ ★ ★
DIVIDEND GROWTH	★ ★ ★ ★
SHAREHOLDER PERKS	★ ★ ★ ★
NYSE—WWY	**19 points**

Every holiday season, William Wrigley finds himself in the throes of what has become an increasingly sticky dilemma. For it is the onus of Mr. Wrigley, 55-year-old grandson of the founder of the Wm. Wrigley Jr. Company, to decide which flavors of the company's gum should be included in its annual gift box for shareholders. The Yuletide offering, which usually numbers about 20 packs (100 sticks in all), is mailed out along with seasons's greetings from Mr. Wrigley to all 9,000 of the company's shareholders of record.

The selection process has become doubly difficult for Mr. Wrigley in recent years, as his company continues to add new brands and new flavors. Through most of the Wrigley Company's 97 years, Juicy Fruit, Doublemint and Spearmint were about the only gums the company put on the market. Now Wrigley fields some 20 different flavors, including Freedent (spearmint, peppermint and cinnamon), Extra (bubble, spearmint, peppermint, cinnamon and Winterfresh), Big Red, Hubba Bubba (original, cola, strawberry, raspberry, blueberry, grape) and Sugarfree Hubba Bubba (original and grape). Shareholders who attended a recent annual meeting got a taste of all 20 flavors when the company passed out free tote bags containing a pack of each.

But even Wrigley shareholders who don't chew the stuff have to be pleased with the company's rising stock price and juicy dividends. Over the past three years, Wrigley shareholders have doubled their pleasure and tripled their investment with a total return of nearly 50 percent per year (from 1985 to 1988).

Even in what many consider to be a mature market, Wrigley continues to find ways to increase its gum sales and profits year after year. The company now holds about a 47 percent share of the country's chewing gum market and continues to stretch its presence worldwide. It is the world's leading gum manufacturer. Of the company's $788 million a year in annual sales, U.S. sales account for about 66 percent, European sales make up 21 percent and other foreign sales comprise the remaining 14 percent. Wrigley owns subsidiaries in 16 foreign countries and sells its gum in more than 100 countries.

Wrigley also owns Amurol Products, which manufactures children's novelty bubble gum and other confectionery products, including Big League Chew and baseball trading cards.

EARNINGS GROWTH

Wrigley's earnings have been fairly consistent over the past decade, with increased earnings per share eight of those ten years. Total earnings per share growth during that period was 172 percent.

Wrigley has a total annual revenue of $788 million, 5,500 employees and 9,000 shareholders of record. Insiders hold about 47 percent of the stock.

STOCK GROWTH

The company's stock price has experienced strong, consistent growth, with ten consecutive years of stock price increases. The stock has had one 2-for-1 stock split and a 3-for-1 split since 1986. Over the past ten years the stock has increased 561 percent (21 percent per year) from its median of $5.75 in 1978 to its recent 1988 price of $38 a share.

Including reinvested dividends, a $10,000 investment in Wrigley stock at its median price in 1978 would have grown to about $110,000 ten years later. Average annual compounded rate of return (including stock growth and reinvested dividends): about 27 percent.

DIVIDEND YIELD

The company generally pays a very good dividend, which has averaged more than 5 percent over the past ten years. During the three-year rating period from 1985 to 1987, the stock paid an average annual current return of 3.5 percent.

DIVIDEND GROWTH

The company raises its dividend most years. The dividend increased 103 percent over the four-year rating period from 1983 to 1987.

SHAREHOLDER PERKS

In addition to the annual Christmas gift boxes, the company hands out a box of about 20 packs of gum each year to all the shareholders who attend the annual meeting.

The company also offers its shareholders of record a good dividend reinvestment and voluntary stock purchase plan. There are no fees or commissions, and shareholders of record may purchase $50 to $1,000 per month in additional shares through the voluntary stock purchase plan.

SUMMARY

Total revenues: $788 million, 1987. Earnings per share: $1.69, 1987; $0.62, 1977; 172% increase. Stock price: $38, 11/3/88; $5.75 (median), 1978; 561% increase (21% per year); price rose 10 of 10 years, 1978–88. Dividend: $0.85, 1987; $0.42, 1983; 4-year increase: 103%. Dividend yield: 3.5% average, 1985–87. P/E ratio: 17, 1/3/89. Average annual total return to investors, 1978–88: about 27%.

H.J. HEINZ COMPANY
600 Grant St.
P.O. Box 57
Pittsburgh, PA 15230-0057
(412) 456-5700
Chairman, President and CEO: Anthony J.F. O'Reilly.

EARNINGS GROWTH	★ ★ ★ ★
STOCK GROWTH	★ ★ ★ ★ ★
DIVIDEND YIELD	★ ★ ★
DIVIDEND GROWTH	★ ★ ★
SHAREHOLDER PERKS	★ ★ ★ ★
NYSE—HNZ	**19 points**

When Americans reach for the ketchup bottle, more often than not, the name on the bottle is "Heinz." The Pittsburg food producer holds a remarkable 55 percent share of the U.S. consumer ketchup market. But ketchup is not the only food group in which the 120-year-old company excels. The Heinz "Mr. Aristocrat Tomato Man" must share the corporate spotlight with a cat named Morris and a tuna named Charlie.

Actually, Heinz's tuna division accounts for a slightly higher percentage (18 percent) of the company's $5.2 billion a year in total revenues than its ketchup division (15 percent). Star-Kist ("Sorry, Charlie") holds an imposing 40 percent share of the U.S. tuna market.

Heinz has also achieved a growing presence in the pet food market. Its 9 Lives brand—Morris' personal favorite—holds a 27 percent share of its market. The company also makes Jerky Treats and Meaty Bones snack foods for dogs.

The company's other major food group is its Ore-Ida frozen potato products, which account for about 9 percent of the company's total revenue.

Heinz is also a leading producer of baby food, canned soup, lower-calorie frozen meals and desserts, beans, sauces and condiments, pasta, candy, pickles, chilled salads, rice cakes, frozen meats, vinegar, flavored rice products and other processed foods.

The company does business around the world. Its strongest areas outside the U.S. and Canada include the United Kingdom, western Europe, Australia, Venezuela and Japan.

Heinz is also the parent company of Weight Watchers, the international diet and fitness organization. Weight Watchers has been in business for more than 25 years. It operates branches in 22 countries and boasts 600,000 members worldwide. The company reports total annual revenues of nearly $1 billion from its service and franchise fees and its licensed product sales.

EARNINGS GROWTH

Heinz has had ten consecutive years of increased earnings. Earnings per share jumped 310 percent during that period.

With total revenues of $5.2 billion a year, Heinz is one of the nation's 15 largest food companies. It has 50,000 employees and 33,000 shareholders.

STOCK GROWTH

The company's stock price has climbed steadily through the past decade, with two 2-for-1 stock splits and one 3-for-1 split since 1981. Over the past ten years the stock has increased 623 percent (22 percent per year) from its median of $6.50 in 1978 to its recent 1988 price of $47 a share.

Including reinvested dividends, a $10,000 investment in Heinz stock at its median price in 1978 would have grown to about $105,000 ten years later. Average annual compounded rate of return (including stock growth and reinvested dividends): about 26.5 percent.

DIVIDEND YIELD

The company generally pays a good dividend yield, which has averaged about 4 percent over the past 10 years. During the three-year rating period from 1986 to 1988, the stock paid an average annual current return of 2.8 percent.

DIVIDEND GROWTH

Heinz has raised its dividend each year for more than a decade. Its dividend has increased 79 percent over the four-year rating period from 1983 to 1987.

SHAREHOLDER PERKS

New shareholders of record who buy 30 shares or more of Heinz stock receive a welcome gift from the company. One year the gift was an old style crock pot, another time it was a Heinz clock, and one year the company sent out a Heinz toy truck.

Shareholders who attend the annual meeting also receive a gift package of some of the company's newer products.

The company puts out one of corporate America's best quarterly reports. They generally run about 30 pages and are packed with new product information and company developments. They occasionally carry special offers for Heinz shareholders. One recent report offered a subscription to the *Morris Report* (for cat lovers) for $6 a year and an opportunity to buy a Heinz "Mr. Aristocrat Tomato Man" talking alarm clock for $25.

Heinz provides a good dividend reinvestment and voluntary stock purchase plan for its shareholders. There are no fees or commissions, and shareholders of record may purchase $25 to $1,000 per quarter in additional shares through the voluntary stock purchase plan.

SUMMARY

Total revenues: $5.2 billion, fiscal 1988 (ended 4/29/88). Earnings per share: $2.91, 1988; $0.71, 1978; 310% increase. Stock price: $47, 11/3/88; $6.50 (median), 1978; 623% increase (22% per year); price rose 9 of 10 years, 1977–87. Dividend: $1.21, 1988; $0.68, 1984; 4-year increase: 78%. Dividend yield: 2.8% average, 1986–88. P/E ratio: 15, 1/3/89. Average annual total return to investors, 1978–88: 26.5%.

UST

UST INC.

100 West Putnam Ave.
Greenwich, CT
(203) 661-1100
Chairman and CEO: Louis F. Bantle.
President and COO: Nicholas A. Buoniconti.

EARNINGS GROWTH	★ ★ ★ ★
STOCK GROWTH	★ ★ ★ ★ ★
DIVIDEND YIELD	★ ★ ★ ★
DIVIDEND GROWTH	★ ★ ★ ★
SHAREHOLDER PERKS	★ ★
NYSE—UST	**19 points**

Pinch by pinch, UST has become one of the most profitable businesses in the tobacco industry. The maker of Skoal, Copenhagen and other "smokeless" and pipe tobaccos keeps adding to its earnings, dividends and revenues year after year. In all, UST sells nearly half a billion cans a year of its tobaccos.

In addition to Skoal and Copenhagen, UST (formerly United States Tobacco Company) produces Skoal Bandits (tobacco pouches), Red Seal, Rooster, Standard, Bruton, CC and Devoe dry tobaccos, WB Cut chewing tobacco, Borkum Riff, Amphora and Alsbo pipe tobaccos and Don Tomas and La Regenta cigars. Copenhagen is UST's oldest product; it was introduced in 1822.

Tobacco accounts for more than 95 percent of UST's earnings, but the Connecticut-based firm is beginning to branch into other areas. The company has already taken aim at both ends of the alcohol market—it produces and sells a line of wines through its wholly owned subsidiary, International Wines and Spirits Ltd., and it recently bought a small group of health care centers that specialize in the treatment of drug and alcohol addiction.

Most of its wines are made in the states of Washington and sold under the labels of Chateau Ste. Michelle, Columbia Crest, Conn Creek and Villa Mt. Eden.

Some of UST's other products include Dr. Grabow pre-smoked pipes, Mastercraft imported pipes, Dill's pipe cleaners, National Pen and Pencil Company writing instruments and Zig-Zag cigarette papers. The company also operates some agricultural properties.

EARNINGS GROWTH

With total annual revenues of $576 million, UST is relatively small by tobacco industry standards. (By comparison, total revenues for industry leader Philip Morris exceed $22 billion a year.) But over the past ten years UST has given its investors the best total return of all tobacco companies. In fact, UST has been one of the better-performing stocks among all Fortune 500 companies, ranking fourth in 1988 in net profit as a percent of assets and sixth in net profit as a percent of sales.

However, like all tobacco companies, UST faces some tough opposition from consumer groups. How dramatically that will affect its sales and profits remains to be seen. So far UST has had no problem continuing its string of more than 15 consecutive years of record earnings.

The company has, however, experienced a modest decline in the sale of its domestic moist tobaccos over the past four years. Since 1987, government regulators have banned TV and radio ads for chewing tobaccos and have required tobacco producers to print alternating warnings on their packages informing consumers that "This product is not a safe alternative to cigarettes," or, more bluntly, "This product may cause mouth cancer."

UST has had more than 15 consecutive years of increased earnings. The company's earnings per share increased 389 percent from 1977 to 1987.

UST has 3,500 employees and about 9,500 shareholders of record.

STOCK GROWTH

UST's stock price has climbed fairly steadily through the past decade, rising 464 percent (19 percent per year) from a median of $5.50 per share in 1978 to its recent 1988 price of $31. The stock has had one 2-for-1 split and one 3-for-1 split since 1983.

Including reinvested dividends, a $10,000 investment in UST stock at its median price in 1978 would have grown to about $86,000 ten years later. Average annual compounded rate of return (including stock growth and reinvested dividends): about 24 percent.

DIVIDEND YIELD

The company generally pays a very good yield, which has averaged about 5 percent over the past ten years. During the three-year rating period from 1985 to 1987, the stock paid an average annual current return of 4.9 percent.

DIVIDEND GROWTH

UST has paid a dividend each year since 1912, with increases each of the past 17 years. The dividend increased 106 percent over the four-year rating period from 1983 to 1987.

SHAREHOLDER PERKS

UST provides an excellent dividend reinvestment and voluntary stock purchase plan for its shareholders. There are no fees or service charges, and shareholders may contribute $10 to $10,000 per month to the stock purchase plan.

At its annual meeting, the company hands out samples of its products, such as cigars and smokeless tobacco, and small gifts such as UST potholders and keychains.

SUMMARY

Total revenues: $576 million, fiscal 1987. Earnings per share: $2.25, 1987; $0.46, 1977; 389% increase. Stock price: $31, 9/1/88; $5.50 (median), 1978 (464% total increase; 19% annual increase); price rose 8 of 10 years, 1977–87. Dividend: $1.20, 1987; $0.58, 1983; 4-year increase: 106%. Dividend yield: 4.9%, 1985–1987. P/E ratio: 15, 1/3/89. Average annual total return to investor, 1978–88: about 24%.

11

WASTE MANAGEMENT, INC.

3003 Butterfield Road
Oak Brook, IL 60521
(312) 572-8800
Chairman: Dean L. Buntrock.
President: Phillip B. Rooney.

EARNINGS GROWTH	★ ★ ★ ★ ★
STOCK GROWTH	★ ★ ★ ★ ★
DIVIDEND YIELD	★ ★
DIVIDEND GROWTH	★ ★ ★ ★
SHAREHOLDER PERKS	★ ★
NYSE—WMX	**18 points**

It's not a very glamorous name—Waste Management, Inc.—but then it's not a very glamorous calling. The Chicago-based waste treatment company has carved out its niche amidst slime, sludge, toxic chemicals and low-grade nuclear wastes. Vile as it may sound, however, refuse has its rewards. Waste Management's willingness to take on America's ignoblest endeavors has made it one of the most successful businesses in U.S. industry.

The company has increased its earnings and revenues every year since it went public in 1971. Over the past ten years, its shareholders have received an average annual return on investment of about 37 percent.

Waste Management is the largest provider of solid waste management services in North America. It manages more than 100 landfills in the U.S., with 40 more under development. It provides trash collection services for half a million commercial and industrial customers and nearly seven million homes and apartments. The company recently began recycling programs in 15 U.S. and Canadian communities, collecting about 300,000 tons a year of recyclable materials.

Waste Management has also entered the waste-to-energy market. It constructed a $75 million waste-to-energy facility in Tampa, Florida, in 1985 that is capable of burning 1,000 tons of waste per day for conversion to steam and electricity. It recently began construction of a second waste-to-energy facility near Fort Lauderdale, Florida, that will have twice the capacity of the first facility.

Through its Chemical Waste Management subsidiary (of which Waste Management owns 81 percent), the company provides disposal and treatment of hazardous chemical wastes and low-level radioactive wastes. Its Chem-Nuclear Systems subsidiary is the largest provider of low-level radioactive waste management services in the U.S.

Waste Management is also involved in several related ventures. It provides street-sweeping services for municipal and commercial customers and operates municipal water and wastewater treatment plants through its Envirotech Operating Services group. It markets Port-O-Let portable lavatories and has entered lawn-care service through its recent acquisition of Tru Green Corp., and pest control service through the acquisition of several small regional firms.

The company has expanded its services beyond North America, with operations in Argentina, Australia, Europe, New Zealand and Saudi Arabia.

EARNINGS GROWTH

Waste Management has had exceptional earnings growth, with increases for 16 consecutive years. Its earnings per share have increased 873 percent over the past ten years.

The company has annual revenues of $2.76 billion. It has about 30,000 employees and 12,000 shareholders.

Waste treatment is a business that is largely immune to trends and economic cycles. And mounting problems in the waste treatment area, with landfill shortages and new restrictions on disposal of hazardous waste, could make Waste Management's services all that much more valuable in the years ahead.

The business is, however, subject to great public scrutiny and potential legal liability if hazardous wastes are improperly treated. So far, though, the company reports that there are no pending cases that would have "a material adverse effect on its operations or financial condition."

STOCK GROWTH

The company's stock price has climbed quickly through the past decade, with two 2-for-1 stock splits and one 3-for-1 split since 1981. Over the past ten years the stock has increased 1900 percent (35 percent per year) from its median of $2 in 1978 to its recent 1988 price of $40 a share.

Including reinvested dividends, a $10,000 investment in Waste Management stock at its median price in 1978 would have grown to about $230,000 ten years later. Average annual compounded rate of return (including stock growth and reinvested dividends): about 36.5 percent.

DIVIDEND YIELD

The company generally pays a low dividend yield, which has averaged about 1.5 percent over the past ten years. During the three-year rating period from 1985 to 1987, the stock paid an average annual current return of 1.2 percent.

DIVIDEND GROWTH

Waste Management has increased its dividend 13 consecutive years. The dividend was raised 113 percent over the four-year rating period from 1983 to 1987.

SHAREHOLDER PERKS

Waste Management offers its shareholders a good dividend reinvestment and voluntary stock purchase plan. There are no fees or service charges, and shareholders may contribute $25 to $2,000 per month to the stock purchase plan.

SUMMARY

Total revenues: $2.8 billion, 1987. Earnings per share: $1.46, 1987; $0.15, 1977; 873% increase. Stock price: $40, 11/9/88; $2.10 (median), 1978; 1900% increase (35% per year); price rose 9 of 10 years, 1977–87. Dividend: $0.34, 1987; $0.16, 1983; 4-year increase: 113%. Dividend yield: 1.2% average, 1985–87. P/E ratio: 22, 1/3/89. Average annual total return to investors, 1978–88: 36.5%.

12

THE LIMITED, INC.

THE LIMITED, INC.

Two Limited Parkway
P.O. Box 16000
Columbus, OH 43216
(614) 479-7000
Chairman and President: Leslie H. Wexner

EARNINGS GROWTH	★ ★ ★ ★ ★
STOCK GROWTH	★ ★ ★ ★ ★
DIVIDEND YIELD	★
DIVIDEND GROWTH	★ ★ ★ ★ ★
SHAREHOLDER PERKS	★ ★
NYSE—LTD	**18 points**

The Limited has tied its fortunes over the years to the fickle nature of the fashion industry. Since 1963, when Leslie Wexner opened his first women's clothing store, hemlines have advanced, retreated and, on occasion, gone both ways at once, but The Limited's revenues just keep moving up.

Even at that, the 51-year-old Mr. Wexner, who still serves as chairman, president and chief executive officer of the 3,100-store women's apparel chain, might be a little surprised to see his company ranked so high on this list.

The fashion industry has been in a slump the past couple of years, particularly following the October 1987 stock market crash, and The Limited has suffered along with the rest of the trade. While its revenues continue to climb, the company's profits have been a little shaky. In its first quarter after the crash, The Limited's earnings were down nearly 50 percent from the previous year.

But clothing sales are cyclical, and when the cycle returns, The Limited should be poised to exploit it. The Columbus, Ohio-based clothier has continued its aggressive policy of adding new stores (448 new stores in 1987) and acquiring smaller chains. Its recent acquisitions include Abercrombie & Fitch, a 25-store sportswear and gifts chain, Lerner Stores, a 750-unit chain of fashionable, budget-priced clothing stores, and Henri Bendel, an upscale apparel store in New York City.

Among The Limited's other leading clothing store chains are:

- The Limited. The original Limited clothing store chain has grown to more than 700 stores. In 1988, the company opened about 20 "super-stores" that are large enough to carry some additional lines of clothing.
- Victoria's Secret. The chain of designer lingerie stores was expected to increase its outlets from 236 stores to about 336 stores during 1988. This is the fastest growing segment of all of The Limited's holdings.
- Lerner. Lerner is geared to the "off-price" customer. With 770 Lerner stores, this is the largest women's apparel business under one name in the country. The Limited acquired Lerner in 1985.
- Lane Bryant. The chain of apparel stores for large-size women has grown from 222 stores in 1982 to more than 600 stores by 1988.
- Lerner Woman (which merged with Sizes Unlimited to form a 338-store chain). The stores sell women's clothing in sizes 14 and up.
- Brylane. This is the second largest fashion catalog retailer in the U.S.

EARNINGS GROWTH

The Limited's growth over the past ten years has been nothing short of spectacular. From (split-adjusted) earnings of 6 cents per share in 1978, earnings have rocketed 20-fold (1983 percent total; 36 percent per year) to $1.25 per share in 1987.

The company has 25,000 employees and 15,000 shareholders. Insiders own about 36 percent of the stock.

STOCK GROWTH

The company's stock price growth has been every bit as spectacular as its earnings growth, although its recent 1988 price of $25 per share is less than half of its peak price of $52 prior to the 1987 crash. Since 1983, the stock has split 2-for-1 twice and 3-for-2 once. Over the past 10 years the stock has increased 1,900 percent (35 percent per year) from its median of $1.25 in 1978 to its recent 1988 price of $25 a share.

Including reinvested dividends, a $10,000 investment in Limited stock at its median price in 1978 would have grown to about $220,000 ten years later. Average annual compounded rate of return (including stock growth and reinvested dividends): about 36 percent.

DIVIDEND YIELD

Dividends have never been a strong point for The Limited, but with the kind of stock price appreciation the company has had, its shareholders should be willing to forgive the meager dividends. Over the past three years the stock has paid an annual current return of 0.6 percent.

DIVIDEND GROWTH

Even though the current return is low, the dividend payments have been increasing rapidly over the past few years. The dividend has grown from (split-adjusted) 4 cents per share in 1983 to 24 cents per share in 1987, a 500 percent total increase over the four-year rating period.

SHAREHOLDER PERKS

The company offers an excellent dividend reinvestment and voluntary stock purchase plan. There are no fees or commissions, and shareholders of record may buy $30 to $6,000 per quarter in additional shares through the voluntary stock purchase program.

SUMMARY

Total revenues: $3.5 billion, 1987. Earnings per share: $1.25, 1987; $0.06, 1977; 1983% increase. Stock price: $25, 10/20/88; $1.25 (median), 1978 (1,900% total increase; 35% annual increase); price rose 9 of 10 years, 1977–87. Dividend: $0.24, 1987; $0.04, 1983; 4-year increase: 500%. Dividend yield: 0.6% average, 1985–1987. P/E ratio: 26, 1/3/89. Average annual total return to investor, 1978–88: about 36%.

VF CORPORATION

1047 North Park Road
Wyomissing, PA 19610
(215) 378-1151
Chairman and CEO: Lawrence R. Pugh
President: Robert E. Gregory, Jr.

EARNINGS GROWTH	★ ★ ★ ★ ★
STOCK GROWTH	★ ★ ★ ★ ★
DIVIDEND YIELD	★ ★ ★
DIVIDEND GROWTH	★ ★ ★
SHAREHOLDER PERKS	★ ★
NYSE—VFC	**18 points**

VF Corp. was founded in 1899 as Vanity Fair, a Pennsylvania-based garment manufacturer that was to become a leading producer of "intimate apparel." VF still carries the Vanity Fair line of "body fashions, daywear, sleepwear and loungewear," but in VF's corporate hierarchy, silk and satin has taken a back seat to denim and twill.

VF is the world's largest publicly owned apparel company, thanks in part to its acquisition in 1986 of garment giant Blue Bell, Inc. The acquisition, which brought Wrangler and Rustler jeans into VF's corporate fold, enabled the company to sew up a 25 percent share of the lucrative U.S. jeans market. Three of the top four U.S. brands—Lee, Wrangler and Rustler—are now manufactured by VF.

The company is also a major player in the sportswear market. VF owns Bassett-Walker, a designer and manufacturer of "knitted, fleeced active-wear," and Jantzen (which it acquired as part of Blue Bell) a leading maker of swimwear, sweaters, tennis attire and other sportswear.

Other VF brands include Red Kap and Big Ben "occupational and career apparel," Modern Globe and Lollipop underwear, Pepsi Apparel America and Girbaud jeans.

VF Corp. is structured essentially as a holding company of each of its brand-name manufacturers. The subsidiaries operate independently of one another and may handle every aspect of their own operations, from the processing of raw cotton and synthetic fibers to the designing, manufacturing and marketing of the finished garment.

Among the four divisions, jeanswear accounts for 60 percent of VF's $2.6 billion a year in total annual revenue, sportswear accounts for about 20 percent, and intimate apparel and occupational apparel each make up about 10 percent.

The company sells its apparel in a number of foreign countries (including South Africa). Foreign sales account for 7 percent of the VF's total revenue.

EARNINGS GROWTH

VF has had excellent earnings growth, increasing its earnings per share nine of the past ten years (through 1987). Earnings per share have climbed 636 percent over the past decade.

The company has about 50,000 employees and 11,000 shareholders of record.

STOCK GROWTH

The company's stock price has increased rapidly in recent years, with three 2-for-1 stock splits since 1982. Over the past ten years the stock has increased 1,100 percent (28 percent per year) from its median of $2.50 in 1978 to its recent 1988 price of $30 a share.

Including reinvested dividends, a $10,000 investment in VF stock at its median price in 1978 would have grown to about $180,000 ten years later. Average annual compounded rate of return (including stock growth and reinvested dividends): about 33.5 percent.

DIVIDEND YIELD

The company has traditionally paid a very good dividend yield, which has averaged about 5 percent over the past ten years. During the three-year rating period from 1985 to 1987, the stock paid an average annual current return of 2.4 percent.

DIVIDEND GROWTH

VF has raised its dividend for more than 15 consecutive years. The dividend increased 74 percent over the four-year rating period from 1983 to 1987.

SHAREHOLDER PERKS

The company provides a dividend reinvestment and voluntary stock purchase plan for its shareholders of record. Shareholders may purchase up to $3,000 per quarter in additional shares through the voluntary stock purchase plan. Participating shareholders are assessed a small service fee and commission.

SUMMARY

Total revenues: $2.6 billion, 1987. Earnings per share: $2.65, 1987; $0.36, 1977; 636% increase. Stock price: $30, 8/4/88; $2.50 (median), 1978; 1,100% increase (28% per year); price rose 8 of 10 years, 1977–87. Dividend: $0.75, 1987; $0.43, 1983; 4-year increase: 74%. Dividend yield: 2.4% average, 1985–87. P/E ratio: 11, 1/3/89. Average annual total return to investors, 1978–88: 33.5%.

14

CONAGRA, INC.

ConAgra Center
One Central Park Plaza
Omaha, NE 68102
(402) 978-4000
Chairman and CEO: Charles M. Harper

EARNINGS GROWTH	★ ★ ★
STOCK GROWTH	★ ★ ★ ★ ★
DIVIDEND YIELD	★ ★ ★
DIVIDEND GROWTH	★ ★ ★
SHAREHOLDER PERKS	★ ★ ★ ★
NYSE—CAG	**18 points**

ConAgra—as its name would imply—is a consolidated agricultural conglomerate that seems to encompass every furrow and fowl of the farming industry. By its own definition, the Omaha-based operation is "a diversified family of companies operating across the entire food chain—from farm to table."

ConAgra sells fertilizer, pesticides, livestock feed and even tractor tires, and operates about 170 rural retail stores. It owns a network of slaughtering operations and corn, flour and oat mills. It is also a major food processor. Its greatest strength is meats, but it also does a good business in seafoods, cheese, peanut butter, jelly, frozen dinners, pet foods and other grocery products. ConAgra is also a major commodity futures trader, operating about 120 comodities brokerage offices.

ConAgra owns Banquet (frozen dinners, pot pies, chicken, etc.), Armour, Country Pride, Decker, Golden Star, Monfort and Pfaelzer meats, King Midas, Diamond and High Altitude flour, Real peanut butter, Maple Rich syrup, Morton and Chun King frozen foods.

It also owns Country General Stores, Wheelers, S&S, Sandvig's, Peavey Ranch and Home stores and Northwest Fabrics and Crafts stores.

In all, ConAgra operates more than 40 different companies with locations throughout North and South America, Europe, Asia and Australia.

The company divides its business into three segments: prepared foods (65 percent of its $9.5 billion in annual revenue), agriculture (20 percent of total revenue) and trading and processing (15 percent of revenues).

EARNINGS GROWTH

ConAgra has had steady earnings growth, with increased earnings nine of the past ten years. Earnings per share have climbed 341 percent through its fiscal 1988.

The company ranks as one of the nation's five largest food-related corporations. It has 40,000 employees and 15,000 shareholders of record.

STOCK GROWTH

The company's stock price has had outstanding appreciation, increasing 12 consecutive years through 1987. ConAgra has had two 2-for-1 stock splits and one 3-for-2 split since 1980. Over the past ten years the stock has increased 1,100 percent (28 percent per year) from its median of $2.50 in 1978 to its late 1988 price of $30 a share.

Including reinvested dividends, a $10,000 investment in ConAgra stock at its median price in 1978 would have grown to about $175,000 ten years later. Average annual compounded rate of return (including stock growth and reinvested dividends): about 33 percent.

DIVIDEND YIELD

The company generally pays a fairly good yield, which has averaged about 4 percent over the past ten years. During the three-year rating period from fiscal 1986 to 1988, the stock paid an average annual current return of 2.3 percent.

DIVIDEND GROWTH

ConAgra has raised its dividend 12 consecutive years. The dividend has increased 75 percent over the four-year rating period from 1984 to 1988.

SHAREHOLDER PERKS

ConAgra provides a couple of perks for its shareholders. At its annual meetings, the company serves up a generous smorgasboard of ConAgra foods and passes out coupons to its shareholders for such items as free packages of hotdogs, free frozen dinners or substantial discounts on products at ConAgra's retail stores.

The company also includes discount offers in some of its quarterly earnings reports. One report had an offer for 15 percent off anything in Pfaelzer Brothers gourmet foods catalog (plus two free filet mignons with the first meat order), another had a coupon for 50 cents off a package of frozen chicken, and a recent fall earnings report offered savings of 25 to 40 percent on Armour meats holiday gift boxes.

ConAgra has a good dividend reinvestment and voluntary cash contribution plan that is entirely free to shareholders of record. Shareholders can contribute $10 to $3,000 per quarter to the stock purchase plan.

SUMMARY

Total revenues: $9.47 billion, for fiscal 1988 (ended 5/31/88). Earnings per share: $1.94, 1988; $0.44, 1978; 341% increase. Stock price: $30, 11/9/88; $2.50 (median), 1978 (1,100% total increase; 28% annual increase); price rose 10 of 10 years, 1977–87. Dividend: $0.65, 1988; $0.37, 1984; 4-year increase: 76%. Dividend yield: 2.3% average, 1986–1988. P/E ratio: 13, 1/3/89. Average annual total return to investor, 1978–88: about 33%.

15

LOEWS

LOEWS CORPORATION

667 Madison Avenue
New York, NY 10021
(212) 545-2000
Chairman: Laurence A. Tisch
President: Preston R. Tisch

EARNINGS GROWTH	★ ★ ★ ★ ★
STOCK GROWTH	★ ★ ★ ★ ★
DIVIDEND YIELD	★ ★ ★
DIVIDEND GROWTH	★ ★ ★ ★ ★
SHAREHOLDER PERKS	(no points)
NYSE—LTR	**18 points**

Like most U.S. cigarette manufacturers, Loews has been burning a path to other markets to temper the slow fade in domestic tobacco sales. The maker of Old Gold, Kent, True and Newport cigarettes has become part broadcaster, part watchmaker, part insurer and part innskeeper.

In addition to its Lorillard cigarette subsidiary, the New York-based conglomerate owns a 25 percent stake in the CBS television network (Loews' chairman and co-CEO, Laurence A. Tisch, now doubles as president and CEO of CBS). Loews also holds a 95 percent share of Bulova watches, an 80 percent stake of CNA Financial (insurance) and a 100 percent share of the 13-unit Loews Hotel chain.

Loews' cigarette operation and its CNA insurance division constitute about 85 percent of the company's total earnings.

Loews is the fourth largest cigarette manufacturer in the U.S., with an 8 percent share of the domestic market. Cigarettes account for only about 18 percent of Loews' $9.2 billion a year in total revenue, but contribute about 35 percent of the company's total profit.

The company sells about 46 billion cigarettes a year. Newport is Loews' leading brand, claiming about a 4.2 percent share of the U.S. market. Newport ranks sixth in sales among all U.S. brands.

CNA Financial, which is a major underwriter of property, casualty, life, accident and health insurance, contributes about 75 percent of Loews' total revenues and about 50 percent of its total profit.

Loews owns a chain of 13 hotels and motels in the U.S. and abroad. In addition to six Loews hotels in the U.S., the company owns luxury hotels in the Bahamas, France, Canada and Monte Carlo, Monaco. It also owns two Ramada Inns, two Howard Johnson's and a Regency Hotel in New York. The company's hotel operations account for about 2 percent of its total revenues.

The company's Bulova subsidiary, which makes watches and clocks, accounts for just under 2 percent of Loews' total revenues.

EARNINGS GROWTH

Loews has had excellent earnings growth throughout the past decade. Earnings per share have increased nine of the past ten years, from 1977 to 1987. Earnings per share jumped a total of 546 percent during that period.

Like other cigarette manufacturers, Loews has been named as a defendant in a number of lawsuits alleging liability for smoking-related deaths. While the cigarette companies had survived dozens of such suits without ever being assessed a penny of damages, the story changed in 1988. For the first time in history, a jury ruled against a cigarette company (Liggett Group, maker of L&Ms), and awarded $400,000 in damages to the husband of the late Rose Cipollone, who died of lung cancer in 1984. While the $400,000 settlement may seem like a drop in the spittoon to the cash-rich tobacco companies, the case could open the floodgates to a rush of new liability suits. At this point, however, it is impossible to say whether such litigation will have a significant impact on the profitability of American tobacco companies.

Loews has about 23,000 employees and 6,600 shareholders of record. Insiders (primarily the Tisch family) control about 24 percent of the common shares.

STOCK GROWTH

The company's stock price has climbed steadily, with 14 consecutive years of stock price increases through 1987. The stock has increased 1,309 percent (30 percent per year), from its median of $5.75 in 1978 to its recent 1988 price of $81 a share.

Including reinvested dividends, a $10,000 investment in Loews stock at its median price in 1978 would have grown to about $160,000 ten years later. Average annual compounded rate of return (including stock growth and reinvested dividends): about 32 percent.

DIVIDEND YIELD

Loews normally pays a fairly low dividend yield—generally under 2 percent. Over the three-year rating period from 1985 to 1987, the stock paid an average annual current return of 3.1 percent—which is deceptively high because the company paid an unusually high dividend in 1985 (6.4 percent yield) that boosted the three-year average. In 1986 and 1987 the yield was just 1.6 percent and 1.4 percent, respectively.

DIVIDEND GROWTH

Loews does not make a habit of raising its dividend. From 1973 to 1983 it paid 16 cents per year, and not a penny more. But it has since raised its dividend to $1 a year—giving the company an astronomical 525 percent increase in its dividend over the four-year rating period from 1983 to 1987.

SHAREHOLDER PERKS   (no points)

The company offers no dividend reinvestment plan, nor does it provide any other perks for its shareholders.

SUMMARY

Total revenues: $9.3 billion, 1987. Earnings per share: $8.92, 1987; $1.38, 1977; 546% increase. Stock price: $81, 10/26/88; $5.75 (median), 1978 (1,309% total increase; 30% annual increase); price rose 10 of 10 years, 1977-87. Dividend: $1.00, 1987; $0.16, 1983; 4-year increase: 525%. Dividend yield: 3.1% average, 1985-1987. P/E ratio: 6, 1/3/89. Average annual total return to investor, 1978-88: about 32%.

16

BROWNING-FERRIS INDUSTRIES

757 North Eldridge
P.O. Box 3151
Houston, TX 77079
(713) 870-8100
Chairman and CEO: William D. Ruckelshaus
President: John E. Drury

EARNINGS GROWTH	★ ★ ★ ★ ★
STOCK GROWTH	★ ★ ★ ★ ★
DIVIDEND YIELD	★ ★
DIVIDEND GROWTH	★ ★ ★ ★
SHAREHOLDER PERKS	★ ★
NYSE—BFI	**18 points**

Browning-Ferris Industries recently began construction of a series of waste disposal facilities designed to turn trash into energy. Such sleight of hand is really nothing new for Browning-Ferris, however. The Houston-based waste management firm has been turning garbage into gold for many years.

Browning-Ferris (B-F) is one of two refuse firms to rank among the nation's best publicly traded companies. Like its contemporary in the waste disposal business, Waste Management, Inc. (see page 33), B-F has enjoyed outstanding earnings and stock price growth over the past ten years.

The company provides waste collection and disposal services for homes, businesses and factories in 700 communities in 43 states, Canada and several other countries. It operates 87 solid waste landfills and manages hazardous waste disposal sites in Ohio, New York, Texas and Louisiana.

The firm's latest venture is the construction of waste-to-energy plants through a partnership with Air Products and Chemicals, Inc. The companies, which are marketing their services under the name American Ref-Fuel, have completed construction of a plant in Hempstead, New York and are currently developing several other plants in communities in New York, Pennsylvania, Massachusetts and Connecticut. Construction costs range from $100 million to $350 million per plant, with plant capacities of 600 to 3,000 tons per day.

B-F also does a business in street and parking lot sweeping, portable restroom rental and bus and van transportation services.

EARNINGS GROWTH

The company has had excellent earnings growth, with 12 consecutive years of increased earnings. Earnings per share have increased 576 percent over the past ten years.

The firm has annual revenues of $1.66 billion. It has about 20,000 employees and 10,000 shareholders.

The waste disposal business is a growing industry that seems to remain strong through good economic times and bad. And Browning-Ferris's foray into the waste-to-energy market could prove to be a timely and profitable move. But, as the company is well aware, the waste disposal business carries with it some inherent risks. Waste disposal companies are subject to the constant threat of legal liability due to environmental problems from their waste disposal sites. B-F and its subsidiaries are currently involved in several such legal suits and government investigations regarding its hazardous waste disposal sites.

STOCK GROWTH

Browning-Ferris has had excellent stock price appreciation over the past decade, with two 2-for-1 stock splits and one 3-for-2 split since 1983. Over the past ten years the stock has increased 1,100 percent (28 percent per year) from its (split-adjusted) median of $2.25 in 1978 to its late 1988 price of $27 a share.

Including reinvested dividends, a $10,000 investment in Browning-Ferris stock at its median price in 1978 would be worth about $150,000 ten years later. Average annual compounded rate of return (including stock growth and reinvested dividends): about 31 percent.

DIVIDEND YIELD

The company has traditionally paid a low to moderate yield, averaging around 3 percent over the past ten years. During the three-year rating period from 1985 to 1987, the stock paid an average annual current return of 1.9 percent.

DIVIDEND GROWTH

Browning-Ferris has raised its dividend 12 consecutive years. The dividend was increased 100 percent over the four-year rating period from 1983 to 1987.

SHAREHOLDER PERKS

The company offers its shareholders a good dividend reinvestment and voluntary stock purchase plan. There are no fees or service charges, and shareholders may contribute $25 to $1,000 per month to the stock purchase plan.
    The company offers no other perks.

SUMMARY

Total revenues: $1.66 billion, 1987. Earnings per share: $1.15, 1987; $0.17, 1977; 576% increase. Stock price: $27, 9/9/88; $2.25 (median), 1978 (1,100% total increase; 28% annual increase); price rose 8 of 10 years, 1977–87. Dividend: $0.40, 1987; $0.20, 1983; 4-year increase: 100%. Dividend yield: 1.9% average, 1985–1987. P/E ratio: 18, 1/3/89. Average annual total return to investor, 1978–88: about 31%.

17

5 3

FIFTH THIRD BANK

FIFTH THIRD BANCORP

38 Fountain Square Plaza
Cincinnati, OH 45263
(513) 579-5300
President and CEO: Clement L. Buenger

EARNINGS GROWTH	★ ★ ★ ★ ★
STOCK GROWTH	★ ★ ★ ★ ★
DIVIDEND YIELD	★ ★ ★
DIVIDEND GROWTH	★ ★ ★
SHAREHOLDER PERKS	★ ★
OTC—FITB	**18 points**

Fifth Third Bancorp is a Cincinnati-based bank-holding company that has not only one of the most unusual names in the banking business, but also one of the most enviable growth records. The company's earnings have increased 14 consecutive years, and its stock price has climbed ninefold in the past ten years.

Fifth Third got its name early in this century as the result of a merger of the Fifth National Bank and the Third National Bank of Ohio. "Bancorp" was added in the late 1970s. Fifth Third Bancorp officials now commonly refer to the company as "Bancorp."

Bancorp has been rapidly acquiring banks throughout Ohio, northern Kentucky and southeastern Indiana. It now owns about 150 bank offices (including branch offices) in the three-state area and is adding a number of new banks each year.

Not all of the additions are the result of acquisitions, however. The company has been opening about 20 to 25 branch offices per year for its existing systems. After less than three years of operation, the Fifth Third Bank in Columbus, Ohio, had already expanded to more than a dozen branch offices.

Bancorp has also entered into a new hybrid of banking services—the "bank mart." Bank marts are small full-service banking centers located in retail outlets. The company opened bank marts in seven Kroger grocery stores in the Cincinnati area in 1987.

Bancorp has launched several specialty credit card ventures, including the Gold Circle/Richway Shoppers Bonus card, which the company claims is the first such credit card arrangement between a bank and a major retailer. The cards can be used in eight states.

Although Bancorp owns banks in only three states, it does business in 27 states, operating a network of more than 1,500 automatic teller machines. The company processes more than 15 million electronic transactions each month.

By bank-holding company standards, Fifth Third Bancorp is a minor player. Its largest subsidiary, Fifth Third Bank, is ranked among the largest 150 banks in the U.S. based on assets. Bancorp's $2.8 billion in annual loans and leases pales in comparison to such holding company heavey-hitters as First Chicago ($27 billion in loans), BankAmerica ($61 billion) and Chase Manhattan ($65 billion). But Bancorp is quickly carving out a profitable niche in the fertile Ohio-Indiana-Kentucky area.

EARNINGS GROWTH

Fifth Third has had increased earnings for 14 consecutive years. The company's earnings per share have increased 400 percent over the past decade.

The company has 2,500 employees and 5,500 shareholders of record. Cincinnati Financial Corp. owns about 20 percent of the company stock, and Western-Southern Life Insurance Company owns nearly 10 percent.

STOCK GROWTH

The company's stock price has climbed quickly through the past decade, with three 3-for-2 stock splits and one 2-for-1 split since 1983. Over the past ten years the stock has increased 788 percent (24 percent per year) from its median of $4.50 in 1978 to its recent 1988 price of $40 a share.

Including reinvested dividends, a $10,000 investment in Fifth Third stock at its median price in 1978 would have grown to about $140,000 ten years later. Average annual compounded rate of return (including stock growth and reinvested dividends): about 30 percent.

DIVIDEND YIELD

The company generally pays a good yield, which has averaged about 5 percent over the past ten years. During the three-year rating period from 1985 to 1987, the stock paid an average annual current return of 2.9 percent.

DIVIDEND GROWTH

Fifth Third has increased its dividend for more than a dozen consecutive years. The dividend increased 85 percent over the four-year rating period from 1983 to 1987.

SHAREHOLDER PERKS

The company provides a dividend reinvestment and voluntary stock purchase plan for its shareholders of record. Shareholders, who are assessed a small fee not to exceed $3 per month for the voluntary cash purchase plan, may purchase $25 to $1,000 per month in additional shares.

SUMMARY

Total loans and leases: $2.8 billion, 1987. Assets: $4.05 billion, 1987. Earnings per share: $3.05, 1987; $0.61, 1977; 400% increase. Stock price: $40, 8/17/88; $4.50 (median), 1978; 788% increase (24% per year); price rose 9 of 10 years, 1977–87. Dividend: $1.02, 1987; $0.55, 1983; 4-year increase: 85%. Dividend yield: 2.9% average, 1985–87. P/E ratio: 12, 1/3/89. Average annual total return to investors, 1978–88: about 30%.

18

QUAKER OATS

321 North Clark Street
P.O. Box 9001
Chicago, IL 60604-9001
(312) 222-7111
Chairman and CEO: William D. Smithburg
President: Frank J. Morgan

EARNINGS GROWTH	★ ★ ★
STOCK GROWTH	★ ★ ★ ★ ★
DIVIDEND YIELD	★ ★ ★
DIVIDEND GROWTH	★ ★ ★
SHAREHOLDER PERKS	★ ★ ★ ★
NYSE—OAT	**18 points**

In this era of high-glitz marketing, it's comforting to know that one major corporation still ties its image to the countenance of a kindly, white-haired Quaker. With his rosy cheeks and blue eyes peering out from beneath his black brimmed hat, the Quaker has symbolized oatmeal and other Quaker Oats foods for generations. But while its trademark Quaker remains the same, the Quaker Oats Company itself has become a lot more than oats.

Quaker has grown from within—through an ongoing program of new product introductions—and from without—through the acquisition of smaller companies. In 1988, 49 percent of its sales came from new brands developed or acquired since 1983.

Quaker puts its own label on such products as Chewy Granola Bars, Rice Cakes and its growing line of hot and cold cereals (including Instant Oatmeal, Fruit & Cream, Cap'n Crunch, Oh!s and Life). Quaker also owns Gatorade; Van Camp's pork and beans; Aunt Jemima pancakes and syrups; Golden Grain Rice-A-Roni; and Ken-L-Ration, Gravy Train and other popular pet food brands. In all, Quaker produces about 400 items for the grocery and food services market. Fisher-Price toys is also part of the Quaker conglomerate.

With total annual revenues of $5.3 billion, the Chicago-based corporation ranks among the nation's 15 largest food producers. It has production facilities in 17 states plus Canada, Latin America and Western Europe. Foreign sales account for about 22 percent of Quaker's total revenues.

The company divides its domestic business into several key divisions:

- U.S. foods group (24 percent of sales). This group includes hot and ready-to-eat cereals, wholesome snacks, Aunt Jemima products, Celeste Pizza and corn products.
- Diversified grocery products (27 percent of sales). Included in this group are Golden Grain products (Rice-A-Roni, Noodle-Roni and Ghirardelli Chocolates), pet foods (Ken-L-Ration, Puss 'n Boots, Gravy Train, Cycle, Gaines•Burgers and Top Choice) and Quaker food services, which supplies Quaker foods to the institutional food services market.
- Grocery specialties (11 percent of sales). This division includes Gatorade, Van Camp's beans and other products.
- Fisher-Price (15 percent of sales). The company is a major force in the U.S. toy market. It makes toys for infants, pre-school-aged children and juveniles.

EARNINGS GROWTH

Quaker Oats has had increased earnings for 13 consecutive years through fiscal 1988. Earnings per share have climbed 286 percent over the past decade.

The company, which was founded in 1901, has 34,000 employees and 31,000 shareholders of record.

STOCK GROWTH

The company's stock price growth has also been steady, with rising prices ten consecutive years through 1987. Quaker has had two 2-for-1 stock splits since 1984. Over the past ten years the stock has increased 822 percent (25 percent per year) from its median of $5.75 in 1978 to its recent 1988 price of $53 a share.

Including reinvested dividends, a $10,000 investment in Quaker stock at its median price in 1978 would have grown to about $128,000 ten years later. Average annual compounded rate of return (including stock growth and reinvested dividends): about 29 percent.

DIVIDEND YIELD

The company generally pays a fairly good yield, which has averaged about 4 percent over the past ten years. During the three-year rating period from 1986 to 1988, the stock paid an average annual current return of 2.2 percent.

DIVIDEND GROWTH

Quaker has raised its dividend for 21 consecutive years. The dividend was increased 82 percent over the four-year rating period from 1984 to 1988.

SHAREHOLDER PERKS

Coupons for a percentage off some of Quaker's new products are often sent to shareholders along with their dividend checks.

Shareholders who attend the annual meeting are given a sample packet that includes a variety of Quaker products.

Quaker offers an excellent dividend reinvestment plan for its shareholders. There are no commissions or service fees, and shareholders may contribute as little as $10 or as much as $30,000 a year to the voluntary cash stock purchase plan.

SUMMARY

Total revenues: $5.3 billion, fiscal 1988 (ended 6/30/88). Earnings per share: $3.20, 1988; $0.83, 1978; 286% increase. Stock price: $53, 11/9/88; $5.75 (median), 1978; 822% increase (25% per year); price rose 10 of 10 years, 1977–87. Dividend: $1.00, 1988; $0.55, 1984; 4-year increase: 82%. Dividend yield: 2.2% average, 1986–88. P/E ratio: 16, 1/3/89. Average annual total return to investors, 1978–88: about 29%.

19

MARRIOTT CORPORATION

Marriott Drive
Washington, D.C. 20058
(301) 380-9000
Chairman, President and CEO: J.W. Marriott, Jr.

EARNINGS GROWTH	★ ★ ★ ★ ★
STOCK GROWTH	★ ★ ★ ★ ★
DIVIDEND YIELD	★
DIVIDEND GROWTH	★ ★ ★ ★
SHAREHOLDER PERKS	★ ★ ★
NYSE—MHS	**18 points**

It's not easy to escape the shadow of the Marriott.

The Washington, D.C.-based accommodations colossus has motels and hotels in 50 states and 24 foreign countries. It runs a food-catering business that prepares the in-flight meals for 140 airlines worldwide, and it caters the cafeterias of about 1,000 businesses, 600 schools and 400 health care facilities. Marriott also operates more than 100 food and gift travel plazas along 15 eastern highway systems, manages airport cafeterias in more than 50 cities worldwide and owns or franchises hundreds of Roy Rogers, Howard Johnson's and Bob's Big Boy restaurants.

Marriott was founded by the late J. Willard Marriott, who started it all in 1927 when he opened a small root beer stand in Washington, D.C. The company initially made its name in the food services industry and began its airline in-flight catering service in 1937. Not until 1957 did Marriott open its first hotel. Now Marriott claims to manage more hotel rooms than any other company in the country. Marriott's annual revenues of $6.5 billion represents more than twice the revenues of the Hilton, Holiday and Ramada corporations combined. Marriott has more than 200,000 employees, serves five million meals a day and develops more than $1 billion a year in real estate.

The company has been honored three consecutive years as best overall U.S. hotel system by *Business Travel News,* and its hotels have earned more

American Automobile Association Four and Five Diamond awards than any other chain in the U.S.

There are about 165 Marriott hotels and resorts in the U.S., plus another 15 Marriotts in Bermuda, Canada, Central America, the Caribbean, Europe and the Middle East. The company owns about 20 of the hotels outright, and operates 110 hotels owned by independent investors. The remainder are franchise operated.

Marriott has also opened about 100 less expensive hotels ($40 to $70 per night) called Courtyard by Marriott, and has purchased the Residence Inn chain of more than 100 extended-stay hotels. Residence Inns feature studio suites with kitchens and two-story penthouse suites that are geared to travelers who are staying more than five consecutive nights.

The company opened about 20 Fairfield Inns in 1987 and 1988. Fairfield Inn is a new economy motel chain with room rates that range from $30 to $40 per night. Marriott also entered the time-sharing resorts market by opening new developments at Hilton Head, South Carolina, and Orlando, Florida. It has recently built two large senior living centers, one near Washington, D.C. and the other near Philadelphia.

Among Marriott's three principal business segments, lodging accounts for about 42 percent of its $6.5 billion in total revenues, contract food services account for about 45 percent of revenues and restaurants account for the remaining 13 percent.

EARNINGS GROWTH

Marriott has had 13 consecutive years of earnings growth. The company's earnings per share has jumped 735 percent over the past ten years.

The company has about 200,000 employees and 38,000 shareholders of record.

STOCK GROWTH

The company's stock price has risen quickly and consistently the past decade, increasing 991 percent (27 percent per year) from its median of $2.75 in 1978 to its late 1988 price of $30 a share. The stock was split 5-for-1 in 1986.

Including reinvested dividends, a $10,000 investment in Marriott stock at its median price in 1978 would have grown to about $115,000 ten years later. Average annual compounded rate of return (including stock growth and reinvested dividends): about 28 percent.

DIVIDEND YIELD

The company has traditionally paid a very low dividend yield, averaging under 1 percent over the past ten years. During the three-year rating period from 1985 to 1987, the stock paid an average annual current return of 0.5 percent.

DIVIDEND GROWTH

Marriott has raised its dividend nine consecutive years dating back to the first year the company paid a dividend. The dividend increased 147 percent over the four-year rating period from 1983 to 1987.

SHAREHOLDER PERKS

Marriott offers one of the best shareholder perks programs in America. Shareholders can get special rates on resort packages and discount rates of up to 50 percent off per night at more than 100 Marriott-owned or managed motels and hotels in about 40 states and a dozen foreign countries. For shareholders who do a lot of traveling, the discounts could add up to savings of hundreds of dollars a year.

Marriott also sponsors an annual shareholder suggestion program to encourage suggestions from its investors. The shareholder who offers the best suggestion receives ten free shares of Marriott stock, and the runner-up receives five shares.

The company offers no dividend reinvestment or voluntary stock purchase plan.

SUMMARY

Total revenues: $6.5 billion, 1987. Earnings per share: $1.67, 1987; $0.20, 1977; 735% increase. Stock price: $30, 11/9/88; $2.75 (median), 1978; 991% increase (27% per year); price rose 9 of 10 years, 1977–87. Dividend: $0.17, 1987; $0.07, 1983; 4-year increase: 142%. Dividend yield: 0.5% average, 1985–1987. P/E ratio: 17, 1/3/89. Average annual total return to investors, 1978–88: about 28%.

20

SHERWIN-WILLIAMS COMPANY

101 Prospect Ave. Northwest
Cleveland, OH 44115-1075
(216) 566-2000
Chairman and CEO: John G. Breen
President: Thomas A. Commes

EARNINGS GROWTH	★ ★ ★ ★ ★
STOCK GROWTH	★ ★ ★ ★ ★
DIVIDEND YIELD	★ ★ ★
DIVIDEND GROWTH	★ ★ ★
SHAREHOLDER PERKS	★ ★
NYSE—SHW	**18 points**

Sherwin-Williams is one company that's true to its corporate motto. The Cleveland-based manufacturer has more than 1,800 paint stores in 48 states, subsidiaries and joint ventures in 10 countries, and licensees in 25 countries. From Chile to China, Jordan to Japan, Belgium to Bolivia, Sherwin-Williams really does "cover the earth."

Sherwin-Williams is the world's largest producer of paints and varnishes. It has been in business for more than 120 years. In addition to its own Sherwin-Williams brand of paints and coatings, the company manufactures Dutch Boy, Martin-Senour, Kem-Tone and a number of private label paints for independent dealers, mass merchandisers and home-improvement centers.

The company's network of paint stores, which has been growing at about 100 per year, should eclipse the 2,000 mark by 1990. The stores sell paints, wall and floor coverings, industrial finishes, window treatments, brushes, scrapers, rollers, spray equipment and other products and tools. Its primary customers are professional painters, contractors and maintenance people; do-it-yourself homeowners and small- to medium-sized manufacturers of products requiring a factory finish.

The paint stores account for about 65 percent of the company's $1.8 billion in total revenue and 44 percent of its total profit.

Sherwin-Williams' other segment, coatings, accounts for the remaining 35 percent of revenues and 56 percent of total profit. The coatings segment is divided into four primary U.S. divisions:

- Consumer division. Manufactures the company's line of consumer paints (such as Dutch Boy and Sherwin-Williams brands), as well as some industrial maintenance products, labels, adhesives and color cards.
- Automotive division. Makes auto finishes and refinishing coatings for body shops and other refinishers. The company operates more than 100 distribution branches throughout the U.S.
- Chemical coatings. Makes finishes for original equipment manufacturers of metal, plastic and wood products.
- Spray-on division. Makes custom and industrial aerosols for paints and Dupli-Color spray paints for automobile touch-ups. It also makes coatings, and automotive, sanitary supply, institutional, pest control and industrial products.

EARNINGS GROWTH

Sherwin-Williams reported an earnings deficit in 1977, but the paint maker has been rolling along smoothly ever since, with ten consecutive years of earnings growth. The company's earnings per share increased 481 percent in the 11 years from 1976 to 1987 (17.5 percent per year).

The company has annual revenues of $1.8 billion. It has 16,000 employees and 12,500 shareholders of record.

STOCK GROWTH

Sherwin-Williams has had excellent stock growth over the past decade, with three 2-for-1 stock splits since 1982. Over the past ten years the stock has increased 762 percent (24 percent per year) from its median of $3.25 in 1978 to its recent 1988 price of $28 a share.

Including reinvested dividends, a $10,000 investment in Sherwin-Williams stock at its median price in 1978 would have grown to about $100,000 ten years later. Average annual compounded rate of return (including stock growth and reinvested dividends): about 26 percent.

DIVIDEND YIELD

The company generally pays a fairly good dividend. Over the past three years the stock has paid an average annual current return of 2.1 percent.

DIVIDEND GROWTH

Sherwin-Williams has raised its dividend nine consecutive years, including an 87 percent increase over the four-year rating period from 1983 to 1987.

SHAREHOLDER PERKS

The company offers a very good dividend reinvestment and voluntary stock purchase plan. There are no fees or commissions, and shareholders of record may buy $10 to $1,000 per month in additional shares through the voluntary cash purchase plan.

SUMMARY

Total revenues: $1.8 billion, 1987. Earnings per share: $2.15, 1987; $0.37, 1976 (1976 earnings were inserted here because the company had a loss in 1977); 481% increase. Stock price: $28, 10/25/88; $3.25 (median), 1978 (762% total increase; 24% annual increase); price rose 8 of 10 years, 1977–87. Dividend: $0.56, 1987; $0.30, 1983; 4-year increase: 87%. Dividend yield: 2.1% average, 1985–1987. P/E ratio: 11, 1/3/89. Average annual total return to investor, 1978–88: about 26%.

21 BARD

C.R. BARD, INC.

730 Central Ave.
Murray Hill, NJ 07974
(201) 277-8000
Chairman: Robert H. McCaffrey
President and CEO: George T. Maloney

EARNINGS GROWTH	★ ★ ★ ★ ★
STOCK GROWTH	★ ★ ★ ★ ★
DIVIDEND YIELD	★ ★
DIVIDEND GROWTH	★ ★ ★ ★
SHAREHOLDER PERKS	★ ★
NYSE—BCR	**18 points**

C. R. Bard may well hold the key to your heart. The company makes angioplasty catheters—tiny tubular devices used to slide through arteries and blood vessels to dislodge lesions that may block the flow of the blood to the heart.

Bard develops and manufactures a wide range of sophisticated cardiovascular, urological and surgical equipment. The company also characterizes itself as a "pioneer in the development of single-use medical products"— surgical instruments and other medical devices that can be used once and thrown away.

The Murray Hill, New Jersey, firm also manufactures prosthetic devices (such as artificial hip replacements), medication-dispensing systems and skin care and wound management products.

Bard, which has been in business for 81 years, has enjoyed exceptionally consistent growth for an emerging medical technology company. It has posted increased sales and earnings for 15 consecutive years.

Bard is little known outside of the medical profession because its products tend to be highly technical. Its primary market is the health-care profession—hospitals, extended-care homes and physicians. It develops and manufactures products such as angioplasty and angiographic catheters and Foley catheters, cardiotomy reservoirs, hemo-concentrators, extracorporeal cannulae, urine-collection systems and implantable blood vessel replacements—not the kind of products you're likely to find on the shelves of your local 7-Eleven.

The company has a strong international presence, particularly in Europe, Japan, Canada and the United Kingdom. International sales account for 19 percent of the company's $641 million in total annual revenue.

Bard's largest division is its cardiovascular group, which accounts for 43 percent of domestic sales.

Its other three product groups include:

- Urological (22 percent of domestic sales). In addition to its Foley catheters and related products, the company makes specialty products such as devices for stone removal, prostate cancer detection, ureteroscopic procedures, incontinence and impotence.
- Surgical (21 percent of domestic sales). The company manufactures systems for electrosurgery, suction and irrigation. It also makes wound drainage and single-use surgical instruments and implantable blood vessel replacements.
- General health (14 percent). Bard makes syringe infusion pumps, medication dispensing pumps, skin-care and wound-management products and disposable obstetrical instruments.

EARNINGS GROWTH

Bard has had 15 consecutive years of record annual sales and earnings. Earnings per share have climbed 478 percent over the past ten years.

The company has 7,200 employees and 5,300 shareholders.

STOCK GROWTH

The company has had excellent stock growth the past decade, with two 2-for-1 stock splits since 1986. The stock price increased eight of ten years from 1977 to 1987. Over the past ten years the stock has soared 740 percent (24 percent per year), from its median of $2.50 in 1978 to its recent 1988 price of $21 a share.

Including reinvested dividends, a $10,000 investment in Bard stock at its median price in 1978 would have grown to about $98,000 ten years later. Average annual compounded rate of return (including stock growth and reinvested dividends): about 25.5 percent.

DIVIDEND YIELD

The company tends to pay a relatively low yield, which has averaged about 1.5 percent over the past ten years. During the three-year rating period from 1985 to 1987, the stock paid an average annual current return of 1.2 percent.

DIVIDEND GROWTH

Bard has raised its dividend more than 15 consecutive years. The dividend was increased 120 percent over the four-year rating period from 1983 to 1987.

SHAREHOLDER PERKS

The company offers its shareholders a good dividend reinvestment and voluntary stock purchase plan. There are no fees or commissions, and shareholders of record may purchase $10 to $1,000 per month in additional shares through the voluntary stock purchase plan.

Aside from a letter of welcome, the company offers its shareholders no other perks. As one company spokesperson put it, "I'm not sure what we could hand out to our stockholders. I don't think anyone would want an artificial hip or a disposable syringe."

SUMMARY

Total revenues: $641 million, 1987. Earnings per share: $1.07, 1987; $0.18, 1977; 478% increase. Stock price: $21, 11/7/88; $2.50 (median), 1978; 740% increase (24% per year); price rose 8 of 10 years, 1977–87. Dividend: $0.22, 1987; $0.10, 1983; 4-year increase: 120%. Dividend yield: 1.2% average, 1985–87. P/E ratio: 18, 1/3/89. Average annual total return to investors, 1978–88: 25.5%.

Kellogg's

KELLOGG COMPANY

Battle Creek, MI 49016-3599
(616) 961-2000
Chairman and CEO: William E. LaMothe

EARNINGS GROWTH	★ ★ ★
STOCK GROWTH	★ ★ ★ ★ ★
DIVIDEND YIELD	★ ★ ★
DIVIDEND GROWTH	★ ★ ★
SHAREHOLDER PERKS	★ ★ ★ ★
NYSE—K	**18 points**

W. K. Kellogg first test-marketed his toasted flake cereals in the late 1880s on the patients of the Battle Creek Sanitarium. The cereal was such a hit with patients that many of them wrote the sanitarium after their release to ask where they might buy more of Kellogg's flakes.

Mr. Kellogg, recognizing a classic market opportunity when he saw one, founded the Battle Creek Toasted Corn Flake Company in 1906, and, as one fabled Kellogg's spokesman would put it, business has been "Grrrreat" ever since.

The Kellogg Company has been one of the most successful corporations in the history of U.S. business. It has had 43 consecutive years of increased sales, 36 straight years of increased earnings and 31 years of increased dividends. Its cereals are sold in about 130 countries.

While W.K. Kellogg will be remembered most for his pioneering efforts in the development of cold cereals, it was his shrewd, aggressive marketing efforts that set his company apart from the competition. A full-page ad in the *Ladies Home Journal* shortly after the company opened in 1906 helped propel his corn flakes sales to 2,900 cases a day. By 1911, Kellogg's advertising budget had swelled to more than $1 million a year. And in 1912 the company erected the world's largest sign on Times Square in New York City—an 80-foot high, 100-foot wide "Kellogg's."

Kellogg introduced 40% Bran Flakes in 1915 and All-Bran in 1916. Rice Krispies first began to snap, crackle and pop on American breakfast tables in 1928.

Through the years, Kellogg has remained primarily a breakfast foods company. In addition to its original favorites, Kellogg produces almost 30 other varieties, including Froot Loops, Frosted Flakes, Nut & Honey Crunch, Special K, Apple Jacks and Fruity Marshmallow Krispies.

Kellogg also owns Mrs. Smith's Frozen Foods, Eggo and Nutri-Grain frozen waffles, Whitney's Yogurt, Salada teas and LeGout soups.

The company has production operations in 17 countries on six continents, including Canada, Australia, Japan, Mexico, the United Kingdom and South Africa (where its wholly owned subidiary, Kellogg Company of South Africa, Ltd., has annual revenues of $18.5 million). U.S. sales account for 66 percent of Kellogg's $3.8 billion in total annual sales, Canada accounts for 5 percent, Europe for 21 percent and all other areas for 8 percent.

EARNINGS GROWTH

Kellogg's string of 36 consecutive earnings increases is among the longest in U.S. business. The company's earnings per share have climbed 253 percent over the past 10 years.

Kellogg has about 17,000 employees and 23,000 shareholders of record.

STOCK GROWTH

Kellogg's stock price growth has not been as consistent as its earnings—increasing eight of the past ten years through 1987—but it has been impressive. Over the past ten years the stock price has climbed 481 percent (19 percent per year), from its median of $10.50 a share in 1978 to its late 1988 price of $61 a share.

Including reinvested dividends, a $10,000 investment in Kellogg stock at its median price in 1978 would have grown to about $95,000 ten years later. Average annual compounded rate of return (including stock growth and reinvested dividends): about 25 percent.

DIVIDEND YIELD

The company generally pays a good yield, which has averaged about 5 percent over the past ten years. During the three-year rating period from 1985 to 1987, the stock paid an average annual current return of 2.6 percent.

DIVIDEND GROWTH

Kellogg has raised its dividend each year for 31 consecutive years. The company increased the dividend 59 percent over the four-year rating period from 1983 to 1987.

SHAREHOLDER PERKS

All new shareholders of record of Kellogg Company receive a welcome kit with brochures and reports on the company along with a pair of coupons for free grocery products such as cereal, frozen waffles or one of Kellogg's newer products.

Those attending the annual meetings in Battle Creek, Michigan, also receive a package of product samples and coupons for other Kellogg's products. The company may also hand out special gifts, such as the decorative plates that were given to shareholders at the 1988 meeting.

Kellogg has a good dividend reinvestment and stock purchase plan. There is no fee, and shareholders may contribute $25 to $2,500 per month to the stock purchase plan.

SUMMARY

Total revenues: $3.8 billion, 1987. Earnings per share: $3.20, 1987; $0.91, 1977; 252% increase. Stock price: $61, 11/9/88; $10.50 (median), 1978 (481% total increase; 19% annual increase); price rose 8 of 10 years, 1977–87. Dividend: $1.29, 1987; $0.81, 1983; 4-year increase: 59%. Dividend yield: 2.6%, 1985–1987. P/E ratio: 17, 1/3/89. Average annual total return to investor, 1978–88: about 25%.

23

TORCHMARK CORPORATION

2001 Third Ave. South
Birmingham, AL 35233
(205) 325-4200
Chairman and CEO: R. K. Richey
President: Jon W. Rotenstreich

EARNINGS GROWTH	★ ★ ★ ★
STOCK GROWTH	★ ★ ★ ★
DIVIDEND YIELD	★ ★ ★
DIVIDEND GROWTH	★ ★ ★ ★ ★
SHAREHOLDER PERKS	★ ★
NYSE—TMK	**18 points**

Torchmark is your one-stop, all-purpose financial services supermarket. Through its small battery of subsidiaries—including Liberty National Insurance and Waddell & Reed financial services—the company manages its own family of mutual funds; oversees several limited partnerships; handles a wide range of life, health and casualty insurance policies and offers a number of other investment services for individuals and institutions. In the process, Torchmark has managed to turn a few of those investment dollars its own way: The company has had a remarkable string of 36 consecutive years of increased earnings and dividends.

Liberty National Insurance is Torchmark's largest subsidiary, with nearly $20 billion of life insurance in force and annual total premiums of more than $400 million. Liberty employs 2,500 agents in 109 sales offices throughout the Southeast. The company sells a complete line of life and health insurance and annuity policies.

Liberty's casualty insurance arm, Liberty National Fire, offers a range of fire, property and casualty insurance for individuals and businesses.

Waddell & Reed (which is a branch of United Investors Management Company, a Torchmark subsidiary) offers financial planning services for individual investors and investment management services for large institutional investors. The company manages 16 mutual funds with assets of $6 billion and offers a number of other investment products, including real estate and equipment leasing limited partnerships. Waddell & Reed reps also sell life and health insurance policies from one of its affiliate companies, United Investors Life, and oil and gas limited partnerships managed by another affiliate, Torch Energy.

Waddell & Reed's national sales force of about 5,000 representatives (covering all 50 states) attracts its client base, in large part, through public seminars on money management aimed at individual investors. The company's representatives conduct nearly 4,000 seminars a year, which draw about 100,000 prospective clients.

Torchmark's other two major subsidiaries are United American Insurance, which sells Medicare supplement insurance through some 58,000 independent agents nationwide, and Globe Life and Accident Insurance, which markets its policies through 1,500 independent agents in 73 branch offices.

EARNINGS GROWTH

Torchmark has had a flawless record of earnings growth for more than three decades, with 36 consecutive years of increased earnings. Its earnings per share have climbed 324 percent over the past ten years.

Torchmark reported total revenues of $1.6 billion in 1987. The company has 6,250 employees (2,300 home office employees, 550 field clerical workers, and 3,400 agency personnel). The company also uses the services of about 72,000 independent agents and brokers. Torchmark has 10,000 shareholders of record.

STOCK GROWTH

The company's stock price has appreciated steadily the past decade, with two 2-for-1 stock splits since 1984. Over the past ten years the stock has increased 439 percent (18.5 percent per year), from its median of $5.75 in 1978 to its recent 1988 price of $31 a share.

Including reinvested dividends, a $10,000 investment in Torchmark stock at its median price in 1978 would have grown to about $82,000 ten years later. Average annual compounded rate of return (including stock growth and reinvested dividends): about 23.5 percent.

DIVIDEND YIELD

The company generally pays a good dividend yield, which has averaged about 4.5 percent over the past ten years. During the three-year rating period from 1985 to 1987, the stock paid an average annual current return of 3 percent.

DIVIDEND GROWTH

Torchmark has increased its dividend 36 consecutive years. The dividend surged 150 percent over the four-year rating period from 1983 to 1987.

SHAREHOLDER PERKS

The company offers its shareholders of record a dividend reinvestment and voluntary stock purchase plan. Shareholders of record may purchase up to $3,000 per quarter in additional shares through the voluntary purchase plan. Participants are charged a small service fee.

SUMMARY

Total revenues: $1.6 billion, 1987. Earnings per share: $2.80, 1987; $0.66, 1977; 324% increase. Stock price: $31, 11/4/88; $5.75 (median), 1978 439% increase (18.5% per year); price rose 9 of 10 years, 1977–87. Dividend: $1, 1987; $0.40, 1983; 4-year increase: 150%. Dividend yield: 3% average, 1985–1987. P/E ratio: 10, 1/3/89. Average annual total return to investors, 1978–88: 23.5%.

24

ALEXANDER & BALDWIN

822 Bishop St.
P.O. Box 3440
Honolulu, HA 96801
(808) 525-6611
Chairman and CEO: R. J. Pfeiffer
President: John C. Couch

EARNINGS GROWTH	★ ★ ★ ★ ★
STOCK GROWTH	★ ★ ★ ★ ★
DIVIDEND YIELD	★ ★ ★
DIVIDEND GROWTH	★ ★ ★ ★
SHAREHOLDER PERKS	(no points)
OTC—ALEX	**17 points**

In 1870, long before the Hawaiian islands were to become America's paradise in the Pacific, Alexander & Baldwin began harvesting sugarcane in the fertile fields of the Maui and Kauai islands. Today, the company's 13 Hawaiian plantations supply nearly 300,000 tons of sugar a year to mainland America.

The Honolulu-based firm has experienced exceptional growth over the past decade, with an average annual return to shareholders of 34 percent.

In recent years, Alexander & Baldwin has sweetened its corporate balance sheet considerably by expanding into ocean shipping and property development. Through its Matson Navigation subsidiary, Alexander & Baldwin has become the principal carrier of ocean cargo between Hawaii and the West Coast.

Its shipping business has become the company's primary source of income, accounting for 66 percent of its $655 million in total annual revenue and 60 percent of its operating income. Each year, the company's fleet of container ships and barges haul about 200,000 24-foot containers of cargo and nearly 80,000 automobiles between Hawaii and the West Coast.

Alexander & Baldwin has also been active in the lucrative property development business in Hawaii. Its biggest year was 1987, when it collected total income of $85 million through property sales and commercial and industrial rental. Typically, the company contracts with outside developers to construct housing and resort facilities on its properties. The company then either leases or sells the developed properties. The company owns 95,000 acres of land in Hawaii.

Its sugarcane operation is now the least profitable of the company's three core business segments. Sugar and molasses sales account for about 20 percent of total revenue, but only about 10 percent of operating income.

EARNINGS GROWTH

Alexander & Baldwin has posted excellent earnings growth over the past decade, with earnings gains eight of ten years through 1987 and a 519 percent earnings per share increase over the ten-year period.

The company employs about 350 people and has 7,000 shareholders.

STOCK GROWTH

Alexander & Baldwin's stock has experienced exceptional growth over the past decade, rising nearly 1,064 percent (28 percent per year), from its median of $2.75 a share in 1978 to its late 1988 price of $32.

The stock has had two 2-for-1 splits and one 3-for-2 split since 1984.

Including reinvested dividends, a $10,000 investment in Alexander & Baldwin stock at its median price in 1978 would be worth about $190,000 ten years later. Average annual compounded rate of return (including stock growth and reinvested dividends): about 34 percent.

DIVIDEND YIELD

The company has traditionally paid a very good dividend, with an average annual yield over the past ten years of just over 5 percent. During the three-year rating period from 1985 to 1987, the stock paid an average annual current return of 3.3 percent.

DIVIDEND GROWTH

Alexander has not made a habit of raising its dividend each year, although it has raised it the past five consecutive years. The dividend was increased 109 percent during the four-year rating period from 1983 to 1987.

SHAREHOLDER PERKS   (no points)

The company provides no dividend reinvestment plan for its shareholders, nor does it offer any other shareholder perks.

SUMMARY

Total revenues: $655 million, 1987. Earnings per share: $2.23, 1987; $0.36, 1977; 519% increase. Stock price: $32, 9/13/88; $2.75 (median), 1978 (1,064% total increase; 28% annual increase; price rose 8 of 10 years, 1978-88. Dividend: $0.68, 1987; $0.33, 1983; 4-year increase: 109%. Dividend yield: 3.3% average, 1985-1987. P/E ratio: 11, 1/3/89. Average annual total return to investor, 1978-88: about 34%.

25

SAFETY-KLEEN CORP.

777 Big Timber Road
Elgin, IL 60123
(312) 697-8460
Chairman: Russell A. Gwillim
President and CEO: Donald W. Brinckman

EARNINGS GROWTH	★ ★ ★ ★ ★
STOCK GROWTH	★ ★ ★ ★ ★
DIVIDEND YIELD	★ ★
DIVIDEND GROWTH	★ ★ ★ ★ ★
SHAREHOLDER PERKS	(no points)
NYSE—SK	**17 points**

To anyone who thought "waste" was a dirty word, Safety-Kleen offers a fresh perspective. The upstart Elgin, Illinois, waste treatment company has become a world leader in recycling hazardous solutions. It collects millions of gallons of used cleaning solvent, paint thinner and motor oil each year; cleans it, processes it and returns it to useable form; then routes it back to its clients for repeated use.

The company's process has not only been a boon for the environment, it's also been a windfall for Safety-Kleen. The firm's earnings have grown more than 20 percent per year for 17 consecutive years—a growth rate the company claims is an American business record.

Safety-Kleen's primary clients include auto repair and body shops, manufacturing facilities and dry cleaning services. Although the company has been in business only since 1969 (and publicly traded since 1979), it already has more than 300,000 customers worldwide. It has more than 160 branch offices in the U.S., plus wholly owned subsidiaries in Canada, Puerto Rico and the United Kingdom; joint ventures in France and Spain: and licensees in Australia, Japan, New Zealand and West Germany.

The company's largest concentration of business is in the auto repair services industry. Safety-Kleen provides parts cleaning services for more than 200,000 automotive businesses such as service stations, car dealers, small engine repair shops and fleet maintenance shops. The company leases and services parts cleaning equipment designed to remove the build-up of gum and varnish from carburetors, fuel injection ports, transmission parts and other engine components. Safety-Kleen makes regular service visits to clean and maintain the cleaning equipment, and to replace the spent material with fresh solvent. The spent solvent is then returned to one of Safety-Kleen's recycling centers where it is cleaned and prepared for use again.

Safety-Kleen provides a similar service for 16,000 dry cleaning shops that use the company's recycled cleaning solution.

Another Safety-Kleen sideline is a paint refinishing service the company offers for automotive body shops, dealerships and manufacturing plants. As part of the service, the company supplies cleaned buffing pads, offers spray gun cleaning assistance, and removes and recycles used paint thinner.

In 1987, the company acquired Breslube Enterprises of Breslau, Ontario, the leading re-refiner of used lubricating oils in North America. While oil refining is, at best, only marginally profitable at this time, as oil prices rise and re-refining techniques become more efficient, the service could become increasingly lucrative.

EARNINGS GROWTH

Safety-Kleen has had a sensational record of growth, with 17 consecutive years of record earnings. Earnings per share have increased 715 percent over the past 10 years.

With total annual revenues of $334 million, Safety-Kleen is one of the smallest company's on the *Best 100* list, but it is the world market leader in all of the services it offers. The company has about 3,500 employees and an equal number of shareholders of record.

STOCK GROWTH

The company did not go public until 1979, but since then its stock has split 3-for-2 four times and 2-for-1 once. The stock price has climbed steadily, soaring 1,060 percent (31 percent per year) over the nine-year period from 1979 to 1988.

Including reinvested dividends, a $10,000 investment in Safety-Kleen stock at its median price in 1979 would have grown to about $120,000 nine years later. Average annual compounded rate of return (including stock growth and reinvested dividends): about 31 percent.

DIVIDEND YIELD

Safety-Kleen has traditionally paid a fairly low dividend yield. Over the past three years the stock has paid an average annual current return of 1 percent.

DIVIDEND GROWTH

The company has increased its dividend each year since it went public in 1979. Over the four-year rating period from 1983 to 1987, the dividend jumped 167 percent, from (a split-adjusted) 9 cents per year to 24 cents.

SHAREHOLDER PERKS   (no points)

The company does not offer a dividend reinvestment plan, nor does it offer any other perks.

SUMMARY

Total revenues: $334 million, 1987. Earnings per share: $1.06, 1987; $0.13, 1977; 715% increase. Stock price: $29, 10/21/88; $2.50 (median), 1979 (1,060% total increase; 31% annual increase); price rose 7 of 8 years, 1979–87 (the company was not taken public until 1979). Dividend: $0.24, 1987; $0.09, 1983; 4-year increase: 167%. Dividend yield: 1% average, 1985–1987. P/E ratio: 21, 1/3/89. Average annual total return to investor, 1978–88: about 32%.

26 *Walgreens*

WALGREEN CO.

200 Wilmot Road
Deerfield, IL 60015
(312) 940-2500
Chairman and CEO: Charles R. Walgreen III
President: Fred F. Canning

EARNINGS GROWTH	★ ★ ★ ★
STOCK GROWTH	★ ★ ★ ★ ★
DIVIDEND YIELD	★ ★
DIVIDEND GROWTH	★ ★ ★
SHAREHOLDER PERKS	★ ★ ★
NYSE—WAG	**17 points**

It's hard to get a fix on Walgreen. The company describes itself as "first and foremost a drugstore," but only 25 percent of its revenues actually come from prescription drugs. Instead, many of its 1,450 stores carry a seemingly disjointed array of general merchandise—clocks, calculators, costume jewelry, artwork, pop, beer, lunch buckets, wastebaskets, coffee makers, mixers, telephones, tape decks and TV sets along with the usual line of cosmetics, toiletries and tobacco.

But, in truth, there is nothing disjointed about Walgreen's prescription for succcess in the highly competitive retail drugstore market. Any doubts about that are quickly dispelled by one look at the company's growth record, which includes 14 consecutive years of record sales and earnings.

With its spacious stores—which average about 9,500 square-feet—and broad line of merchandise, Walgreen is targeting the convenience shopper. In addition to the usual drugs and general merchandise, more than 500 Walgreen stores now carry dairy products, frozen foods and other grocery items. Walgreen has also extended its store hours in recent years. In fact, about 75 Walgreen outlets now offer 24-hour service.

The company has been expanding rapidly, adding about 100 new stores per year. More than half of Walgreen's stores have opened since 1982. But unlike many growing retail chains, most of Walgreen's growth has come internally by building its own stores, rather than through an aggressive acquisition policy. It has, however, deviated from tradition in a couple of cases recently, acquiring the 66-store Medi Mart chain in the Northeast and the 26-store Ribordy chain in northern Indiana.

Walgreen's stores are located in 30 states and Puerto Rico. Its biggest concentration is in and around its Chicago home base, where Charles R. Walgreen, Sr. opened his first store in 1901. (His grandson, 52-year-old Charles R. Walgreen III, is currently the company's chairman and chief executive officer.) The company operates about 250 stores in the Chicago area, 80 in Wisconsin and 60 in Indiana. Walgreen is also big in Texas, where it owns about 180 stores, and it is staking out a growing presence in Arizona, where it owns about 80 stores. The company's biggest growth area is Florida, where it operates about 220 stores and has another 50 locations under consideration.

Walgreen leads all U.S. retail stores in terms of prescriptions filled. The company fills nearly 5 percent of all prescriptions, while operating about 2.5 percent of all U.S. drugstores. Walgreen management credits its "Intercom" on-line pharmacy computer system with part of its success in bolstering its prescription trade—which has been growing at nearly 30 percent per year the past several years. The Intercom system maintains customer records, offers simplified transferability of prescriptions between stores and automatically alerts pharmacists to the availability of less-expensive generic prescriptions.

Walgreen's drugstore operations account for about 97 percent of its $4.9 billion a year in total sales. The company also owns about 90 Wag's 24-hour family restaurants, which are located primarily in Florida and the Chicago area.

EARNINGS GROWTH

Walgreen has had excellent earnings growth, with 14 consecutive years of increased earnings. Earnings per share have climbed 367 percent over the past decade.

Walgreen has 45,000 employees and 21,000 shareholders of record.

STOCK GROWTH

The company's stock price has climbed quickly through the past decade, with two 2-for-1 stock splits since 1981. Over the past ten years the stock has increased 967 percent (26.5 percent per year), from its median of $3 in 1978 to its recent 1988 price of $31 a share.

Including reinvested dividends, a $10,000 investment in Walgreen's stock at its median price in 1978 would have grown to about $140,000 ten years later. Average annual compounded rate of return (including stock growth and reinvested dividends): about 30 percent.

DIVIDEND YIELD

The company's dividend yield has been steadily declining since the mid-1970s, when the yield reached a peak of just over 8 percent. During the three-year rating period from 1986 to 1988, the stock paid an average annual current return of 1.6 percent.

DIVIDEND GROWTH

While the yield has been dropping nearly every year, the actual cash pay-out has increased each year for more than a decade. The dividend increased 67 percent over the four-year rating period from 1984 to 1988.

SHAREHOLDER PERKS

Shareholders who attend the Walgreen annual meeting usually receive one or two Walgreen products. At a recent annual meeting, the company passed out a bottle of 160 Super Aytinal multi-vitamin pills.

The company also offers its shareholders of record a good dividend re-investment and voluntary stock purchase plan. There are no fees or commissions, and shareholders of record may contribute $10 to $1,000 to the voluntary stock purchase plan up to eight times per year.

SUMMARY

Total revenues: $4.88 billion, fiscal 1988 (ended 8/31/88). Earnings per share: $2.10, 1988; $0.45, 1978; 367% increase. Stock price: $32, 11/3/88; $3.00 (median), 1978; 967% increase (26.5% per year); price rose 10 of 10 years, 1977–87. Dividend: $.60, 1988; $0.36, 1984; 4-year increase: 67%. Dividend yield: 1.6% average, 1986–1988. P/E ratio: 14, 1/3/89. Average annual total return to investors, 1978–88: about 30%.

27

Shaw Industries, Inc.

SHAW INDUSTRIES, INC.
P.O. Drawer 2128
Dalton, GA 30722-2128
(404)-278-3812
Chairman: J.C. Shaw
President and CEO: Robert E. Shaw

EARNINGS GROWTH	★★★★★
STOCK GROWTH	★★★★
DIVIDEND YIELD	★★★
DIVIDEND GROWTH	★★★★★
SHAREHOLDER PERKS	(no points)
NYSE—SHX	**17 points**

It's not easy being a high-flier in the kind of low-to-the-ground business that Shaw Industries is in. Its competition is always under foot; its customers are constantly calling it on the carpet.

But Shaw doesn't mind. The Georgia-based manufacturer is in the carpet business. In fact, with sales of nearly $1 billion a year, Shaw is the largest carpet manufacturer in the U.S.

Shaw Industries is a relatively young company, formed in 1967 by brothers J.C. and Robert E. Shaw. The brothers, now in their late fifties, still serve as chairman and president, respectively, and control about 15 percent of the stock.

In an era of rampant diversification, Shaw has stuck to its knitting. Carpet is not only Shaw's principal business, it's its only business. Shaw's carpeting is marketed under the Magee, Philadelphia and Cabin Craft labels, as well as some private labels for distributors and retailers. The company sells carpeting through about 20,000 retail stores and 300 wholesale distributors in the United States. It also claims some foreign sales, although its foreign business accounts for less than 1 percent of the company's total revenue.

Like 95 percent of the U.S. carpeting industry, Shaw makes "tufted" carpet from nylon yarn. Shaw is vertically integrated, handling every step of the carpet-making process—spinning the fiber, dyeing it, weaving the rug and cutting it to size. In all, Shaw makes nearly 300 styles of tufted carpet for residential and commercial customers.

A couple of other factors have helped Shaw rise to top of the carpet industry over its roughly 250 U.S. competitors. Through its rather aggressive acquisitions program, the company has been able to bring some of the best-known carpet brands into its fold. By integrating those operations and marketing them through one sales force, it has been able to reduce overhead and sales costs. It also attempts to provide more efficient and timely distribution through its 10 regional distibution centers.

EARNINGS GROWTH

Shaw Industries has had excellent earnings growth, with earnings increases nine of the past ten years (through fiscal 1988). The company's earnings per share have jumped 526 percent over the past decade.

Shaw has nearly 10,000 employees and 1,500 shareholders of record.

STOCK GROWTH

Shaw's stock price has been erratic but dramatic the past decade, with increases only six of the past ten years, but with a total increase over the period of 820 percent (25 percent per year). The company has had one 4-for-3 stock split and one 2-for-1 split since 1983.

Including reinvested dividends, a $10,000 investment in Shaw stock at its median price in 1978 would have grown to about $140,000 ten years later. Average annual compounded rate of return (including stock growth and reinvested dividends): about 30 percent.

DIVIDEND YIELD

The company generally pays a fairly good dividend yield, which has averaged about 4.5 percent over the past ten years. During the three-year rating period from 1985 to 1987, the stock paid an average annual current return of 2.6 percent.

DIVIDEND GROWTH

Shaw has not made a habit of raising its dividend each year, although it has had increased dividends the past five years. Over the four-year rating period from 1984 to 1988, the company raised its dividend 170 percent, from 24 cents to 65 cents.

SHAREHOLDER PERKS (no points)

Shaw Industries offers no dividend reinvestment plan for its shareholders, nor does it provide any other perks.

SUMMARY

Total revenues: $958 million, for fiscal 1988 (ended 5/31/88). Earnings per share: $2.13, 1988; $0.34, 1978; 526% increase. Stock price: $23, 8/17/88; $2.50 (median), 1978 (820% total increase; 25% annual increase); price rose 6 of 10 years, 1977-87. Dividend: $0.65, 1988; $0.24, 1984; 4-year increase: 170%. Dividend yield: 2.6%, 1986-1988. P/E ratio: 10, 1/3/89. Average annual total return to investor, 1978-88: about 30%.

SARA LEE CORPORATION

SARA LEE CORPORATION

Three First National Plaza
Chicago, IL 60602-4260
(312) 726-2600
Chairman and CEO: John H. Bryan, Jr.
President: Paul Fulton

EARNINGS GROWTH	★ ★ ★
STOCK GROWTH	★ ★ ★ ★ ★
DIVIDEND YIELD	★ ★ ★
DIVIDEND GROWTH	★ ★ ★
SHAREHOLDER PERKS	★ ★ ★
NYSE—SLE	**17 points**

Sara Lee is the market leader in America's fast and fattening trade. The Chicago-based sweets specialist has built its business by aggressively marketing its line of prebaked frozen cheese cakes, pound cakes, snack cakes, coffee cakes, muffins, cinnamon rolls and other baked goods to consumers who want to have their cake and their free time, too. The company holds a 38 percent share of the U.S. frozen pastries market. And its string of 13 years of earnings increases—and a 28 percent average annual return to its shareholders over the past ten years—has been the icing on the cake.

But Sara Lee is a lot more than just desserts. Through acquisitions and internal growth, the company has mustered a broad line of other well-known food and consumer products. With annual revenues of $10.4 billion, Sara Lee ranks as one of the three or four largest food companies in the U.S.

The company is particularly strong in the frozen meats market. Its Jimmy Dean breakfast sausage is the U.S. market leader in its segment, and the company's Hillshire Farm smoked sausage is the national leader in its category. Hillshire also markets a number of other packaged meats, including ham, bacon and Chi-Town Franks. Bil Mar Foods, another Sara Lee subsidiary, is the country's third largest retail turkey producer. Sara Lee's packaged meats and bakery division accounts for about one-third of the company's $10.4 billion a year in total revenue.

In addition to its packaged meats and bakery division, Sara Lee breaks its operations down into four other key segments:

- Packaged consumer products (20 percent of sales). Sara Lee is a leading manufacturer of women's hosiery. It owns both Hanes (Isotoner and Silk Reflections) and L'eggs (Sheer Energy and Sheer Elegance). The company also owns Fuller Brush and Coach Leatherware, a 24-store chain of leather goods.
- Food service (22 percent of sales). Sara Lee's PYA/Monarch supplies food and nonfood items to institutional food dining facilities (at hospitals, schools, factories, etc.). PYA/Monarch is the nation's third largest food service operation. Sara Lee also owns Lyon's Restaurants, a chain of 63 24-hour restaurants in the western U.S.
- Household and personal care products (11 percent of sales). Sara Lee recently acquired the Kiwi line of shoe polish, Esquire shoe polish and Ty-D-bol toilet bowl cleaner. The acquisitions make Sara Lee the leading U.S. manufacturer of both shoe polish and toilet bowl cleaner.
- Coffee and grocery products (16 percent of sales). Sara Lee owns Douwe Egbert, one of Europe's leading brands of coffee and tea, Duyvis nuts, the leading retail nut brand in the Netherlands, and Benenuts, France's leading line of nuts.

Sara Lee has operations in more than 30 countries and markets its products in 145 countries. About 26 percent of the company's revenue is generated through sales outside of the U.S.

EARNINGS GROWTH

Sara Lee has had 13 consecutive years of increased earnings. Its earnings per share have climbed 254 percent over the past decade.

The company has annual revenues of $10.4 billion. It has 82,000 employees and 45,000 shareholders of record.

STOCK GROWTH

The company's stock has performed very well over the past decade, particularly since 1980. The stock has had two 2-for-1 splits since 1983. Over the past ten years the stock has increased 636 percent (22 percent per year), from its median of $6.25 in 1978 to its recent 1988 price of $46 a share.

Including reinvested dividends, a $10,000 investment in Sara Lee stock at its median price in 1978 would have grown to about $120,000 ten years later. Average annual compounded rate of return (including stock growth and reinvested dividends): about 28 percent.

DIVIDEND YIELD

The company has traditionally paid a very good dividend, which has averaged about 5 percent over the past ten years. During the three-year rating period from 1986 to 1988, the stock paid an average annual current return of 2.8 percent.

DIVIDEND GROWTH

Sara Lee raises its dividend most years. The dividend increased 80 percent over the four-year rating period from 1984 to 1988.

SHAREHOLDER PERKS

Each year at the annual meeting, Sara Lee shareholders receive a gift box of Sara Lee products, including such items as Kiwi shoe polish and L'eggs or Hanes hosiery, plus a handful of coupons for foods such as Jimmy Dean and Hillshire Farm meats and Sara Lee frozen desserts.

The company also offers its shareholders of record a dividend reinvestment and voluntary stock purchase plan. There are no fees or commissions, and shareholders of record may purchase $5 to $1,500 per quarter in additional shares through the voluntary stock purchase plan.

SUMMARY

Total revenues: $10.4 billion, fiscal 1988 (ended 7/2/88). Earnings per share: $2.83, 1988; $0.80, 1978; 254% increase. Stock price: $46, 11/7/88; $6.25 (median), 1978; 636% increase (22% per year); price rose 8 of 10 years, 1977–87. Dividend: $1.15, 1988; $0.64, 1984; 4-year increase: 80%. Dividend yield: 2.8% average, 1985–1987. P/E ratio: 14, 1/3/89. Average annual total return to investors, 1978–88: about 28%.

29

STANHOME, INC.

333 Western Ave.
Westfield, MA 01085
(413) 562-3631
Chairman, President and CEO: H.L. Tower

EARNINGS GROWTH	★ ★ ★
STOCK GROWTH	★ ★ ★ ★ ★
DIVIDEND YIELD	★ ★ ★ ★
DIVIDEND GROWTH	★ ★ ★
SHAREHOLDER PERKS	★ ★
NYSE—STH	**17 points**

One of Stanhome's key ventures is a Tupperware-style direct sales venture for homemakers called the "Famous Stanley Hostess Party Plan." The program has indeed had its share of success, but "famous" may be stretching things a bit. As a recent research report from Shearson Lehman Hutton notes, "To say that Stanhome is an obscure company is to shout the obvious."

Stanhome is, however, beginning to draw a following on Wall Street thanks to its outstanding stock and earnings growth over the past few years.

The company has two primary lines of business: its direct sales program and a giftware business. The giftware business, which Stanhome handles through its wholly owned subsidiary, Enesco Imports (acquired in 1983), accounts for about 47 percent of the company's earnings.

Enesco's line of giftware includes porcelain figurines, brassware, tinware, music boxes, dolls and ornaments produced primarily in the Far East. Trademarks include Country Cousins, Treasured Memories, Growing Up, Precious Moments, Garfield, Lucy and Me, '57 Heaven and Superman.

Its giftware is sold in 50,000 retail stores and through the Precious Moments collectors club, which has more than 300,000 members.

Stanhome's direct selling business is a worldwide venture that has had excellent success in Europe. The company uses its direct selling network to market a wide line of household and personal care products, including brooms, brushes, mops, pesticides, cosmetics, toiletries, weight loss products and vitamins.

Most of the sales are made through the Famous Stanley Hostess parties, in which homemakers invite friends and neighbors to their homes for a demonstration of the products by an independent Stanley dealer. The sponsoring hostess generally receives prizes or gifts from the dealer for organizing the gathering.

The direct sales business accounts for just over 50 percent of the company's operating earnings.

The company also has a small industrial business that supplies cleaning systems and products to industrial clients.

The Westfield, Massachusetts, company does business throughout the world, including France, Spain, Canada, Mexico, Hong Kong, West Germany and Central America.

EARNINGS GROWTH

Stanhome has had fairly steady earnings growth over the past decade, with earnings gains eight of the past ten years through 1987. Earnings per share have moved up 295 percent over the past decade.

The company has total annual revenues of $433 million. It has about 4,000 employees and a like number of shareholders of record.

STOCK GROWTH

The company's stock price has had excellent growth over the past decade, with three 2-for-1 stock splits since 1984. Over the past ten years the stock has increased 700 percent (21.5 percent per year), from its median of $2.50 in 1978 to its recent 1988 price of $20 a share.

Including reinvested dividends, a $10,000 investment in Stanhome stock at its median price in 1978 would have grown to about $120,000 ten years later. Average annual compounded rate of return (including stock growth and reinvested dividends): about 28 percent.

DIVIDEND YIELD

The company generally pays an excellent dividend yield, which has averaged about 6 percent over the past ten years. During the three-year rating period from 1985 to 1987, the stock paid an average annual current return of 4.1 percent.

DIVIDEND GROWTH

Stanhome raises its dividend most years. The company increased its dividend 71 percent over the four-year rating period from 1983 to 1987.

SHAREHOLDER PERKS

The company offers a good dividend reinvestment and voluntary stock purchase plan for its shareholders. There are no fees or service charges, and shareholders may contribute $10 to $5,000 per quarter to the stock purchase plan.

SUMMARY

Total revenues: $433 million, 1987. Earnings per share: $1.58, 1987; $0.40, 1977; 296% increase. Stock price: $20, 9/6/88; $2.50 (median), 1978 (700% total increase; 21.5% annual increase); price rose 8 of 10 years, 1977–87. Dividend: $0.47, 1987; $0.28, 1983; 4-year increase: 71%. Dividend yield: 4.1% average, 1985–1987. P/E ratio: 10, 1/3/89. Average annual total return to investors, 1978–88: about 28%.

HERSHEY FOODS CORPORATION

100 Mansion Road East
P.O. Box 814
Hershey, PA 17033-0810
(717) 534-7500
Chairman and CEO: Richard A. Zimmerman
President: Kenneth L. Wolfe

EARNINGS GROWTH	★ ★
STOCK GROWTH	★ ★ ★ ★ ★
DIVIDEND YIELD	★ ★ ★
DIVIDEND GROWTH	★ ★ ★
SHAREHOLDER PERKS	★ ★ ★ ★
NYSE—HSY	**17 points**

For decades, the sweet smell of chocolate has wafted like a steady sea breeze over Hershey, Pennsylvania. This is Chocolatetown, USA, hometown of the nation's leading producer of chocolates and confectionary products.

A simple listing of the Hershey's leading products is enough to send even the most devoted dieters back on a bender. The list includes: Big Block, Special Dark, Golden Almond, Kit Kat, Rolo Caramels, Mr. Goodbar, Hershey's Kisses, Marabou Mint Crisp, Reese's Pieces, 5th Avenue, Twizzlers, Krackel, Bar None, Queen Anne chocolate cherries, Skor, the original Hershey's chocolate bar and Hershey's chocolate bar with almonds.

About two-thirds of Hershey's $2.4 billion in annual revenue comes from its candy operations. The company has maintained strong growth the past few years through some strategic acquisitions and new product introductions.

Among the company's most significant recent acquisitions were Luden's (Luden's cough drops, 5th Avenue and Luden's Mello Mints) and Queen Anne (chocolate-covered cherries). In 1987, the company also acquired Nabisco's Canadian confectionary operations, which includes (for the Canadian market only) Life Savers, Oh Henry, Planters nuts, Bubble Yum bubble gum, Care Free chewing gum and several other candies.

Hershey has improved its candy sales in recent years through a beefed-up advertising budget. In 1970, advertising and promotional expenses amounted to about 4 percent of revenues. By contrast, in 1987 the company devoted 11.5 percent of revenues—$31 million—to its advertising program.

The company's other key group is its pasta division. With such brands as American Beauty, San Giorgio, Skinner, Delmonico, P & R and Light 'N Fluffy, the pasta group accounts for 9 percent of Hershey's total annual revenue.

Hershey sold its chain of Friendly's restaurants in September 1988 to the Tennessee Restaurant Company, which also owns Perkins Restaurants. Friendly's, which operates about 850 family restaurants throughout the Northeast and parts of the Midwest, accounted for about 25 percent of Hershey's total revenue. Friendly's had turned in some disappointing results in recent years, with declining sales and earnings.

EARNINGS GROWTH

Hershey has had nine consecutive years of increased earnings per share. Earnings per share have moved up 230 percent over the past decade.

The company has 16,000 employees and 24,000 shareholders. Milton Hershey School owns 99 percent of the voting stock and 31 percent of Hershey common stock.

STOCK GROWTH

The company's stock price has climbed quickly through the past decade, with one 2-for-1 stock split and one 3-for-1 split since 1983. Over the past ten years the stock increased 614 percent (22 percent per year), from its median of $3.50 in 1978 to its late 1988 price of $25 a share.

Including reinvested dividends, a $10,000 investment in Hershey stock at its median price in 1978 would have grown to about $110,000 ten years later. Average annual compounded rate of return (including stock growth and reinvested dividends): about 27 percent.

DIVIDEND YIELD

The company generally pays a fairly good yield, which has averaged about 4.5 percent over the past ten years. During the three-year rating period from 1985 to 1987, the stock paid an average annual current return of 2.6 percent.

DIVIDEND GROWTH

Hershey has increased its dividend 13 consecutive years. The dividend was raised 57 percent over the four-year rating period from 1983 to 1987.

SHAREHOLDER PERKS

Hershey makes Christmas shopping a lot easier for shareholders with chocolate-loving friends. Each year Hershey mails its Christmas gift catalog exclusively to shareholders of record. Shareholders may purchase special gift packages from the catalog and have them wrapped and mailed directly to their friends by Hershey.

Shareholders who attend the annual meeting are treated to a packet of Hershey goodies. At the 1988 annual meeting shareholders received some coupons for Friendly Restaurants, a Golden Almond bar, a Symphony chocolate and toffee bar, a six-pack of Bar None bars, a box of pasta and a few other samples.

Hershey also offers a good dividend reinvestment and voluntary stock purchase plan. Shareholders may buy up to $20,000 in additional stock each year through the company plan with no commission or fees.

SUMMARY

Total revenues: $2.4 billion, 1987. Earnings per share: $1.64, 1987; $0.50, 1977; 230% increase. Stock price: $25, 11/9/88; $3.50 (median), 1978; 614% increase (22% per year); price rose 9 of 10 years, 1977-87. Dividend: $0.58, 1987; $0.37, 1983; 4-year increase: 57%. Dividend yield: 2.6% average, 1985-1987. P/E ratio: 11, 1/3/89*. Average annual total return to investors, 1978-88: about 27%.

---

*Includes earnings of $53.4 million from sale of Friendly's restaurants. P/E based on earnings from continuing operations is about 16.

31

RALSTON PURINA COMPANY

Checkerboard Square
St. Louis, Missouri 63164
(314) 982-1000
Chairman and CEO: William P. Stiritz

EARNINGS GROWTH	★ ★ ★
STOCK GROWTH	★ ★ ★ ★ ★
DIVIDEND YIELD	★ ★
DIVIDEND GROWTH	★ ★ ★
SHAREHOLDER PERKS	★ ★ ★ ★
NYSE—RAL	**17 points**

Ralston Purina. The name has long been synonymous with dog chow, chicken feed and checkerboards. And indeed, the St. Louis-based food processor still leads the world in dried pet-food production. But it is Ralston's bakery goods division—Twinkies, Cupcakes, Suzy Q's, Choco-Bliss, Ding Dongs and Fruit Pies from Hostess, and Wonder bread from Continental Baking Company—that now takes the cake in total sales among all of the company's product groups.

Ralston Purina is among the ten largest food products companies in the U.S. Nearly one-third of its $5.9 billion in annual sales come from Ralston's Continental Bakery Company, which it acquired in 1984. In addition to its famed snack cakes, Continental operates about 600 Thrift stores that serve as outlets for its surplus bakery goods.

Among Ralston's brand name foods, the most recognizable are Wheat Chex, Rice Chex and Corn Chex. Ralston also has its own versions of corn flakes, sugar frosted flakes, raisin bran, fig bars, graham crackers, saltines and other packaged foods products. Cereals account for about 5 percent of total revenue.

Ralston continues its dominance in the world pet-foods market. Some of its more familiar brands include Purina Dog and Cat Chow, Butcher's Blend, Chuck Wagon, Fit & Trim, Grrravy, Lucky Dog, Moist & Meaty, Hearty Chews, Cheesedawgs, Meow Mix, Thrive, Special Dinners, Tender

Vittles and Smart Cat. Pet-foods account for about one-quarter of total sales.

Not all of Ralston's offerings are edible—for man or beast. In 1986, Purina purchased Union Carbide's Eveready Battery division, which manufactures the Energizer and Eveready batteries. The acquisition makes Ralston the world's largest manufacturer of dry cell batteries. The battery division now accounts for nearly 20 percent of Ralston's total revenue.

In 1986, Ralston Purina parted company with part of its heritage when it sold Purina Mills. Since the turn of the century, Purina Mills had served as a symbol of rural American, a beacon to farmers across the fertile plain. In Ralston's 1987 annual report, the company paid its final homage this way: "In October, 1986, the Company sold its domestic agricultural products business (Purina Mills), recognizing an after-tax gain of $209.3 million or $2.89 per share." So much for sentiment.

Ralston still maintains a strong foreign market in livestock and poultry feed. It has 74 processing facilities outside the U.S. and distributes its products through about 3,400 independent foreign dealers. Foreign sales account for about 11 percent of the company's pretax earnings.

EARNINGS GROWTH

Ralston has had earnings increases eight of the past ten years. During that period its earnings per share increased 291 percent.

Ralston, which was founded in 1984, has about 60,000 employees and 34,000 shareholders of record.

STOCK GROWTH

The company has had excellent stock price growth. Over the past ten years the stock increased 482 percent (19 percent per year) from its median of $13.75 in 1978 to its recent 1988 price of $80 a share.

Including reinvested dividends, a $10,000 investment in Ralston stock at its median price in 1978 would have grown to about $85,000 ten years later. Average annual compounded rate of return (including stock growth and reinvested dividends): about 24 percent.

DIVIDEND YIELD

The company has traditionally paid a good dividend yield, averaging about 4 percent over the past ten years. But with its rising stock price, the yield has dropped off considerably in the past few years. During the three-year rating period from fiscal 1986 to 1988, the stock paid an average annual current return of 1.9 percent.

DIVIDEND GROWTH

Ralston Purina has raised its dividend for more than 15 consecutive years. The dividend increased 57 percent over the four-year rating period from 1984 to 1988.

SHAREHOLDER PERKS

At the Ralston annual meeting shareholders can feast on Twinkies, Cup Cakes, Ding Dongs and other Hostess snacks, and then take home a grab bag of several Ralston products such as cereal, Energizer batteries, Chicken of the Sea tuna and coupons for pet food.

The company, which is part owner of Keystone ski resort in Colorado, also sends a discount coupon for a percentage off of Keystone lodging, ski rental and lift tickets to shareholders in September along with their dividend checks.

Ralston provides an excellent dividend reinvestment plan for its shareholders. There are no commissions or service fees, and shareholders may contribute any amount up to $60,000 a year to the voluntary cash stock purchase plan.

SUMMARY

Total revenues: $5.9 billion, fiscal 1988 (ended 9/30/88). Earnings per share: $5.63, 1988; $1.44, 1978; 291% increase. Stock price: $80, 11/9/88; $13.75 (median), 1978; 482% increase (19% per year); price rose 8 of 10 years, 1977–87. Dividend: $1.44, 1988; $0.92, 1984; 4-year increase: 57%. Dividend yield: 1.9% average, 1986–88. P/E ratio: 15, 1/3/89. Average annual total return to investors, 1978–88: about 24%.

FORD MOTOR COMPANY
American Road
P.O. Box 1899
Dearborn, MI 48121
(313) 322-3000
Chairman and CEO: Donald E. Petersen
Vice Chairman and COO: Harold A. Poling

EARNINGS GROWTH	★ ★
STOCK GROWTH	★ ★ ★ ★
DIVIDEND YIELD	★ ★ ★ ★
DIVIDEND GROWTH	★ ★ ★ ★ ★
SHAREHOLDER PERKS	★ ★
NYSE—F	**17 points**

It's been a fitful journey the past decade for Henry Ford's corporate legacy. Like all Yankee automakers, Ford Motor Company had been throttled by some imposing market forces that the late Mr. Ford never had to contend with—namely: Toyota, Honda, Nissan, Mazda, Mitsubishi, Isuzu, Subaru, Hyundai.

But Detroit's number two automaker appears to be back on the high road. After several years of stinging losses, Ford finally found a better idea: "If you can't beat 'em, join 'em." Now, thanks in part to a series of joint ventures with Japan-based Mazda and Nissan, Ford is steadily reclaiming lost market share.

Ford's 20 percent stake of the U.S. auto market in 1987 was its highest level since 1979. The company also sold 29 percent of the new trucks purchased in the U.S., its largest share since 1983. By comparison, General Motors has been losing ground in both categories. GM's share of the U.S. auto market dropped from 44.5 percent in 1984 to 37 percent in 1987, and its share of the truck market dropped from 39.5 percent in 1983 to 31 percent in 1987.

Ford sells about 3.5 million cars and trucks in the U.S. each year, and about 2.5 million outside the U.S. Ford actually has a higher market share in Great Britain (29 percent) and Australia (28.6%) than it does in the U.S.

Worldwide, Ford accounts for about 15 percent of all car and truck sales. (By comparison, GM accounts for 18.5 percent, Toyota accounts for 9.4 percent; Nissan for 6.6 percent, Volkswagen for 6.5 percent, Chrysler for 5.7 percent and all others for about 40 percent.)

Ford has manufacturing plants and distributorships throughout the world. (It recently sold out its South African operation but maintains distribution agreements there, according to the Investor Responsibility Research Center.)

The company conducts joint operations with Mazda in the Asia-Pacific region and has agreed to a joint manufacturing arrangement with Nissan's Australian division. The Ford Festiva, introduced here in 1987, was built through a cooperative venture between Ford, Mazda and Kia Motors Corporation in South Korea.

Among Ford's best-selling automobiles in the U.S. are Escort, Lincoln Continental, Mustang, Tempo, Festiva, Taurus, Thunderbird and Bronco trucks. The company also sells farm and industrial tractors through its Ford New Holland subsidiary.

More than 90 percent of Ford's total revenue is generated by sales from its automotive group. Its two other key subsidiaries are:

- Ford Financial Services Group. The company operates Ford Credit and Insurance Subsidiaries, First Nationwide Finance Corporation and United States Leasing International.
- Ford Aerospace. The company manufactures missiles and missile control systems, ammunition satellites, ground stations, communication systems and air defense systems.

EARNINGS GROWTH

With total annual revenue of about $72 billion, Ford is the nation's third largest company (behind General Motors and Exxon). The company has about 400,000 employees and 300,000 shareholders. Over the past ten years, Ford has had three years of earnings losses (1980–82). But it has rebounded well with five consecutive years of earnings gains from 1983 to 1987. Earnings have grown from $31.5 per share in 1977 to $9.05 per share in 1987, a 187 percent increase for the period.

While profits have been good recently, Ford officials worry about heightened foreign competition in the future. With the increasing capacity of Japanese assembly plants in North America, and the growing influx of Korean autos, Ford predicts an increase in the availability of new cars in the U.S. beginning in about 1990. The increased competition, claims Ford, "could adversely affect the company's sales and profits."

STOCK GROWTH

After declining dramatically from 1978 to 1981, Ford's stock price has increased steadily through most of the decade, with one 2-for-1 stock split and two 3-for-2 splits since 1983. The stock price has increased seven of the past ten years. From its 1978 median ($10) to its recent 1988 price of $50 a share, the stock price has increased an average of 17.5 percent per year.

When you add in reinvested dividends, a $10,000 investment in Ford stock in 1978 would have grown to about $76,000 in 1988. Average annual compounded return (including stock growth and reinvested dividends): about 23.5 percent.

DIVIDEND YIELD

Ford has traditionally paid a fairly high yield. Over the past three years the stock has paid a current return of 4.3 percent.

DIVIDEND GROWTH

Like its stock price and earnings, Ford's dividend growth has had some ups and downs over the past ten years. The company paid no dividend in 1982, but since then the dividend has increased 829 percent, from 17 cents in 1983 to $1.58 in 1987.

SHAREHOLDER PERKS

Ford assesses its shareholders a small fee for participation in the company's dividend reinvestment and voluntary stock purchase plan. Investors may contribute $10 to $1,000 per month to the stock purchase plan.

The company offers no other perks.

SUMMARY

Total revenues: $71.6 billion, 1987. Earnings per share: $9.05, 1987; $3.15, 1977; 187% increase. Stock price: $50, 9/22/88; $10 (median), 1978 (400% total increase; 17.5% annual increase); price rose 6 of 10 years, 1977–87. Dividend: $1.58, 1987; $0.17, 1983; 4-year increase: 829%. Dividend yield: 4.3%, 1985–87. P/E ratio: 5, 1/3/89. Average annual total return to investor, 1978–88: about 23.5%.

33

DELUXE CORPORATION

P.O. Box 64399
St. Paul, MN 55164-0399
(612) 483-7111
Chairman: Eugene R. Olson
President and CEO: Harold V. Haverty

EARNINGS GROWTH	★ ★ ★ ★ ★
STOCK GROWTH	★ ★ ★ ★ ★
DIVIDEND YIELD	★ ★ ★
DIVIDEND GROWTH	★ ★ ★ ★
SHAREHOLDER PERKS	(no points)
NYSE—DLX	**17 points**

Deluxe Corporation is an excellent example of a company that has found its niche and exploited it to the fullest. Deluxe has turned bank check printing into a billion dollar-a-year business. The company so dominates the field that it controls a greater market share of the nation's check printing business than all of its competitors combined. Deluxe does business with more than 90 percent of the banks in the U.S. and controls about a 52 percent share of the check printing market.

The company (formerly Deluxe Check Printers) has had a phenomenal record of growth, with 49 consecutive years of increased sales and 35 consecutive years of record earnings.

It's not hard to see why Deluxe has developed such a loyal and widespread clientele. Despite its huge volume of business (410,000 check orders received each working day; more than 100 million annually), Deluxe is able to print and ship 97 percent of its orders within two days of the time they're received. And 99 percent of those orders are shipped without error. To help keep the orders flowing out, the St. Paul-based company has a network of more than 60 electronically linked printing plants located throughout the country.

About 80 percent of Deluxe's revenue comes from its check and related forms printing business. Its business systems group, which is a major supplier of short-run computer and business forms and record-keeping systems, accounts for just under 10 percent of total revenue.

Deluxe, which has been in business since 1915 (incorporated in 1920), has spent most of those years doing what it does best—printing checks. But in recent years, the company has caught the acquisitions fever and has ventured outside its specialty.

One of its most significant acquisitions was that of A.O. Smith Data Systems, which Deluxe acquired in 1936. Data Systems is the nation's leading processor of third-party automatic teller machine (ATM) interchange transactions. ATMs—also known as "cash machines"—represent one of the fastest growing segments of the banking industry, and Data Systems' specialty, which is to process transactions in which customers of one financial institution use the ATMs of another, is the fastest growth segment of the ATM market.

Deluxe also acquired Chex Systems (in 1984), which helps financial companies verify new accounts and identify individuals whose checking accounts have been "involuntarily" closed. It handles 800,000 inquiries each month from 38,000 financial offices that subscribe to the service.

In late 1987, Deluxe acquired Current, Inc., the nation's largest direct-mail marketer of greeting cards, stationery and related consumer products. Current's sales, along with other sales in the company's consumer specialty products group, account for 10 percent of the company's total revenue.

EARNINGS GROWTH

Few companies in the U.S. can match Deluxe's string of 35 consecutive years of record earnings. Its earnings per share have increased 453 percent over the past ten years.

Deluxe has total annual revenues of $948 million. The company has 13,000 employees and 18,000 shareholders of record.

STOCK GROWTH

Much like its earnings growth, Deluxe's stock growth has been consistent and sustained over the past ten years, increasing 513 percent (20 percent per year) from its median of $3.75 in 1978 to its recent 1988 price of $23 a share.

Including reinvested dividends, a $10,000 investment in Deluxe stock at its median price in 1978 would have grown to about $82,000 ten years later. Average annual compounded rate of return (including stock growth and reinvested dividends): about 23.5 percent.

DIVIDEND YIELD

The company has traditionally paid a moderately low dividend, averaging just over 3 percent during the past ten years. During the three-year rating period from 1985 to 1987, the stock paid an average annual current return of 2.3 percent.

DIVIDEND GROWTH

Deluxe has raised its dividend every year for many years. The company increased its dividend 145 percent, from 31 cents to 76 cents per share, over the four-year rating period from 1983 to 1987.

SHAREHOLDER PERKS   (no points)

Deluxe offers no dividend reinvestment plan, nor does it provide any other perks for its shareholders.

SUMMARY

Total revenues: $948 billion, 1987. Earnings per share: $1.55, 1987; $0.28, 1977; 453% increase. Stock price: $23, 7/25/88; $3.75 (median), 1978; 513% increase (20% per year); price rose 10 of 10 years, 1977–87. Dividend: $0.76, 1987; $0.31, 1983; 4-year increase: 145%. Dividend yield: 2.3% average, 1985–87. P/E ratio: 15, 1/3/89. Average annual total return to investors, 1978–88: 23.5%.

34 Noxell

NOXELL CORPORATION

11050 York Road
Hunt Valley, MD 21030-2098
(301) 785-7300
Chairman and CEO: George L. Bunting, Jr.
President: Marvin L. Hathaway

EARNINGS GROWTH	★ ★ ★ ★ ★
STOCK GROWTH	★ ★ ★ ★ ★
DIVIDEND YIELD	★ ★
DIVIDEND GROWTH	★ ★ ★ ★
SHAREHOLDER PERKS	★
OTC—NOXLB	**17 points**

Noxell Corporation is not just another pretty face, but the company has spent the past 70 years helping millions of American woman attain that distinction. Noxell is a major manufacturer of skin care and cosmetics products, including Cover Girl makeup, the nation's number-one selling cosmetics line.

Cover Girl markets a broad line of facial creams, lipsticks, eye shadows, lining pencils, nail polishes, mascaras and blushers. It holds down half the U.S. market for facial powders.

Noxell also manufactures cosmetics skin care products under the Rain Tree (moisturizing cream), Clarion and Noxema labels. Clarion specializes in facial powders, eye makeup, lipstick and skin creams.

Noxema is known most for its medicated skin lotions, including Noxema Antiseptic Skin Cleanser, Clear-ups Medicated Cleansing Pads and Complexion Therapy Peel-Off Mask. The company also markets a line of medicated shaving creams.

The company's line of cosmetics and beauty creams accounts for about 95 percent of its $490 million in annual revenue.

While the Maryland-based manufacturer focuses primarily on the cosmetics market, it has strayed into the household products sector with its Lestoil all-purpose liquid cleaner and a rug shampoo. It also owns Caliente

Foods, a specialty foods distributor. Lestoil accounts for about 3 percent of total sales, and Caliente accounts for only about 1 percent.

Although the company does most of its business in the U.S. and Canada, Noxell also markets its products in Europe (about 5 percent of sales) and Latin America (about 2.5 percent). Noxell has manufacturing plants in Hunt Valley, Maryland (near Baltimore), Mississauga, Ontario (Canada) and Wakefield, Yorkshire (England).

EARNINGS GROWTH

Noxell has had 12 consecutive years of earnings increases. Earnings per share have climbed 470 percent over the past decade.

Founded in 1917, the company has 20,000 employees and 4,500 shareholders of record. Insiders hold 24 percent of Noxell common stock and 85 percent of the voting stock.

STOCK GROWTH

The company's stock price has climbed steadily through the past decade, with three 2-for-1 stock splits since 1983. Over the past ten years the stock increased 700 percent (20 percent per year), from its median of $2.50 in 1978 to its recent 1988 price of $20 a share.

Including reinvested dividends, a $10,000 investment in Noxell stock at its median price in 1978 would have grown to about $80,000 ten years later. Average annual compounded rate of return (including stock growth and reinvested dividends): about 23 percent.

DIVIDEND YIELD

The company has paid a moderate yield, averaging just under 3 percent over the past ten years. During the three-year rating period from 1985 to 1987, the stock paid an average annual current return of 1.6 percent.

DIVIDEND GROWTH

The company has raised its dividend 11 consecutive years. The dividend was increased 100 percent over the four-year rating period from 1983 to 1987.

SHAREHOLDER PERKS

At its annual meeting, shareholders are given a sample packet of Noxell products, including lipstick, nail polish, mascara, eye shadow, Caliente chili and Lestoil liquid cleaner.

The company offers no dividend reinvestment plan.

SUMMARY

Total revenues: $490 million, 1987. Earnings per share: $1.08, 1987; $0.23, 1977; 470% increase. Stock price: $20, 11/6/88; $2.50 (median), 1978; 600% increase (20% per year); price rose 10 of 10 years, 1977–87. Dividend: $0.36, 1987; $0.18, 1983; 4-year increase: 100%. Dividend yield: 1.6% average, 1985–87. P/E ratio: 16, 1/3/89. Average annual total return to investors, 1978–88: about 23%.

RITE AID CORPORATION

P.O. Box 3165
Harrisburg, PA 17105
(717) 761-2633
Chairman and President: Alex Grass

EARNINGS GROWTH	★ ★ ★ ★
STOCK GROWTH	★ ★ ★ ★ ★
DIVIDEND YIELD	★ ★
DIVIDEND GROWTH	★ ★ ★ ★
SHAREHOLDER PERKS	★ ★
NYSE—RAD	**17 points**

Rite Aid stores have never professed to be your one-stop Christmas shopping spot. They don't carry manger scenes nor mistletoe. No Easter baskets either. And you can't buy shoes for the children, rakes for the lawn or parts for your car at a Rite Aid store. The company has grown to become the biggest drugstore chain in America by clinging to a simple philosophy: stay small.

In an era of drug superstores, probably the most glaring statistic that emerges from Rite Aid's balance sheet is that 40 percent of its revenue is generated by prescription drug sales.

The company sticks to a basic formula for nearly all of its stores. Each store encompasses approximately 6,500 square feet of floor space—about a third smaller than many of its competitors. (By comparision, the average store size for Walgreen, another top 100 company, is about 10,000 square feet.) Rite Aid's merchandise is limited primarily to health and beauty aids, proprietary drugs, housewares, tobacco products, sundries and prescription medicine.

Rite Aid attracts its customers through discount prices. About 1,000 of its standard products are cut-rate Rite Aid private label brands. Low-priced generic drugs account for about 30 percent of the more than 60 million prescriptions Rite Aid stores fill each year.

The company was founded in 1962 when Alex Grass opened Thrif D Discount Center in Scranton, Pennsylvania. Grass continues to serve as chairman and president of Rite Aid, but the company has since moved its headquarters to nearby Harrisburg. In all, Rite Aid now operates more than 2,100 drug stores in 22 eastern, midwestern and southern states. Most of the company's growth has come through acquisitions. Its most notable recent acquisitions include the 113-store SupeRX chain (from the Kroger Company) in 1987 and the 356-store Gray Drug Fair chain (from Sherwin-Williams) in 1988.

Rite Aid's drugstores account for about 95 percent of its $2.5 billion in annual revenues. The company also owns a chain of 65 ADAP auto parts stores and 40 Encore bookstores. It also owns Sera-Tec Biologicals, which provides plasma for use in therapeutic and diagnostic products, and it holds a 47 percent interest in Super Rite Foods.

EARNINGS GROWTH

Rite Aid's earnings-per-share have grown steadily over the past decade with increases in nine of the past ten years. During that period, its earnings per share increased 354 percent (16 percent per year).

The company has about 30,000 employees and 9,000 shareholders of record. Founder Alex Grass and his family hold about 10 percent of the common stock.

STOCK GROWTH

The company's stock price increased ten consecutive years through 1987. The stock has had one 2-for-1 split, one 3-for-2 split and one 4-for-3 split since 1981. Over the past ten years the stock has increased 500 percent (20 percent per year), from its median of $5.50 in 1978 to its recent 1988 price of $33 a share.

Including reinvested dividends, a $10,000 investment in Rite Aid stock at its median price in 1978 would have grown to about $75,000 ten years later. Average annual compounded rate of return (including stock growth and reinvested dividends): about 22 percent.

DIVIDEND YIELD

The company generally pays a fairly low yield, which has averaged just over 2 percent over the past ten years. During the three-year rating period from 1985 to 1987, the stock paid an average annual current return of 1.9 percent.

DIVIDEND GROWTH

Rite Aid has raised its dividend for more than 15 consecutive years. The company increased the dividend 100 percent over the four-year rating period from 1983 to 1987.

SHAREHOLDER PERKS

Rite Aid offers its shareholders a good dividend reinvestment and voluntary stock purchase plan. There are no fees or service charges, and shareholders may contribute up to $25,000 per year to the stock purchase plan.

SUMMARY

Total revenues: $2.5 billion, 1987. Earnings per share: $2.27, 1987; $0.50, 1977; 354% increase. Stock price: $33, 9/8/88; $5.50 (median), 1978; (500% total increase; 20% annual increase); price rose 10 of 10 years, 1977–87. Dividend: $0.68, 1987; $0.34, 1984; 4-year increase: 100%. Dividend yield: 1.9% average, 1985–87. P/E ratio: 14, 1/3/89. Average annual total return to investor, 1978–88: about 22%.

PALL CORPORATION

2200 Northern Blvd.
East Hills, NY 11548
(516) 484-5400
Chairman: Dr. David B. Pall
CEO: Abraham Krasnoff
President: Maurice G. Hardy

EARNINGS GROWTH	★ ★ ★ ★ ★
STOCK GROWTH	★ ★ ★ ★ ★
DIVIDEND YIELD	★ ★
DIVIDEND GROWTH	★ ★ ★
SHAREHOLDER PERKS	★ ★
ASE—PLL	**17 points**

Dr. David B. Pall has spent most of his life fighting an invisible enemy. Sometimes destructive, sometimes deadly, Pall's microscopic adversaries can wreak havoc in blood streams, in equipment, in medications and in foods and beverages. Dr. Pall, the 74-year-old founder and chairman of the board of the Pall Corporation, has made a career—and built a $400 million-a-year corporate empire—by finding ways to eradicate these menacing intruders.

Pall Corporation manufactures special filtering systems for a variety of applications, including the purification of medical and pharmaceutical products, foods, beverages, aerospace and industrial equipment, fluids, chemicals, gas, oil and steel.

The company divides its business into three principal segments:

- Health care. Pall makes prefilters and sterilizing filters to remove germs from fluids and from the air. Its filters are used to cleanse blood for transfusions, tissue culture, vaccines, intravenous fluids, breathing gases and other health care-related products. Its advanced blood filters can reportedly reduce the risk of AIDS and hepatitis significantly for patients receiving blood transfusions—an area that could promise outstanding future growth for the company.

Pall also supplies filters for the beverage industry that remove bacteria, yeast and other contaminants from wine, beer, water and other products. This sector accounts for about one-third of Pall's total annual revenue.

- Aeropower. The company makes hydraulic, fuel and lube filters for military combat vehicles, aircraft, helicopters and ships. It also makes filters for industrial customers who use or manufacture steel, paper, plastics, automobiles and other machinery. The company also produces devices used to "protect against nuclear-biological chemical warfare (NBC) contamination." The aeropower division accounts for about 37 percent of the company's revenue.

- Fluid processing. Pall sells filtration and sterilizing systems to advanced technology companies engaged in a variety of pursuits including the manufacture of microelectronic components, magnetic tape, film, fiber, paint and chemicals. Fluid processing accounts for about 29 percent of Pall's revenue.

The company has a strong worldwide market. Foreign sales account for about 40 percent of the company's $425 million in annual revenue.

EARNINGS GROWTH

Pall has had more than 15 consecutive years of earnings growth (through fiscal 1988). Over the past ten years, earnings per share have climbed 400 percent.

The company has about 5,000 employees and 3,500 shareholders of record.

STOCK GROWTH

Pall has had excellent stock price growth over the past decade, including two 3-for-2 stock splits and two 4-for-3 splits since 1980. Over the past ten years the stock price has increased 535 percent (20 percent per year), from its median of $4.25 in 1978 to its late 1988 price of $27 a share.

Including reinvested dividends, a $10,000 investment in Pall stock at its median price in 1978 would have grown to about $75,000 ten years later. Average annual compounded rate of return (including stock growth and reinvested dividends): about 22 percent.

DIVIDEND YIELD

The company has traditionally paid a very low dividend yield, averaging just over 1 percent over the past ten years. During the three-year rating period from 1986 to 1988, the stock paid an average annual current return of 1.2 percent.

DIVIDEND GROWTH

Pall has raised its dividend 13 consecutive years (dating back to the first year the company paid a dividend). The company increased its dividend 95 percent over the four-year rating period from 1984 to 1988.

SHAREHOLDER PERKS

Pall has an excellent dividend reinvestment and voluntary stock purchase plan for its shareholders. There are no commissions or service charges, and shareholders may contribute up to $60,000 per year to the stock purchase plan.

SUMMARY

Total revenues: $425 million, for fiscal 1988 (ended 7/30/88). Earnings per share: $1.60, 1988; $0.32, 1978; 400% increase. Stock price: $27, 9/9/88; $4.25 (median), 1978; (535% total increase; 20% annual increase); price rose 8 of 10 years, 1977–87. Dividend: $0.39, 1988; $0.20, 1984; 4-year increase: 95%. Dividend yield: 1.2%, 1986–88. P/E ratio: 18, 1/3/89. Average annual total return to investor, 1978–88: about 22%.

BROWN-FORMAN CORPORATION

850 Dixie Highway
Louisville, KY 40210
(502) 585-1100
Chairman and CEO: W. L. Lyons Brown, Jr.
President: Owsley Brown II

EARNINGS GROWTH	★ ★ ★
STOCK GROWTH	★ ★ ★ ★
DIVIDEND YIELD	★ ★ ★
DIVIDEND GROWTH	★ ★ ★ ★
SHAREHOLDER PERKS	★ ★ ★
ASE-BF.B	**17 points**

Its detractors portray it as "alcohol disguised as Kool Aid." Its boosters say it's sweeter, lighter and punchier than traditional wine. Highbrow connoisseurs won't touch the stuff. But the imbibing public once embraced the "wine cooler" with staggering alacrity—just as it now seems to be discarding it with sobering resolve.

California Cooler, a leading line of wine coolers that Brown-Forman acquired in 1985, had been one of the company's sparkling success stories. In fiscal 1987, Brown-Forman sold the equivalent of 12 million nine-liter cases of California Cooler—a remarkable volume considering that the company sold less than 2 million cases each of its much more esablished Bolla wines, Cella wines and Southern Comfort. Wine coolers were not introduced on a national basis until 1984, but by 1986 cooler sales accounted for about one-fourth of all wine sales in the United States.

The American tippler, however, is a fickle creature, given to sudden changes in taste. (Remember Boone's Farm Wine?) Market observers believe that wine cooler sales have already peaked. In fact, Brown-Forman reported a decline of about 25 percent in sales of its California Cooler in fiscal 1988. Fortunately, for Brown-Forman, the company distills and markets a solid stable of other well-established wines and spirits to keep its profits up while cooler sales cool.

Brown-Forman's other leading alcoholic beverage brands include Jack Daniel's Tennessee Whiskey, Early Times Old Style Kentucky Whisky, Old Forester Kentucky Straight Bourbon Whiskies, Canadian Mist Whisky, Martell Cognacs, Usher's Green Stripe Scotch Whisky, Old Bushmills Irish Whiskey, Pepe Lopez Tequilas, Korbel champagnes, Fontana Candida Italian wines, Parducci Premium California wines, and Black Bush malt whiskey from Ireland.

Brown-Forman's wine and spirits segment accounts for about 76 percent of its total sales.

The Louisville-based distiller also owns Lenox, a manufacturer of fine china, crystal and giftware; ArtCarved, a manufacturer of jewelry and class rings, and Hartman Luggage. Its housewares segment accounts for about 14 percent of sales, and its personal products (luggage and jewelry) contribute about 10 percent of total sales.

EARNINGS GROWTH

With annual revenues of $1.35 billion, Brown-Forman is the largest distiller of wine and distilled spirits in the U.S. (Seagram's of Canada is the largest in the world.) The company has about 7,000 employees, and 2,300 holders of Class A stock and about 4,000 holders of Class B stock. (Class B is the more widely traded stock.)

The company has enjoyed consistent earnings growth, with earnings increases nine of the past ten years. Earnings per share have increased a total of 296 percent, from 82 cents a share in fiscal 1978 to $3.25 per share in 1988.

STOCK GROWTH

Brown-Forman's (Class B) stock price has made a fairly steady climb the past decade, increasing 430 percent (18 percent per year) from its median of $9.25 in 1978 to its recent 1988 price of $49 a share.

Including reinvested dividends, a $10,000 investment in Brown-Forman stock at its median price in 1978 would have grown to about $67,000 ten years later. Average annual compounded rate of return (including stock growth and reinvested dividends): about 21 percent.

DIVIDEND YIELD

Brown-Forman tends to pay an average dividend. Over the past three years, the stock has paid an annual current return of 2.7 percent.

DIVIDEND GROWTH

The company raises its dividend most years—unless earnings are flat. It has increased its dividend eight of the past ten years. The dividend jumped 110 percent over the four-year rating period from 1984 to 1988.

SHAREHOLDER PERKS

During the holiday season the past few years, Brown-Forman has offered its shareholders a special 50 percent discount on Lenox china and crystal dinnerware and Christmas tree ornaments.

The company also offers a dividend reinvestment and voluntary stock purchase plan. The plan carries a small fee. Shareholders of record may buy $50 to $3,000 per quarter in additional shares through the voluntary stock purchase plan.

SUMMARY

Total revenues: $1.35 billion, for fiscal 1988 (ended 4/30/88). Earnings per share: $3.25, 1988; $0.82, 1978; 296% increase. Stock price (Class B): $49, 10/5/88; $9.25 (median), 1978 (430% total increase; 18% annual increase); price rose 8 of 10 years, 1977–87. Dividend: $1.24, 1988; $0.59, 1984; 4-year increase: 110%. Dividend yield: 2.7%, 1986–88. P/E ratio: 14, 1/3/89. Average annual total return to investor, 1978–88: about 21%.

38

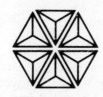

BRISTOL-MYERS COMPANY

345 Park Avenue
New York, NY 10154
(212) 546-4000
Chairman and CEO: Richard L. Gelb

EARNINGS GROWTH	★ ★ ★
STOCK GROWTH	★ ★ ★ ★
DIVIDEND YIELD	★ ★ ★
DIVIDEND GROWTH	★ ★ ★ ★
SHAREHOLDER PERKS	★ ★ ★
NYSE—BMY	**17 points**

Knee acting up again? Bristol-Myers can set you up with a new one. Hip out of joint? The company makes those, too. Hearing on the blink? A Bristol-Myers implantable magnetic disc can carry the sound directly to your inner ear. Got a headache that's "THIS BIG?" The firm's Excedrin pain reliever can probably stop it. (If not, you might try its Bufferin or Nuprin brands.) Hair losing body, shape, style? Bring Miss Clairol to the rescue. Drowsy? Try No-Doz. Cholesterol level on the rise? Anxiety got you down? Bristol-Myers' pharmaceutical division makes some medications that just might help.

Bristol-Myers, the nation's third largest pharmaceuticals company, has ridden its broad range of pharmaceutical and consumer health care products to 15 consecutive years of earnings increases.

The new York-based manufacturer divides its domestic operations into four core business segments, including:

- Non-prescription health products (accounts for 28 percent of the company's $5.4 billion in annual sales). Bristol-Myers makes Excedrin, Nuprin, Bufferin, Comtrex (cold reliever), Ammens Medicated Powder and No-Doz.
- Toiletries and beauty aids (22 percent of sales). The company makes Clairol hair products, including Nice 'n Easy, Loving Care, Miss Clairol,

Ultress, Clairesse, Silk & Silver, and several other products. It also makes Ban anti-perspirants and Vitalis men's hair formulas.

- Household products (9 percent of sales). The company makes Drano, VANiSH bowl cleaner, Renuzit air fresheners, O-Cedar mops and brooms, Endust cleaning aids and Behold furniture polishes.
- Pharmaceuticals and medical products (41 percent of sales). The company makes a wide range of medical products, including artificial hips and knees, implantable hearing devices and compression garments for burn treatments. The company also makes a line of drugs for the treatment of cancer (it markets the broadest range of anti-cancer agents in the U.S.), cardiovascular ailments, high cholesterol, infections, congestion and nervous disorders. The company's Mead Johnson subsidiary makes nutritional formulas for infants, including Enfamil and ProSobee. The company is also at work developing treatments for the AIDS virus.

Bristol-Myers does a strong international business, marketing its products in more than 100 countries. (Among its foreign subsidiaries is B-M Group Ltd. of South Africa, which manufactures pharmaceuticals and consumer products.) Foreign sales account for about 23 percent of the company's total revenue.

EARNINGS GROWTH

Bristol-Myers has had 15 consecutive years of increased earnings. Earnings per share have climbed 260 percent over the past decade.

The company, which was founded in 1887, has 34,000 employees and 54,000 shareholders of record.

STOCK GROWTH

The company has had steady stock price appreciation through the past decade with two 2-for-1 stock splits since 1983. Over the past ten years the stock has increased 353 percent (16 percent per year), from its median of $9.50 in 1978 to its recent 1988 price of $43 a share.

Including reinvested dividends, a $10,000 investment in Bristol-Myers stock at its median price in 1978 would have grown to about $60,000 ten years later. Average annual compounded rate of return (including stock growth and reinvested dividends): about 19.5 percent.

DIVIDEND YIELD

The company generally pays a moderate yield, which has averaged about 3.5 percent over the past ten years. During the three-year rating period from 1985 to 1987, the stock paid an average annual current return of 3 percent.

DIVIDEND GROWTH

Bristol-Myers has raised its dividend for more than 15 consecutive years. The dividend increased 133 percent over the four-year rating period from 1983 to 1987.

SHAREHOLDER PERKS

The company sends all of its new shareholders of record a welcome packet of its consumer products, including small bottles of Excedrin, Bufferin, Nuprin, Clairol, Ban and VANiSH bowl cleaner.

The company also offers its shareholders an excellent dividend reinvestment and voluntary stock purchase plan. There are no fees or commissions, and shareholders of record may purchase $10 to $3,000 per month in additional shares through the voluntary stock purchase plan.

SUMMARY

Total revenues: $5.4 billion, 1987. Earnings per share: $2.47, 1987; $0.68, 1977; 260% increase. Stock price: $43, 11/8/88; $9.50 (median), 1978; 353% increase (16% per year); price rose 9 of 10 years, 1977–87. Dividend: $1.40, 1987; $0.60, 1983; 4-year increase: 133%. Dividend yield: 3% average, 1985–87. P/E ratio: 16, 1/3/89. Average annual total return to investors, 1978–88: 19.5%.

39

WAL-MART

WAL-MART STORES, INC.

Bentonville, AR 72716
(501) 273-4000
Chairman: Sam M. Walton
President and CEO: David D. Glass

EARNINGS GROWTH	★ ★ ★ ★ ★
STOCK GROWTH	★ ★ ★ ★ ★
DIVIDEND YIELD	★
DIVIDEND GROWTH	★ ★ ★ ★ ★
SHAREHOLDER PERKS	(no points)
NYSE—WMT	**16 points**

They dot America's heartland, reaching out to shoppers in small cities and towns that the Sears and K marts and J.C. Penneys have chosen to ignore. You'll find them on the outskirts of communities like Mountain View, Arkansas; Grapevine, Texas; Gallup, New Mexico, and more than 1,100 other out-of-the-way locations from Blue Earth, Minnesota, to Picayune, Mississippi, from Rock Hill, South Carolina, to Broken Bow, Oklahoma.

Wal-Mart opens a new store, on average, about every three days. In 1980 there were 330 Wal-Mart stores in 11 states. Now there are more than three times that number in 23 states. And the rapid growth should continue. Where there's a town that lacks the advantages of a discount retailer, there's yet another Wal-Mart store waiting to be born.

The company has enjoyed spectacular growth, increasing its earnings and revenues every year since 1962, when the first Wal-Mart store was opened. Over the past ten years its stock price, on average, has increased 46 percent per year. A $10,000 investment in Wal-Mart in 1978 would have grown to about $450,000 in 1988.

If you're a city slicker, you may not be familiar with Wal-Mart. Aside from their rural locations, Wal-Mart stores are much the same as any other discount department store. The corporate formula calls for each store to be divided into 36 departments, including apparel, housewares, hardware, appliances, automotive accessories, cameras, toys, sporting goods, health and beauty aids and jewelry.

The company has achieved its success largely by opening stores in locations where there is little competition from other discounters. It buys its merchandise in large volume and, through discount pricing, turns it over quickly at its 1,200 stores, incurring a minimum of overhead in the process.

The first Wal-Mart store (called "Wal-Mart Discount City") was opened in Rogers, Arkansas, in 1962 by Samuel M. Walton. By the time he opened his first Wal-Mart, Mr. Walton was already well schooled in the art of operating discount department stores. His original foray into retailing came in 1945, when he opened a Ben Franklin variety store franchise in Newport, Arkansas. He's been in the discount retailing business ever since and still serves as Wal-Mart's chairman of the board.

In addition to its namesake stores, Wal-Mart also operates Sam's Wholesale Club (about 100 stores), which tend to be located in larger metropolitan markets, and dot Discount Drug, with about a dozen stores in Iowa, Missouri, Kansas and Nebraska. Wal-Mart also operates several Helen's Arts and Crafts stores, and has recently launched a new chain called "Hypermart ★ USA," which is essentially an expanded version of Wal-Mart that includes both groceries and general merchandise.

EARNINGS GROWTH

Although Wal-Mart is a relatively young corporation, it has already become one of the largest retail operations in the United States. With $16 billion in revenue, Wal-Mart has passed J.C. Penney and is quickly creeping up on K mart. The only other larger retail company is Sears.

Wal-Mart has about 150,000 employees and 35,000 shareholders. If the company has a weakness—from an investor's point of view—it may be its high stock price-to-earnings ratio. (Remember, P/E ratios are like golf scores: the lower the better.) Wal-Mart's P/E has been lingering above 20, which is much higher than most companies of comparable size. But with its rapid growth, Wal-Mart could well overcome the high P/E and still prove to be an excellent long-term value.

Wal-Mart's earnings growth has been nothing short of spectacular, with a 2,220 percent increase over the past ten years (36 percent per year). The company has had 25 consecutive years of increased earnings.

STOCK GROWTH

Wal-Mart's stock price growth has been even more spectacular than its earnings growth, increasing 4,167 percent over the past ten years (46 percent per year), from a median of about 75 cents a share in 1978 to its recent price of $32.

Including reinvested dividends, the company's average annual compounded rate of return over the past ten years was about 47 percent.

DIVIDEND YIELD

The company has traditionally paid a very low dividend yield, averaging under 1 percent per year over the past ten years. During the three-year rating period from 1985 through 1988, the stock paid an average annual current return of only 0.4 percent.

DIVIDEND GROWTH

Wal-Mart has raised its dividend every year since it began paying a dividend in 1977. Over the four-year rating period from 1983 to 1987, the company raised its dividend 200 percent.

SHAREHOLDER PERKS (no points)

Wal-Mart offers no dividend reinvestment plan, nor does it offer any other special perks for its shareholder.

SUMMARY

Total revenues: $16 billion, 1987. Earnings per share: $1.11, 1987; $0.05, 1977; 2,220% increase. Stock price: $32, 11/1/88; $0.75 (median), 1978; 4,167% increase (46% per year); price rose 10 of 10 years, 1977–87. Dividend: $0.12, 1987; $0.04, 1983; 4-year increase: 200%. Dividend yield: 0.4% average, 1985–87. P/E ratio: 23, 1/3/89. Average annual total return to investors, 1978–88: about 47%.

TYSON FOODS, INC.

2210 West Oaklawn Dr.
Springdale, AR 72764
(501) 756-4000
Chairman and CEO: Don Tyson
President: Leland Tollett

EARNINGS GROWTH	★ ★ ★ ★ ★
STOCK GROWTH	★ ★ ★ ★ ★
DIVIDEND YIELD	★
DIVIDEND GROWTH	★ ★ ★ ★ ★
SHAREHOLDER PERKS	(no points)
OTC—TYSNA	**16 points**

The typical American carnivore, pinched for cash and wise to the risks of red meat, has been prime plucking the past few years for poultry giant Tyson Foods. The Arkansas meat packer has come up with dozens of new ways to package its fowl—fresh, frozen, mixed and marinated, plus 50 sizes, shapes and styles of boneless breasts and breaded patties—and in the process has managed to flit its way to the top of the roost among the world's poultry producers.

Tyson runs a fully integrated operation, nudging its flock through every phase of the production process—from first cheep to final shipping. The company owns 24 hatcheries, 14 feed mills and 29 processing plants with slaughtering capacity of approximately 15 million head per week.

Tyson markets its poultry to the food services industry (55 percent of sales) and retail stores (45 percent).

In addition to its chicken, turkey, Cornish hens and other poultry products (which account for 90 percent of its $1.8 billion in total revenues), Tyson does a good business in pork (4 percent of revenues), and produces a line of Crispitos flour and corn tortilla chips (2 percent of revenue).

Tyson's management attributes its rapid growth to three primary factors: The U.S. poultry market has exploded in the past ten years as consumers looked for healthier and less expensive meats; the company has expanded from without through a number of acquisitions; and it has expanded from within through ongoing product line extensions.

In 1985 Tyson acquired Valmac Industries, and in 1986 it acquired Lane Processing and Heritage Valley. In 1988 it attempted a hostile takeover of one of its primary competitors, Holly Farms. (The acquisition attempt was still unresolved at this writing.)

The company adheres to a simple philosophy of product development, says Leland Tollett, Tyson's president: "Let the dog have pups. Once we have a winner, we ask ourselves what else we can do with it."

After watching sales of its precooked boneless chicken rise quickly among its food services customers, Tyson began marketing the product to the retail trade, then followed the same strategy with chunks and patties. "And we don't make just one kind of chicken patty," says Tollett. "We make 26. By putting money into products that are basically offshoots of what we've already done, we're able to diversify with minimal risk."

Some of Tyson's leading products include Chick 'N Quick precooked patties, breast strips and chunks; Tyson Chicken Entrees (15 varieties of plated dinners); Cornish game hens (fresh and frozen); Tyson Country Fresh Chicken (prepackaged fresh chicken); Chicken Originals (low-calorie entrees in eight flavors); boneless and breaded breast products.

Tyson is the nation's number one developer of poultry products for fast-food chains and claims to do business with about 80 percent of the country's top restaurant chains.

EARNINGS GROWTH

With total revenues of $1.8 billion a year, Tyson is the world's largest poultry producer. The company has had sensational earnings gains over the past ten years, although its pace of growth appears to be slowing somewhat. Little wonder, though, when you consider that its earnings per share grew 2,500 percent (38 percent per year average) from 1977 to 1987. The company has had earnings gains eight of the past ten years.

Tyson, which was founded in 1935 and first incorporated in 1947, has 25,000 employees and 11,000 shareholders. The Tyson family controls about 60 percent of the company's stock.

STOCK GROWTH

The company's stock price growth has been just as impressive as its earnings growth, with a 5-for-2 stock split in 1985, a 2-for-1 split in 1986 and a 3-for-2 split in 1987. Over the past ten years the stock has increased 2,566 percent (39 percent per year) from its median of 60 cents per share in 1978 to its recent 1988 price of $16 a share. The stock price increased eight of ten years from 1977 to 1987.

Including reinvested dividends, a $10,000 investment in Tyson Foods stock at its median price in 1978 would have grown to about $290,000 ten years later. Average annual compounded rate of return (including stock growth and reinvested dividends): about 40 percent.

DIVIDEND YIELD

Tyson generally pays a very low dividend. Over the past three years the stock has paid an average annual current return of only 0.2 percent.

DIVIDEND GROWTH

While its dividend yield has been quite low, the company has made an effort to beef up its pay-out to shareholders the past few years. It raised the dividend 300 percent during the four-year rating period, from a split-adjusted one cent per share in 1983 to four cents per share in 1987.

SHAREHOLDER PERKS (no points)

The company offers no dividend reinvestment plan, nor does it offer any other shareholder perks.

SUMMARY

Total revenues: $1.8 billion, 1987. Earnings per share: $1.06, 1987; $0.04, 1977; 2,500% increase. Stock price: $16, 10/24/88; $0.60 (median), 1978; (2,566% total increase; 39% annual increase); price rose 8 of 10 years, 1977–87. Dividend: $0.04, 1987; $0.01, 1984; 4-year increase: 300%. Dividend yield: 0.2%, 1985–87. P/E ratio: 14, 1/3/89. Average annual total return to investor, 1978–88: about 40%.

41

PRECISION CASTPARTS CORPORATION

4600 S.E. Harney Drive
Portland, OR 97206-0898
(503) 777-3881
CEO: Edward H. Cooley
President: William C. McCormick

EARNINGS GROWTH	★ ★ ★ ★ ★
STOCK GROWTH	★ ★ ★ ★ ★
DIVIDEND YIELD	★
DIVIDEND GROWTH	★ ★ ★ ★ ★
SHAREHOLDER PERKS	(no points)
OTC—PCST	**16 points**

Precision Castparts Corporation (PCC) is a leading manufacturer of "investment" (molded) castings for aerospace, industrial and medical products. Using designs supplied by its customers, PCC manufactures castings for everything from jet engine parts and fan blades to hip and knee joint implants.

Most of PCC's work, however, is done for the aerospace industry. General Electric has used PCC castings for its jet engines for 20 years. By establishing itself as a leader in its niche—PCC is the world's largest manufacturer of large, complex structural molded castings and the second largest producer overall of investment castings—the Portland-based company has managed to post phenomenal earnings and stock price gains. Over the past ten years, its earnings per share have increased at an average annual rate of 30 percent, and its stock price has grown at a 36 percent average annual rate.

PCC's lightweight, high-strength "superalloy" jet engine castings are expected to be in even greater demand in the next few years as the commercial airline industry attempts to meet increasingly stringent fuel efficiency and noise reduction requirements. The company's backlog of orders has increased 180 percent in the past two years.

PCC's largest customers are General Electric (30 percent of net sales), and Pratt & Whitney (26 percent of net sales). PCC also supplies custom molded parts for Boeing, McDonnell Douglas, Airbus and other aerospace contractors. About 86 percent of the company's total revenue comes from the aerospace industry (nearly 50 percent of its sales are government-related). Foreign sales account for about 20 percent of Precision's $414 million in total revenue.

Part of PCC's success has been its development of new "superalloys"— high-strength blended metals that can endure extreme conditions of temperature and stress.

One of PCC's most recent patented developments is "powder titanium." Titanium is a light, durable metal used for parts in engines and industrial machinery. Normally, titanium products are formed by melting the titanium at extremely high temperatures and pouring it into ceramic shells. In some applications, however, using molten titanium is impractical, so titanium "powder" (which is not really powder, but tiny beads of titanium) are forged through a high-pressure process that does not require the extreme heat of traditionally forged titanium. The company is the world leader in the powder titanium process.

EARNINGS GROWTH

PCC has had earnings gains eight of ten years through fiscal 1988. Earnings per share have soared 1,319 percent over the past decade.

The company has about 5,500 employees and 2,000 shareholders of record.

The one cause for pause with PCC is that almost 90 percent of its business is in the aerospace industry, which relies heavily on the government. Cutbacks in defense and aerospace spending could have an adverse affect on the company's earnings. But PCC has also established a market for its cast-parts in the commercial aircraft manufacturing industry, which could temper potential declines from cutbacks in government contracts.

STOCK GROWTH

The company's stock price has increased rapidly, with four stock splits since 1983. Over the past ten years the stock has increased 2,025 percent (36 percent per year), from its median of $1.60 in 1978 to its late 1988 price of $34 a share.

Including reinvested dividends, a $10,000 investment in PCC stock at its median price in 1978 would have grown to about $220,000 ten years later. Average annual compounded rate of return (including stock growth and reinvested dividends): about 37 percent.

DIVIDEND YIELD

The company traditionally pays a very low yield. During the three-year rating period from 1986 to 1988, the stock paid an average annual current return of 0.3 percent.

DIVIDEND GROWTH

PCC has not made a habit of raising its dividend each year, although it has had increases the past four years. During the four-year rating period, the dividend has gone from (split-adjusted) three cents per share to eight cents per share—an increase of a mere nickel on a $34 stock. But, in percentage terms, it adds up to a 167 percent increase.

SHAREHOLDER PERKS   (no points)

PCC offers no dividend reinvestment plan, nor does it provide any other perks for its shareholders.

SUMMARY

Total revenues: $414 million, fiscal 1988 (ended 3/31/88). Earnings per share: $2.27, 1988; $0.16, 1978; 1,319% increase. Stock price: $34, 11/9/88; $1.60 (median), 1978; 2,025% increase (36% per year); price rose 9 of 10 years, 1977–87. Dividend: $0.08, 1987; $0.03, 1983; 4-year increase: 167%. Dividend yield: 0.3% average, 1985–87. P/E ratio: 13, 1/3/89. Average annual total return to investors, 1978–88: about 37%.

42

FOOD LION, INC.

2110 Executive Drive
P.O. Box 1330
Salisbury, NC 28145-1330
(704) 633-8250
Chairman: Ralph W. Ketner
President and CEO: Tom E. Smith

EARNINGS GROWTH	★ ★ ★ ★ ★
STOCK GROWTH	★ ★ ★ ★ ★
DIVIDEND YIELD	★
DIVIDEND GROWTH	★ ★ ★ ★ ★
SHAREHOLDER PERKS	(no points)
OTC—FDLNB	**16 points**

Most of Food Lion's 500 stores are what you'd call self-service, cash-and-carry, no-frills groceries. They offer no trading stamps, no banking services, no pharmacies, no video rentals, no floral boutiques; just a solid selection of groceries with prices slashed to the nub. The low prices have kept sales roaring and helped Food Lion romp to 17 consecutive years of record earnings. Scant margins and high volume have long been a trademark of the North Carolina grocer, where the corporate philosophy is: "We'd rather make five fast pennies than one slow nickel."

The fast-pennies approach has helped early Food Lion shareholders penny ante their way to a lionly fortune. When the stock was first issued in 1957 (as Food Town), it sold for $10 a share; $1,000 would buy you 100 shares. Food Lion stock still trades at about $10 a share, but the stock has gone through so many splits over the years that by 1988 that original 100 shares would have ballooned to 1.3 million shares, and the original $1,000 investment would now be worth $13 million.

The company has continued its strong growth over the past ten years, with earnings-per-share increases of about 30 percent per year and stock price appreciation of about 35 percent per year.

At one time, Food Lion's battle cry was "Lowest food prices in North Carolina," but the company has long since extended its domain beyond the

Tarheel state. Roughly half of the company's stores are located in North Carolina, and the others are spread through South Carolina, Virginia, Tennessee, Georgia, Florida, Maryland and Delaware. The company opens nearly 100 new stores a year, and expects to have about 800 stores in operation by the end of 1990.

Food Lion's basic format calls for conventional-sized groceries (25,000 square feet) which are relatively small compared with many of the new grocery superstores that other chains are now building. By comparison, Albertson's (another Best 100 entry) is now building 40,000 square-foot groceries—60 percent larger than Food Lion's standard stores.)

Although Food Lion is slowly moving to expand its offerings (and increase its per store margins), the real draw for consumers continues to be its low prices. The company has been able to trim costs even further by operating its own truck fleet and by building its own food warehouse distribution centers in North Carolina, South Carolina, Virginia, Tennessee and Florida.

Tom E. Smith, Food Lion's president and CEO, learned the grocery trade from the ground up. While in high school, he joined the company as a bagger in 1958, then worked his way through college as a store manager.

EARNINGS GROWTH

Food Lion has annual revenues of $3 billion. The company has had increased earnings per share for 17 consecutive years. Earnings have increased 1,250 percent (30 percent per year) over the past ten years.

The company has 27,000 employees. Its stock is evenly divided between Class A (non-voting) and Class B (voting). Class B stock generally trades about 5 to 10 percent higher than Class A stock. The Belgian supermarket company, Establissements Delhaize Frere et Cie, S.A., controls about 50 percent of the Class B voting stock. There are about 14,000 shareholders of record of Class A stock and 9,000 shareholders of Class B stock.

One cautionary note: Food Lion has the highest price-earnings ratio of any company among the Best 100. Its stock is trading at 30 times earnings. That shouldn't be a problem if the company continues its explosive growth, but should its growth flatten out, the stock price could prove volatile.

STOCK GROWTH

The company's stock price has climbed steadily through the past decade with increases eight of the past 10 years (through 1987). The stock has had three 3-for-1 stock splits and two 2-for-1 splits since 1979. Over the past ten years the stock has increased 1,900 percent (35 percent per year) for its (split-adjusted) median of 50 cents in 1978 to its late 1988 price of $10 a share.

Including reinvested dividends, a $10,000 investment in Food Lion stock at its median price in 1978 would have grown to about $205,000 ten years later. Average annual compounded rate of return (including stock growth and reinvested dividends): about 35.5 percent.

DIVIDEND YIELD

Food Lion has traditionally paid a very low dividend yield, which has averaged well under 1 percent over the past ten years. During the most recent three-year period, the stock has paid an annual current return of 0.4 percent.

DIVIDEND GROWTH

Although the dividend yield is still quite low, the company has raised its payout substantially in recent years. The dividend was increased 577 percent over the four-year rating period from 1983 to 1987.

SHAREHOLDER PERKS   (no points)

The company offers no dividend reinvestment plan, nor does it offer any other shareholder perks.

SUMMARY

Total revenues: $3 billion, 1987. Earnings per share: $0.27, 1987; $0.02, 1977; 1,250% increase. Stock price (Class B): $10, 12/16/88; $0.50 (median), 1978; 1,900% increase (35% per year); price rose 8 of 10 years, 1977–87. Dividend: $0.05, 1987; 0.0075, 1983; 4-year increase: 566%. Dividend yield: 0.4% average, 1985–87. P/E ratio: 30, 1/5/89. Average annual total return to investors, 1978–88: 35.5%.

43

PRIME MOTOR INNS, INC.

700 Route 46 East
P.O. Box 2700
Fairfield, NJ 07007
(201) 882-1010
Chairman and CEO: Peter E. Simon

EARNINGS GROWTH	★ ★ ★ ★ ★
STOCK GROWTH	★ ★ ★ ★ ★
DIVIDEND YIELD	★
DIVIDEND GROWTH	★ ★
SHAREHOLDER PERKS	★ ★ ★
NYSE—PDQ	**16 points**

At first blush, Prime Motor Inns may seem a bit out of its league on this list. Not only is it one of the youngest companies to make the *Best 100* (it was incorporated in 1968), it is also one of the smallest (annual revenues of $301 million). And Prime's meager dividend—8 cents on a $30 stock (a 0.2 percent yield)—ranks dead last.

But most investors—especially those who like to travel—should be more than willing to overlook such deficiencies when they get a glimpse of Prime's other numbers.

Prime offers one of the best shareholder perks in America. Shareholders can save up to 50 percent on the cost of a room at Prime's motor lodges throughout the United States. For someone who travels frequently, that type of discount could add up to hundreds of dollars a year in lodging savings.

But you don't have to leave home to appreciate some of Prime's other numbers. The company has had sensational earnings and stock price growth the past ten years. Earnings have increased 23-fold and Prime stock has jumped 20-fold.

Prime owns more than 100 motels and hotels throughout the United States, including 62 Howard Johnson motels, 22 Holiday Inns, 13 Ramada Inns, five Sheraton Inns, two Days Inns, two independent motor inns and a Marriott Hotel. The company also manages more than 20 other motels that are either leased or owned by others and serves as franchisor of more than

450 Howard Johnson motels. As franchisor, Prime provides training, marketing, reservation coordination and other services for the motels in exchange for an up-front fee and annual royalties of about 5 to 7 percent of gross revenue from the motel.

Prime also operates a number of restaurants and bars located adjacent to its inns.

Prime has established itself in what appears to be a profitable niche, enjoying explosive growth during an otherwise disappointing decade for most of its contemporaries in the lodging industry. Jeff Adams, an analyst with PaineWebber, says four factors separate Prime from the competition: "management's construction expertise, aggressive marketing methods, ability to self-finance expansion and ability to do successful acquisitions."

In addition to its lodging business, Prime holds controlling interest in Universal Communication Systems, which sells and services telephone interconnect systems for hotels, hospitals, schools, businesses and governmental offices.

EARNINGS GROWTH

Prime has had sensational earnings growth over the past 10 years. Its earnings per share jumped 2,178 percent, from 9 cents a share in 1978 to $2.05 a share in fiscal 1988. The company has had 12 consecutive years of increased earnings.

The company has 3,400 shareholders and 10,000 employees. Insiders hold about 12 percent of the stock.

STOCK GROWTH

Over the past ten years, Prime's stock has had three 3-for-2 stock splits and two 4-for-3 splits. The stock price has climbed 1,900 percent (35 percent per year) over the past decade, from its median of $1.50 per share in 1978 to its recent 1988 price of $30 per share.

Including reinvested dividends, a $10,000 investment in Prime stock at its median price in 1978 would have grown to about $200,000 ten years later. Average annual compounded rate of return (including stock growth and reinvested dividends): about 35 percent.

DIVIDEND YIELD

Dividends are not a strong point for Prime, averaging well under 1 percent per year since it began paying dividends in 1982. But, with the company's strong stock price appreciation, few of its shareholders would quibble over the low yield. During the three-year rating period from 1986 to 1988, the stock paid an average annual current return of 0.2 percent.

DIVIDEND GROWTH

The company has not made a habit of raising its dividends each year. The dividend was increased 33 percent over the four-year rating period from 1984 to 1988.

SHAREHOLDER PERKS

Prime Motor Inns offers no dividend reinvestment plan but still manages an above average score in this category because of its discount lodging program for shareholders. All shareholders of record receive a "Prime Advantage" card entitling them to 50 percent off on Prime-operated motel and hotel rooms (reserved in advance) taken Friday and Saturday nights, and 25 percent off rooms taken during the week.

SUMMARY

Total revenues: $370 billion, fiscal 1988 (ended 6/30/88). Earnings per share: $2.05, 1988; $0.09, 1978; 2,178% increase. Stock price: $30, 11/8/88; $1.50 (median), 1978; 1,900% increase (35% per year); price rose 9 of 10 years, 1977–87. Dividend: $0.08, 1988; $0.06, 1984; 4-year increase: 33%. Dividend yield: 0.2% average, 1986–88. P/E ratio: 15, 1/3/89. Average annual total return to investors, 1978–88: about 35%.

44

A. Schulman Inc.

A. SCHULMAN, INC.

3550 W. Market St.
Akron, OH 44313
(216) 666-3751
Chairman and President: William C. Zekan

EARNINGS GROWTH	★ ★ ★ ★ ★
STOCK GROWTH	★ ★ ★ ★ ★
DIVIDEND YIELD	★ ★
DIVIDEND GROWTH	★ ★ ★ ★
SHAREHOLDER PERKS	(no points)
OTC—SHLM	**16 points**

In the classic motion picture "The Graduate," Dustin Hoffman's would-be father-in-law tried to steer him to a career of boundless potential with a single word of advice: "Plastics."

He wasn't joking. A. Schulman, an emerging plastics manufacturer based in Akron, Ohio, has borne out that advice over the past decade with a phenomenal record of growth. Schulman, one of the smallest companies on the *Best 100* list, has been one of the most profitable for its shareholders, with an average annual return on investment of about 34.5 percent the past ten years.

Schulman is a leading international supplier of plastics compounds and resins, which it custom-produces for sale to manufacturers. Schulman's plastics are used in a wide range of applications, including consumer products (pens, disposable diapers, shelving, videotape cassettes, batteries, outdoor furniture, lawn sprinklers, artificial turf, skateboards, toys and plastic parts for various household appliances), electronics (telephone parts, wire insulation, transformers), packaging (for such products as food, soap, flowers and other household items), office equipment (computer cases and housings, folders and binders, stack trays), automotive (protective bumper strips and bumper guards, window seals, air ducts, steering wheels, fan shrouds, grills, and body side moldings) and agriculture (greenhouse coverings and protective film for animal feed and agricultural mulch).

Schulman also manufactures flame retardants used in telephone system terminal blocks, color television tube covers, appliance housings and electrical components. And it does a good business in plastic color concentrates used to add color to plastic products such as toys, household goods, automotive parts, cable and packaging material.

The company has three plants in the U.S. plus plants in Belgium, West Germany, South Wales, England, and Canada.

Most of Schulman's sales come from outside the U.S. European sales account for 60 percent of the company's $599 million in total annual revenue, foreign sales outside of Europe account for 9 percent of revenues and U.S. sales account for about 32 percent of the total.

EARNINGS GROWTH

Schulman has had exceptional earnings growth over the past few years and appears to be well-positioned for future growth.

The company has had earnings per share increases 9 of the past ten years through 1988, with a total increase during the period of 472 percent.

Schulman, which has been in business since 1928, has 1,100 employees and a like number of shareholders of record.

STOCK GROWTH

The company's stock price growth has been exceptional over the past decade, with increases nine of the past ten years. During the period, the stock has climbed a total of 1,460 percent (31.5 percent per year), from its 1978 median of $2.50 per share to its recent 1988 price of $39.

Including reinvested dividends, a $10,000 investment in Schulman stock at its median price in 1978 would have grown to about $195,000 ten years later. Average annual compounded rate of return (including stock growth and reinvested dividends): about 34.5 percent.

DIVIDEND YIELD

The company normally pays a fairly low dividend yield, averaging just under 3 percent the past ten years. During the past three years, the stock has paid an average annual current return of only 1.3 percent.

DIVIDEND GROWTH

The company increases its dividend most years and often pays special dividends to its shareholders. Over the four-year rating period from 1983–87, the dividend has increased 129 percent.

SHAREHOLDER PERKS   (no points)

The company has no dividend reinvestment plan, nor does it offer any other shareholder perks.

SUMMARY

Total revenues: $599 million, fiscal 1988 (ended 8/31/88). Earnings per share: $3.09, 1988; $0.54, 1978; 472% increase. Stock price: $39, 10/18/88; $2.50 (median), 1978; 460% increase (31.5% per year); price rose 9 of 10 years, 1977–87. Dividend: $0.48, 1988; $0.21, 1984; 4-year increase: 129%. Dividend yield: 1.3% average, 1986–88. P/E ratio: 14, 1/3/89. Average annual total return to investors, 1978–88: 34.5%.

45

PHILIPS INDUSTRIES, INC.

4801 Springfield St.
P.O. Box 943
Dayton, Ohio 45401
(513) 253-7171
Chairman: Jesse Philips
President and CEO: Robert H. Brethen

EARNINGS GROWTH	★ ★ ★ ★ ★
STOCK GROWTH	★ ★ ★ ★
DIVIDEND YIELD	★ ★ ★
DIVIDEND GROWTH	★ ★ ★ ★
SHAREHOLDER PERKS	(no points)
NYSE—PHL	**16 points**

Philips Industries is a burgeoning manufacturing operation with a diverse range of products and a voracious appetite for acquisitions. The Ohio-based conglomerate has swallowed up more than 20 smaller manufacturers since 1982.

The acquisitions have helped Philips broaden an already crowded—and disparate—line of products. The company's product list includes fans and ventilation components, bathroom sinks and bathtubs, mobile home windows and patio doors, automotive wheels and axles, conveyer assemblies and overhead crane systems.

Among its more recent additions are Dearborn Fabricating & Engineering, Arrowhead Conveyor, Mayfran companies, Midwest Conveyor group and Stearns Airport Equipment.

Not only have its acquisitions kept the company's product line growing, they have also helped Philips keep its flawless record of revenue growth intact. The company has increased its revenues for 30 consecutive years, dating back to 1957, the year the company was founded by Jesse Philips (who continues to serve as the company's chairman of the board). Over the past ten years, the company has provided its shareholders with an excellent average annual return on investment of more than 30 percent.

Philips Industries breaks its operations into five key groups. Its largest is air distribution products, which account for almost one-third of the company's $693 million in total revenue. The air distribution group manufactures components for the heating and air conditioning markets, including blowers, propeller fans, dampers, rooftop fire and smoke hatches, vents, grills and duct heaters.

Other divisions include:

- Molded plastic products (22 percent of total revenues). This group includes Lasco fiberglass and acrylic showers, bathtubs and spas, and fiberglass panels for garage doors, wall liners, patio covers, room dividers and utility sheds.
- Transportation products (22 percent of revenues). Its Dexter Axle division is the leading producer of axles and running gear assemblies for recreational vehicles and light- to medium-duty utility trailers. Its Shelby Wheel subsidiary makes cast aluminum wheels for new and used automobiles.
- Shelter products (22 percent of revenues). This division manufactures a line of aluminum windows, doors and venting products for the manufactured housing and recreational vehicle markets. It also makes windows and doors for standard homes and other buildings.
- Industrial components (4 percent of revenue). This is the newest and smallest of Philips' segments. It makes hoists, overhead conveyor systems for the automotive industry and overhead crane systems for other industrial applications.

EARNINGS GROWTH

Philips Industries has had 12 consecutive years of increased earnings (through fiscal 1988). Over the past ten years, its earnings per share have climbed 533 percent.

The company has total annual revenues of $692 million. It has 10,000 employees and 4,500 shareholders of record.

STOCK GROWTH

The company's stock price has climbed quickly but somewhat erratically over the past decade, with increases only seven of the past ten years. The stock has been split 2-for-1 twice since 1983. Over the past ten years the stock has increased 1,033 percent (27.5 percent per year), from its median of $1.50 in 1978 to its recent 1988 price of $17 a share.

Including reinvested dividends, a $10,000 investment in Philips stock at its median price in 1978 would have grown to about $155,000 ten years later.

Average annual compounded rate of return (including stock growth and re-invested dividends): about 31.5 percent.

DIVIDEND YIELD

The company generally pays a fairly good yield, which has averaged about 3.4 percent over the past ten years. During the three-year rating period from 1986 to 1988, the stock paid an average annual current return of 2.3 percent.

DIVIDEND GROWTH

Philips has increased its dividend 11 consecutive years. The dividend increased 147 percent over the four-year rating period from 1984 to 1988 (from 17 cents to 42 cents).

SHAREHOLDER PERKS   (no points)

Philips offers no dividend reinvestment plan, nor does it provide any other perks for its shareholders.

SUMMARY

Total revenues: $692 million, fiscal 1988 (ended 3/31/88). Earnings per share: $1.52, 1988; $0.24, 1978; 533% increase. Stock price: $17, 11/8/88; $1.50 (median), 1978; 1,033% increase (27.5% per year); price rose 7 of 10 years, 1977–87. Dividend: $0.42, 1988; $0.17, 1984; 4-year increase: 147%. Dividend yield: 2.3% average, 1986–88. P/E ratio: 12, 1/3/89. Average annual total return to investors, 1978–88: 31.5%.

46

KELLY SERVICES, INC.
999 West Big Beaver Road
Troy, MI 48084
(313) 362-4444
Chairman: William Russell Kelly
President: Terence E. Adderley

EARNINGS GROWTH	★ ★ ★ ★ ★
STOCK GROWTH	★ ★ ★ ★ ★
DIVIDEND YIELD	★ ★
DIVIDEND GROWTH	★ ★ ★ ★
SHAREHOLDER PERKS	(no points)
OTC—KELYA	**16 points**

The Kelly Girl was born of an accident, a temporary setback that William Russell Kelly managed to turn into a booming international business.

When Mr. Kelly, the 83-year-old founder and still chairman of the temporary help firm, first opened his "service bureau" in 1946, he sold his customers on the concept of sending their work to him. Companies that were falling behind on their paperwork could get overnight typing and production help from Mr. Kelly's staff (which initially included his wife and one other woman). All the work was done in Kelly's own production office.

But one client, desperate for immediate clerical help, asked Mr. Kelly to send one of his secretaries out to his company for the day to do some in-house work. Kelly grudgingly agreed, charging the client $6.75 for the day's work. The real hitch, however, came the next day when the woman didn't return to work at Kelly's office. Mr. Kelly tracked her down and learned that she had taken a job at his client's office. The client had been so pleased with her work that he hired her on the spot. While Mr. Kelly felt burned by the loss of his typist, the case did open his eyes to a whole new market—the need for clerical workers who could step into a job on short notice to help a company overcome a temporary overload.

Today, Kelly Services does business with 175,000 businesses in the U.S., Canada, the United Kingdom and France. The company, based near Detroit, has 800 offices worldwide. In all, Kelly has more than half a million temporary employees.

The company has expanded beyond secretarial work and now also offers temporary marketing, technical, light industrial and home care services.

Kelly counts on the unpredictable—as well as the predictable—for its steady flow of assignments. Its workers often step in for ailing full-time employees and help businesses out during peak times or during special projects or promotions.

The computer age has posed new problems for Kelly. Whereas at one time its temporary secretaries needed only to be competent typists, now they often must be able to operate a company's computerized word processing system. With so many types of computers and word processing programs on the market, a Kelly Girl might be asked to work on a different system every time she changes assignments.

To address that problem, Kelly introduced a training program in 1987 to help its clerical workers learn twelve different word processing systems and three of the most common software spreadsheet applications. The program also includes a toll-free hotline its workers can call if they run into problems on the job.

EARNINGS GROWTH

Kelly Services has enjoyed excellent earnings growth over the past decade, with a 600 percent increase in earnings per share during the ten-year period.

With total revenues of $1.3 billion, Kelly is one of the two largest temporary help companies in the U.S. Kelly has 3,000 permanent employees and 550,000 temporary employees. The company has 1,500 Class A shareholders of record. Insiders control nearly 60 percent of Class A stock and 83 percent of Class B stock.

STOCK GROWTH

The company's stock price has climbed quickly and consistently, with 13 consecutive years of stock price increases through 1987. Over the past ten years the stock has increased 1,100 percent (28 percent per year), from its median of $3.25 in 1978 to its recent 1988 price of $39 a share.

Including reinvested dividends, a $10,000 investment in Kelly Services stock at its median price in 1978 would have grown to about $150,000 ten years later. Average annual compounded rate of return (including stock growth and reinvested dividends): about 31 percent.

DIVIDEND YIELD

The company generally pays a fairly low yield, which has averaged about 2.5 percent over the past ten years. During the three-year rating period from 1985 to 1987, the stock paid an average annual current return of 1.4 percent.

DIVIDEND GROWTH

Kelly has increased its dividend 16 consecutive years. The dividend rose 104 percent over the four-year rating period from 1983 to 1987.

SHAREHOLDER PERKS   (no points)

The company provides no dividend reinvestment plan nor does it offer any other perks for its shareholders.

SUMMARY

Total revenues: $1.2 billion, 1987. Earnings per share: $2.10, 1987; $0.30, 1977; 600% increase. Stock price: $39, 11/3/88; $3.25 (median), 1978; 1,100% increase (28% per year); price rose 10 of 10 years, 1977–87. Dividend: $0.51, 1987; $0.25, 1983; 4-year increase: 104%. Dividend yield: 1.4% average, 1985–87. P/E ratio: 15, 1/3/89. Average annual total return to investors, 1978–88: about 31%.

47 nordstrom

NORDSTROM, INC.

1501 Fifth Ave.
Seattle, WA 98101-1603
(206) 628-2111
Co-Chairmen: Bruce A. Nordstrom,
John N. Nordstrom and James F. Nordstrom
President: Jack McMillan

EARNINGS GROWTH	★ ★ ★ ★ ★
STOCK GROWTH	★ ★ ★ ★ ★
DIVIDEND YIELD	★
DIVIDEND GROWTH	★ ★ ★ ★ ★
SHAREHOLDER PERKS	(no points)
OTC—NOBE	**16 points**

John W. Nordstrom was a turn-of-the-century prospector who cashed in his gold for a shoe store, then turned his shoe store into a gold mine. Nearly a century later, his descendents, Bruce and John Nordstrom (co-chairmen of the board), and James Nordstrom (president) still rule the company with that golden touch.

Since going public in 1971, the West Coast apparel chain has had 17 consecutive years of record earnings, and its shareholders have earned an average annual return on investment the past ten years of about 30 percent.

Nordstrom's first shoe store was opened in 1901 in Seattle (as Wallin & Nordstrom). Through the years, as the first store grew more profitable, the family decided to open more shoe stores in other northwestern cities. Then, in the early 1960s, the company began to expand its focus, delving into other fashion areas such as clothing and accessories for men, women and children.

When the company went public in 1971, the new infusion of capital opened the door for further growth and expansion.

Nordstrom now claims to be the nation's leading fashion specialty store. The company operates 39 full-line specialty stores, seven Place Two specialty fashion shops, and ten Nordstrom Rack discount clearance outlets.

Until 1988, all of Nordstrom's stores were in the far West (Washington, Oregon, California, Alaska, Utah and Montana). Its first East Coast store, which opened outside of Washington, D.C., in March 1988, is also among its largest—three floors and 208,000 square feet. The company plans to open several more East Coast department stores in the near future.

Nordstrom maintains a decentralized system of operations. Each region has its own buyers to ensure that the merchandise they buy reflects the regional tastes of their customers. Department, store and regional managers are also given great flexibility in their operational decisions.

Nordstrom stores are a favorite of West Coast shoppers because of the quality and wide selection of their apparel offerings.

With annual sales of about $2 billion, Nordstrom has moved into some elite company among the nation's retailers. It is larger than Saks Fifth Avenue, Nieman-Marcus and the Gap, although it still lags far behind other retail chains such as Dayton-Hudson, The Limited, Federated Department stores and J.C. Penney.

EARNINGS GROWTH

Nordstrom has had increased earnings for 17 consecutive years. Earnings per share have climbed 465 percent over the past decade.

The company has 20,000 employees and 31,500 shareholders. The Nordstrom family holds 41 percent of the stock.

STOCK GROWTH

The company's stock price has risen quickly through the past decade, with three 2-for-1 stock splits since 1983. Over the past ten years the stock has increased 1,140 percent (28.5 percent per year) from its median of $2.50 in 1978 to its late 1988 price of $31 a share.

Including reinvested dividends, a $10,000 investment in Nordstrom stock at its median price in 1978 would have grown to about $137,000 ten years later. Average annual compounded rate of return (including stock growth and reinvested dividends): about 30 percent.

DIVIDEND YIELD

The company tends to pay a fairly low dividend yield, which has averaged just over 1 percent during the past ten years. Over the three-year rating period from 1985 to 1987, the stock paid an average annual current return of 0.8 percent.

DIVIDEND GROWTH

Nordstrom has increased its dividend every year since going public in 1971. The dividend was raised 157 percent over the four-year rating period from 1983 to 1987.

SHAREHOLDER PERKS   (no points)

Nordstrom offers no dividend reinvestment plan, nor does it any other perks for its shareholders.

SUMMARY

Total revenues: $1.9 billion, 1987. Earnings per share: $1.13, 1987; $0.20, 1977; 465% increase. Stock price: $30, 10/28/88; $2.50 (median), 1978; 1,140% increase (28.5% per year); price rose 8 of 10 years, 1977–87. Dividend: $0.18, 1987; $0.07, 1983; 4-year increase: 157%. Dividend yield: 0.8% average, 1985–87. P/E ratio: 23, 1/3/89. Average annual total return to investors, 1978–88: about 30%.

48

HARLAND

JOHN H. HARLAND COMPANY

2939 Miller Road
Decatur, GA 30035
(404) 981-9460
Chairman and CEO: J. William Robinson
President: Robert R. Woodson

EARNINGS GROWTH	★ ★ ★ ★ ★
STOCK GROWTH	★ ★ ★ ★ ★
DIVIDEND YIELD	★ ★
DIVIDEND GROWTH	★ ★ ★ ★
SHAREHOLDER PERKS	(no points)
NYSE—JH	**16 points**

By all rights, the electronic age should have leveled a crushing blow to the John H. Harland Company. Harland derives its income from the printing of bank checks, deposit tickets and other standard bank forms. Scribes have long predicted that advances in technology would usher in a paperless society in which financial transactions would be performed almost entirely by credit card and electronic transfer. But so far, the advent of electronic banking has had no effect on Harland's extraordinary record of growth. The Georgia-based printer has had 38 consecutive years of increased sales and 34 straight years of increased earnings and dividends.

While Harland's annual revenue of $288 million pales compared to the nearly $1 billion a year generated by the market leader, Deluxe Corporation (also a *Best 100* company), Harland does command a formidable share of the nation's check printing business.

The company does business with 70,000 banks, savings and loans and other financial institutions. It operates 44 printing plants throughout the U.S., with combined printing capacity of about 400,000 checks per week. In 1987, the company printed a total of 10.3 billion checks, deposit tickets and other forms, with an accuracy rate of 99.2 percent. The company holds about a 23 percent share of the U.S. check printing market.

While Harland's management acknowledges that technological advances have created new alternatives to the check, they point out that electronic payment volume equals only 1 to 2 percent of the number of checks written. They also point out some other factors that would seem to indicate that check printing is by no means a dying art:

- Checks continue to be the primary method of payment in this country, with an estimated 45 billion checks written each year.
- Checking accounts continue to escalate, with the increase of dual-income families.
- Checking accounts remain the primary basis of the relationship between banks and their customers.
- With more new services such as cable TV, day care, mail-ordering and credit card accounts, many consumers are writing more checks now than ever before to pay their bills.

EARNINGS GROWTH

Harland has one of the most impressive records of long-term growth in American industry, with 34 consecutive years of increased earnings. Earnings per share have climbed 563 percent over the past decade.

With annual revenues of $288 million, Harland is the nation's second-largest check printer. The company has 5,200 employees and 5,500 shareholders of record.

STOCK GROWTH

The company's stock price has grown even faster than its earnings over the past decade. During that period, the stock has increased 922 percent (26 percent per year), from its median of $2.25 in 1978 to its recent 1988 price of $23 a share.

Including reinvested dividends, a $10,000 investment in Harland stock at its median price in 1978 would have grown to about $123,000 ten years later. Average annual compounded rate of return (including stock growth and reinvested dividends): about 28.5 percent.

DIVIDEND YIELD

The company traditionally pays a fairly low dividend yield, which has averaged just over 2 percent the past ten years. During the three-year rating period from 1985 to 1987, the stock paid an average annual current return of 1.7 percent.

DIVIDEND GROWTH

Harland has raised its dividend 34 consecutive years. The dividend soared 121 percent during the four-year rating period from 1983 to 1987.

SHAREHOLDER PERKS   (no points)

The company provides no dividend reinvestment plan for its shareholders, nor does it offer any other perks.

SUMMARY

Total revenues: $288 million, 1987. Earnings per share: $1.26, 1987; $0.19, 1977; 563% increase. Stock price: $23, 11/4/88; $2.25 (median), 1978; 922% increase (26% per year); price rose 10 of 10 years, 1977–87. Dividend: $0.42, 1987; $0.19, 1983; 4-year increase: 121%. Dividend yield: 1.7% average, 1985–87. P/E ratio: 16, 1/3/89. Average annual total return to investors, 1978–88: 28.5%.

49

SONOCO PRODUCTS COMPANY

P.O. Box 160
Hartsville, SC 29550
(803) 383-7000
President: Charles W. Coker

EARNINGS GROWTH	★ ★
STOCK GROWTH	★ ★ ★ ★ ★
DIVIDEND YIELD	★ ★ ★
DIVIDEND GROWTH	★ ★ ★
SHAREHOLDER PERKS	★ ★ ★
OTC—SONO	**16 points**

Sonoco Products began in 1899 in Hartsville, South Carolina, as a manufacturer of yarn cones for the textile industry. The company still makes paper cones, cores and tubes for winding yarn, paper, foils and films, and it is still based in Hartsville, but that's where the simliarities end.

Today, Sonoco has manufacturing plants in 200 locations throughout the world. It manufactures a wide range of packages and packaging material, from plastic motor oil containers and Ajax tubes to fiber drums and industrial wire spools. Its earnings and revenues have grown consistently through the years as a result of internal growth and acquisitions. Its annual revenues total about $1.3 billion.

The company divides its domestic business into three key segments:

- Converted products (62 percent of total revenue). In addition to its trademark cones, tubes and cores, Sonoco Products also makes cans and plastic bottles for packaging snack foods, frozen juice concentrates, solid shortening, motor oil, Ajax scouring powder and other consumer products. It manufactures fiber and plastic drums for packaging products such as chemicals, pharmaceuticals and foods, and it makes fiber partitions and packaging forms for shipping cartons.
- Paper (15 percent of revenues). Sonoco produces about 565,000 tons of cylinderboard from recycled waste paper (the company recycles about 800,000 tons of waste paper each year). Most of the cylinderboard is

converted to paperboard packaging products such as tubes, cones and drums for Sonoco's own operations. The company also produces about 150,000 tons per year of corrugated material.

* Miscellaneous (10 percent of revenues). Plastic grocery sacks, produced by Sonoco's Polysack Division, are one of the company's fastest-growing new products. The company also makes metal beams for the textile industry, wood and metal reels for the wire and cable industries, adhesives and coatings, wood chips for pulping, railroad cross-ties and hardwood lumber.

Sonoco's international segment, with operations in England, Canada, Mexico, Australia and 15 other nations, accounts for about 13 percent of the company's total revenue.

The company's most recent acquisitions include Continental Fibre Drum Company, Plasti-Drum and the Consumer Packaging Division of Boise Cascade.

EARNINGS GROWTH

Sonoco Products has had record annual sales and earnings for 19 of the past 20 years. Earnings have climbed 233 percent over the past decade.

Sonoco, with total annual revenues of $1.3 billion, has 14,000 employees and 13,500 shareholders of record.

STOCK GROWTH

The company's stock price has climbed quickly through the past decade, with three 2-for-1 stock splits since 1981. Over the past ten years the stock has increased 728 percent (23.5 percent per year) from its median of $3.50 in 1978 to its recent 1988 price of $29 a share.

Including reinvested dividends, a $10,000 investment in Sonoco Products stock at its median price in 1978 would have grown to about $112,000 ten years later. Average annual compounded rate of return (including stock growth and reinvested dividends): about 27.5 percent.

DIVIDEND YIELD

The company generally pays a fairly good yield, which has averaged about 3.5 percent over the past ten years. During the three-year rating period from 1985 to 1987, the stock paid an average annual current return of 2.3 percent.

DIVIDEND GROWTH

Sonoco traditionally raises its dividend nearly every year. The dividend increased 79 percent over the four-year rating period from 1983 to 1987.

SHAREHOLDER PERKS

Although the company makes no consumer products itself, it does manufacture the packaging for a number of foods and household products. Shareholders who attend Sonoco's annual meetings receive a package of some of these products, such as a can of Crisco shortening (Sonoco makes the cans), a roll of masking tape (the company makes the inner-spools the tape comes on), Pringles potato chips (Sonoco makes the containers), and a can of tennis balls.

The company offers its shareholders of record a dividend reinvestment and voluntary stock purchase plan. There is a small fee and commission charge for participants. Shareholders may contribute $10 to $500 per month to the voluntary stock purchase plan.

SUMMARY

Total revenues: $1.3 billion, 1987. Earnings per share: $1.53, 1987; $0.46, 1977; 233% increase. Stock: $29, 11/3/88; $3.50 (median), 1978; 728% increase (23.5% per year); price rose 8 of 10 years, 1977–87. Dividend: $0.50, 1987; $0.28, 1983; 4-year increase: 79%. Dividend yield: 2.3% average, 1985–87. P/E ratio: 18, 1/3/89. Average annual total return to investors, 1978–88: 27.5%.

CARTER-WALLACE, INC.

767 Fifth Ave.
New York, NY 10153
(212) 758-4500
Chairman and CEO: Henry H. Hoyt, Jr.
President: Daniel J. Black

EARNINGS GROWTH	★ ★ ★ ★ ★
STOCK GROWTH	★ ★ ★ ★ ★
DIVIDEND YIELD	★ ★
DIVIDEND GROWTH	★ ★ ★
SHAREHOLDER PERKS	(no points)
NYSE—CAR	**16 points**

Carter-Wallace has it all for the man on the make: Pearl Drops to brighten his teeth, Rise to lather his beard, Arrid to keep him dry and Trojan condoms to protect him and his partner. (Carter-Wallace also markets a line of "Answer-2" home pregnancy test kits for women.)

The New York-based consumer and health-care products manufacturer also produces a number of other well-known personal care items, including Carter's Little Pills (laxative), Nair (hair remover), H-R lubricating jelly, Sea & Ski and Block Out suncare lotions, Rigident denture adhesives, Triple X pediculicide (for lice) and Deoped footcare products.

Carter-Wallace also has a major presence in the pet-care market. It makes Chirp vitamins for birds, Evict liquid wormers, Bar Flies and Boundary mosquito repellent, Femalt hairball remover, Ear Rite miticide, Victory Veterinary Formula insecticides, Fresh 'N Clean grooming products and stain and odor remover, Medi-Cleen, Huggin' Clean, Snowy Coat and Good Bye Dry shampoos, Shield and Head to Tail flea and tick products, and the Lassie line of pet products.

The company's consumer products segment accounts for about 54 percent of its $483 million in total annual sales. Its most profitable line is its Arrid deodorant, which has been the nation's leading brand for several years, holding an 11 percent market share. Deodorant sales account for about 25 percent of the company's total annual revenue.

Its line of Trojan condoms is also a U.S. market-leader, accounting for more than 50 percent of all condoms sold in the U.S. Sales of condoms have increased substantially in recent years, primarily as a result of fears about the AIDS virus.

Carter's other key segment is health-care products promoted primarily through doctors, pharmacists and hospitals. Its health-care segment makes up about 46 percent of the company's annual sales. The company manufactures tranquilizers, muscle relaxants, antibiotics, laxatives, expectorants, antibacterials and antihypertensive drugs. Carter-Wallace also makes Rynatan and Rynatuss cough and cold products, Bentasil medicated throat lozenges, Aspro aspirins, Peptol antiulcer medication, Diovol and Univol antacid products, Butisol sedative-hypnotic drugs, Atasol analgesics and Jordan toothbrushes.

Its other products include antinauseants, topical analgesics, nasal decongestants and antispasmodics.

The company markets a line of medical testing kits to help detect a number of ailments such as herpes, mononucleosis, influenza, meningitis and rubella.

The firm markets its products throughout the world. Foreign sales account for about 13 percent of its operating income.

EARNINGS GROWTH

Carter-Wallace has had earnings increases for 12 consecutive years. Earnings per share have jumped 558 percent over the past decade.

The company has about 4,000 employees and a like number of shareholders of record.

STOCK GROWTH

The company's stock price growth has been even more dramatic than its earnings growth. Over the past ten years the stock has increased 744 percent (24 percent per year), from its median of $4.50 in 1978 to its late 1988 price of $38 a share.

Including reinvested dividends, a $10,000 investment in Carter-Wallace stock at its median price in 1978 would have grown to about $115,000 ten years later. Average annual compounded rate of return (including stock growth and reinvested dividends): about 27.5 percent.

DIVIDEND YIELD

The company has traditionally paid a fairly good dividend, although the dividend yield has dropped off considerably in the past few years. During the three-year rating period from 1986 to 1988, the stock paid an average annual current return of 1.3 percent.

DIVIDEND GROWTH

Carter-Wallace has raised its dividend for six consecutive years. It has increased its dividend 114 percent over the four-year rating period from 1984 to 1988.

SHAREHOLDER PERKS   (no points)

Carter-Wallace offers no dividend reinvestment plan, nor does it provide any other perks for its shareholders.

SUMMARY

Total revenues: $483 million, for fiscal 1988 (ended 3/31/88). Earnings per share: $2.50, 1988; $0.38, 1977; 558% increase. Stock price: $38, 9/13/88; $4.50 (median), 1978 (744% total increase; 24% annual increase); price rose 8 of 10 years, 1977–87. Dividend: $0.50, 1988; $0.23, 1984; 4-year increase: 114%. Dividend yield: 1.3%, 1986–1988. P/E ratio: 14, 1/3/89. Average annual total return to investor, 1978–88: about 27.5%.

51

DEAN FOODS COMPANY

3600 North River Road
Franklin Park, IL 60131
(312) 625-6200
Chairman and CEO: Howard M. Dean
President: William Fischer

EARNINGS GROWTH	★ ★ ★
STOCK GROWTH	★ ★ ★ ★ ★
DIVIDEND YIELD	★ ★
DIVIDEND GROWTH	★ ★ ★
SHAREHOLDER PERKS	★ ★ ★
NYSE—DF	**16 points**

Milk builds strong bones and robust balance sheets. Chicago-based Dean Foods has fashioned one of the steadiest records of corporate growth in the foods industry while relying on the sale of simple, homogenized milk for more than half of its $1.6 billion in annual revenues.

Dean also does a good business in the traditional dairy sidelines—ice cream, cheese, butter, buttermilk, yogurt, cottage cheese, cream cheese, sour cream, eggnog, coffee creamer and chip dip—as well as some not-so-traditional dairy hybrids of its own. It recently introduced a product called Taste D-Lite, which combines cottage cheese with fresh fruit, and a liquid yogurt called Yogurt To Go, which the company describes as a "drinkable, naturally flavored refrigerated product."

The company also milks some profits from other food groups. About one-third of Dean's annual revenues comes from sales of its non-dairy foods such as canned and frozen vegetables (Veg-All, Freshlike and Larsen brands), pickles, relishes and salad dressings (Peter Piper, Heifetz, Pesta, Atkins and Bond pickles; Hoffman House dressings), sauces and puddings (Amboy Specialty), deli foods (Mrs. Weaver's) and juices (Juice Services and Sun Flo).

Many of Dean's products are sold under private label brands at grocery chains across the country. Jewel stores, for example, carries Dean's products under its own Jewel label. Jewel, a subsidiary of American Stores, is Dean's largest customer, accounting for about 8 percent of Dean's total annual sales.

Dean also operates about 425 Baskin-Robbins ice cream franchises in 11 midwestern and western states.

Dean's growth has come primarily through an aggressive policy of acquisitions. Since 1984, the company has acquired a number of regional food processing companies, including Bluhill-American of Arvada, Colorado; Gilt Edge farms of Norman, Oklahoma; Hart's Dairy of Fort Myers, Florida; Ryan Milk of Murray, Kentucky; Reiter Dairy of Akron, Ohio; Modern Dairy of Elgin, Illinois; Fairmont products of Bellville, Pennsylvania, and Verifine Dairy of Sheboygan, Wisconsin. Through a stock merger agreement, Dean also absorbed Larsen Company, a large producer of canned and frozen vegetables.

Typically, Dean continues to market the products of its subsidiaries under the original names. Among Dean's leading regional dairy brands are Creamland, Fieldcrest, Gilt Edge, McArthur, Hart's, Bowman, Bell, Gandy, Carnival, Calypso and Fitzgerald. Dean also owns Mecadam, the New York state cheese maker. Cheese sales account for about 3 percent of Dean's total revenues. Milk (and related fluid dairy products) accounts for 56 percent of sales, ice cream makes up 8 percent, and other foods account for 33 percent of total sales.

EARNINGS GROWTH

Dean Foods has had 15 consecutive years of record sales and earnings, although its growth has flattened out considerably over the past few years (per share earnings increased only seven cents—from $1.53 to $1.60—from fiscal 1986 to 1988.)

The company has, however, had excellent growth over the past ten years. Earnings per share climbed 264 percent, from 44 cents per share in 1978 to $1.60 in fiscal 1988.

Dean has about 7,000 employees and 8,500 shareholders.

STOCK GROWTH

Dean's stock price growth has fared much better than its earnings growth over the past decade, increasing 731 percent (23.5 percent per year), from its 1978 median of $3.25 to its recent 1988 price of $27. The stock has had four 3-for-2 stock splits and one 2-for-1 split since 1978.

Including reinvested dividends, a $10,000 investment in Dean Foods stock in 1978 would have grown to about $103,000 in 1988. Average annual compounded return (including stock growth and reinvested dividends): about 26.5 percent.

DIVIDEND YIELD

Dean has traditionally paid a moderate to low dividend yield. Over the past three years the stock has paid an average annual current return of about 1.7 percent.

DIVIDEND GROWTH

Dean normally increases its dividends each year. The dividend climbed 74 percent over the four-year period from 1984 to 1988.

SHAREHOLDER PERKS

No one goes home hungry from a Dean Foods annual meeting. The company passes out a small grab bag of groceries that might include a can of vegetables, a jar of pickles, a nondairy creamer, shrimp sauce and coupons for such items as Baskin-Robbins ice cream and Mrs. Weaver's deli foods.

Dean offers a good dividend reinvestment and voluntary stock purchase plan. There are no fees, and shareholders of record may buy $25 to $3,000 per quarter in additional shares.

SUMMARY

Total revenues: $1.56 billion, for fiscal 1988 (ended 5/31/88). Earnings per share: $1.60, 1988; $0.44, 1978; 264% increase. Stock price: $27, 10/4/88; $3.25 (median), 1978 (731% total increase; 23.5% annual increase); price rose 9 of 10 years, 1977–87. Dividend: $0.54, 1988; $0.31, 1984; 4-year increase: 74%. Dividend yield: 1.7%, 1986–1988. P/E ratio: 15, 1/3/89. Average annual total return to investor, 1978–88: about 26.5%.

ALBERTSON'S, INC.

250 Parkcenter Blvd.
P.O. Box 20
Boise, Idaho 83726
(208) 385-6200
Chairman and CEO: Warren E. McCain
President: John B. Carley

EARNINGS GROWTH	★ ★ ★ ★
STOCK GROWTH	★ ★ ★ ★ ★
DIVIDEND YIELD	★ ★ ★
DIVIDEND GROWTH	★ ★ ★
SHAREHOLDER PERKS	★
NYSE—ABS	**16 points**

Joe Albertson started with a single grocery in Boise, Idaho in 1939. Five decades later and 465 stores stronger, the company still keeps its headquarters in Boise, and Mr. Albertson still serves as chairman of the firm's executive committee.

If you live west of the Mississippi, odds are you've bought some groceries at Albertson's. More than 400 of the company's stores are located in 15 western states. The rest are scattered through Florida and Louisiana. Albertson's is strongest on the West Coast. Nearly half its stores are located in California, Washington and Oregon.

The company, now the seventh largest food and drug chain in the United States and the 17th largest retailer overall, has posted 18 consecutive years of record sales and earning.

Albertson's consistent, sustained growth may be due in part to its ability to keep up with changing consumer buying trends. Its stores, on average, are now 50 percent larger than stores of a decade earlier, and four times the size of Albertson's first 10,000 square-foot grocery in Boise. Of the company's 465 stores, 109 would be classified as "combination food-drug units," 152 are "superstores," 25 are "warehouse stores" and 179 are conventional supermarkets.

In 1988, the company began an aggressive five-year, $1.5 billion expansion and remodeling program. Plans call for the opening of 175 new stores, primarily in Idaho, Nevada, Utah, California, Florida, Texas and Arizona. The company also plans to remodel and, in some cases, expand 150 of its existing stores. The company will also be updating its in-store computer systems to help with inventory control.

Albertson has pinned much of its growth not only to its expanding store base, but also to its expanding product base. In addition to its standard grocery offerings, many of its larger stores have five special service departments:

* Pharmacy. Low cost pharmacies in 188 Albertsons stores provide additional convenience for its shoppers.
* Lobby departments. Many of its stores provide services for customers such as money orders, bus passes, lottery tickets, stamps, camera supplies, film developing and videotape rental.
* Service deli. Delicatessens in 355 of its stores offer take-home foods, meats, cheeses, fresh salads and fried chicken. Salad bars have been added in 192 Albertson's stores.
* Service fish and meat departments. About 170 Albertson stores have specialty departments with a full array of fresh fish, shellfish, premium cuts of meat and semi-prepared items such as stuffed pork chops.
* Bakeries. The company is moving towards a partial self-service concept in which customers may pick out the freshly baked breads, pastries, cakes and cookies on their own (or request personal service).

EARNINGS GROWTH

Albertson's has had 18 consecutive years of record earnings. Earnings per share have climbed 359 percent over the past decade.

The company has 43,000 employees and 10,000 shareholders. Insiders hold about 30 percent of the stock.

STOCK GROWTH

The company's stock price has moved up quickly through the past decade with three 2-for-1 stock splits since 1980. Over the past ten years the stock has increased 700 percent (23 percent per year), from its median of $4.50 in 1978 to its late 1988 price of $36 a share.

Including reinvested dividends, a $10,000 investment in Albertson's stock at its median price in 1978 would have grown to about $100,000 ten years later. Average annual compounded rate of return (including stock growth and reinvested dividends): about 26 percent.

DIVIDEND YIELD

The company generally pays a moderate yield, which has averaged about 2.5 percent over the past ten years. During the three-year rating period from 1985 to 1987, the stock paid an average annual current return of 2.1 percent.

DIVIDEND GROWTH

Albertson's has increased its dividend for more than 15 consecutive years. The dividend increased 60 percent over the four-year rating period from 1983 to 1987.

SHAREHOLDER PERKS

Shareholders who attend the annual meeting receive a packet of some of Albertson's private label groceries—cans of vegetables, napkins, paper towels and other samples. What better reason for a trip to Boise?

SUMMARY

Total revenues: $5.9 billion, 1987. Earnings per share: $1.88, 1987; $0.41, 1977; 359% increase. Stock price: $36, 11/8/88; $4.50 (median), 1978; 700% increase (23% per year); price rose 8 of 10 years, 1977–87. Dividend: $0.48, 1987; $0.30, 1983; 4-year increase: 60%. Dividend yield: 2.1% average, 1985–1987. P/E ratio: 17, 1/5/89. Average annual total return to investors, 1978–88: about 26%.

⊞ Pitney Bowes

PITNEY BOWES INC.

One Elmcroft Rd.
Stamford, CT 06926-0700
(203) 356-5000
Chairman, President and CEO: George B. Harvey

EARNINGS GROWTH	★ ★ ★
STOCK GROWTH	★ ★ ★ ★ ★
DIVIDEND YIELD	★ ★ ★
DIVIDEND GROWTH	★ ★ ★
SHAREHOLDER PERKS	★ ★
NYSE—PBI	**16 points**

It is the hottest new toy in corporate America. Its very presence has unleashed an accelerating torrent of inter-office communications. It is known, technically, as a "facsimile transmission machine"—it scans and transmits (or receives) printed material by telephone—but in the common corporate vernacular, this revolutionary new wonderbox is referred to simply as a "fax." Pitney Bowes markets a line of Japanese-made fax machines including a new "9200" laser model that can store to disc and send up to 1,200 pages of printed material automatically—one page every 11 seconds.

But while the fax is Pitney's fastest growing product (sales have increased 150 percent over the past two years), postage meter machines have long been the backbone of the Stamford, Connecticut, firm. With more than a million meters in service at businesses throughout the U.S., Canada and the United Kingdom, Pitney is the world's leading manufacturer of postage meters.

Pitney is also the market leader worldwide for mailing machines, scales, inserting systems, parcel registers, shipping systems and mailroom furniture.

Much of the company's $2.3 billion a year in total revenue comes from rental and service charges for its equipment. In 1987, the company earned $507 million in rental revenue from its postage equipment, plus another $332 million in service charges.

Pitney Bowes manufactures or markets a wide range of other business equipment, including copying machines, dictating machines, telephone answering systems, voice recording loggers and other voice processing systems. Business equipment accounts for about 78 percent of the company's total revenue.

Its two segments include:

- Retail systems (11 percent of revenues). Pitney Bowes makes price-marking and merchandise identification equipment and electronic article surveillance systems through its Monarch Marking Systems subsidiary.
- Business supplies. Business supplies now account for about 11 percent of the company's total revenues, but that will drop in future years due to the sale of its Data Documents subsidiary. However, the company is still involved in the business supplies market through its Wheeler Group subsidiary, which markets 4,000 items such as printed forms, labels, stationery, and office and computer supplies through direct mail and telemarketing.

EARNINGS GROWTH

Pitney Bowes has had earnings increases 13 of the past 14 years (through 1987). Earnings per share have climbed 272 percent over the past decade.

The company has 30,000 employees and 25,000 shareholders of record.

STOCK GROWTH

The company's stock price has experienced exceptional growth over the past decade, with two 2-for-1 stock splits since 1983. Over the past ten years the stock has increased 617 percent (22 percent per year), from its median of $6 in 1978 to its late 1988 price of $43 a share.

Including reinvested dividends, a $10,000 investment in Pitney Bowes stock at is median price in 1978 would have grown to about $100,000 ten years later. Average annual compounded rate of return (including stock growth and reinvested dividends): about 26 percent.

DIVIDEND YIELD

The company generally pays a fairly good yield, which has averaged about 3.5 percent over the past ten years. During the three-year rating period from 1985 to 1987, the stock paid an average annual current return of 2.3 percent.

DIVIDEND GROWTH

Pitney Bowes raises its dividend nearly every year. The dividend increased 69 percent over the four-year rating period from 1983 to 1987.

SHAREHOLDER PERKS

The company offers its shareholders of record a good dividend reinvestment and voluntary stock purchase plan. There are no fees or commissions, and shareholders of record may purchase $100 to $3,000 per quarter in additional shares through the voluntary stock purchase plan.

SUMMARY

Total revenues: $2.25 billion 1987. Earnings per share: $2.53, 1987; $0.68, 1977; 272% increase. Stock price: $43, 11/10/88; $6 (median), 1978; 617% increase (22% per year); price rose 8 of 10 years, 1977–87. Dividend: $0.76, 1987; $0.45, 1983; 4-year increase: 69%. Dividend yield: 2.3% average, 1985–1987. P/E ratio: 14, 1/3/89. Average annual total return to investors, 1978–88: about 26%.

BORDEN, INC.

277 Park Ave.
New York, NY 10172
(212) 573-4000
Chairman and CEO: R. J. Ventres

EARNINGS GROWTH	★ ★
STOCK GROWTH	★ ★ ★ ★ ★
DIVIDEND YIELD	★ ★ ★
DIVIDEND GROWTH	★ ★ ★
SHAREHOLDER PERKS	★ ★ ★
NYSE—BN	**16 points**

If you know Borden, then you know Elsie. Borden is the *créme de la créme* of the dairy business, and Elsie is its original cash cow. Elsie's lovable, bovine mug has smiled out from milk bottles and ice cream cartons for more than 50 years. "If it's Borden," she'll tell you, "it's got to be good."

But while Borden continues its dominance as the world's largest dairy producer (accounting for more than a third of the company's $6.5 billion in total annual revenue), the company has also strayed into other pastures. The New York-based conglomerate is the world's largest pasta producer and the nation's second largest "salty snack" producer. Borden—which acquired 38 smaller companies during 1986 and 1987—owns Cracker Jack, Creamettes and Red Cross pasta brands, Seyferts chips, Kava coffee, Orleans oyster crackers, Doxsee clam juice and Campfire marshmallows.

But Borden's reach goes well beyond the foods industry. It's the number two producer of wall coverings in the world and is a major competitor in spray paints and household glues. It manufactures Rally Car Wash, Rain Dance Glass Cleaner and Krylon paints.

Borden also operates a chemical specialties division that is a major force in the adhesives and forest products resins market, and a niche grocery business that focuses on smaller-volume, higher-margin specialty foods.

Borden's expansive range of products, by segment, includes:

- Dairy products (37 percent of sales). The company produces a full range of dairy products (milk, cottage cheese, sour cream, whipping cream, eggnog, ice cream) under the labels of Borden, Meadow Gold, Mountain High, Viva, Old Fashioned Recipe. It continues to acquire regional creameries. Valley Bell Dairy of West Virginia and Sinton Dairy of Colorado were two of several 1987 acquisitions. The company operates 75 domestic processing facilities and sells its dairy goods in 38 states.
- Snacks (11 percent of sales). The company has acquired a number of regional snack foods manufacturers. Along with its five national brands (Borden, La Famous, New York Deli, Seyfert's and Wise) it owns several large regional snack food companies (Jays, Chesty, Laura Scudder's, Buckeye, Clover Club, Snacktime, Cain's, Geiser's, Guy's) with sales in 46 states.
- Pasta (6 percent of total sales). In addition to its Creamette brand, the company owns 17 regional brands of pasta.
- Niche grocery (17 percent of sales). The company has 28 brands of special grocery such as condensed milk (Eagle Brand), mincemeat (None Such), shakes (Frostee), bouillon (Wyler's) and maple syrup (Cary's). It holds the number one or number two marketing position in 23 product categories.
- Nonfood consumer (8 percent of sales). Includes Elmer's glues, cements and sealants, Krylon paints, Rain Dance and Rally car waxes, and a dozen brands of wall coverings.
- Chemical specialties (16 percent of sales). Makes resins, coatings, specialty adhesives and packaging films.

Borden has operations in 36 foreign countries (including South Africa, where its wholly owned subsidiary, Borden Ltd., is involved in food sales and processing) and sells its products through dozens of countries worldwide.

EARNINGS GROWTH

Borden's earnings growth has not been particularly dramatic over the past decade, but it has been fairly steady, with earnings gains eight of ten years through 1987. During that period earnings per share increased 166 percent.

The company, which was founded in 1857, has 32,000 employees and 40,000 shareholders.

STOCK GROWTH

Borden's stock price has increased seven of ten years through 1988. The company has had one 2-for-1 stock split and one 3-for-2 split since 1985. Over the past ten years the stock has increased 600 percent (20 percent per year), from its median of $9.50 in 1978 to its late 1988 price of $57 a share.

Including reinvested dividends, a $10,000 investment in Borden stock at its median price in 1978 would have grown to about $100,000 ten years later. Average annual compounded rate of return (including stock growth and reinvested dividends): about 25.5 percent.

DIVIDEND YIELD

The company generally pays a good dividend yield, which has averaged about 5 percent over the past ten years. During the three-year rating period from 1985 to 1987, the stock paid an average annual current return of 2.9 percent.

DIVIDEND GROWTH

Borden has a long history of annual dividend increases. The dividend increased 55 percent over the four-year rating period from 1983 to 1987.

SHAREHOLDER PERKS

Shareholders who attend the annual meeting are treated to a small bag of Borden products such as Elmer's glue, Harris crabmeat, popcorn, potato chips, Cheez Doodles and other snacks.

The company offers its shareholders of record a good dividend reinvestment and voluntary stock purchase plan. There are no fees or commissions, and shareholders of record may purchase up to $10,000 per quarter in additional shares through the voluntary stock purchase plan.

SUMMARY

Total revenues: $6.5 billion, 1987. Earnings per share: $3.62, 1987; $1.36, 1977; 166% increase. Stock price: $57, 11/7/88; $9.50 (median), 1978; 600% increase (20% per year); price rose 7 of 10 years, 1977–87. Dividend: $1.24, 1987; $0.80, 1983; 4-year increase: 55%. Dividend yield: 2.9% average, 1985–1987. P/E ratio: 15, 1/5/89. Average annual total return to investors, 1978–88: 25.5%.

55

PPG INDUSTRIES, INC.

One PPG Place
Pittsburgh, PA 15272
(412) 434-3131
Chairman and CEO: Vincent A. Sarni

EARNINGS GROWTH	★ ★ ★
STOCK GROWTH	★ ★ ★ ★ ★
DIVIDEND YIELD	★ ★ ★
DIVIDEND GROWTH	★ ★ ★
SHAREHOLDER PERKS	★ ★
NYSE—PPG	**16 points**

PPG Industries was first incorporated as the Pittsburgh Plate Glass Company in 1883. The name was changed to PPG Industries in 1968, reflecting its broader corporate mission. PPG is now the world's leading supplier of auto and industrial coatings, and a major global supplier of chlorine and caustic soda. Glass products, however, continue to be PPG's prime commodity; it manufactures about one-third of the total North American industry output of flat glass.

The company makes glass for automobiles, homes, commercial buildings, aircraft, furniture and even the electronics industry. PPG does a good business in fiberglass, ranking as the world's second largest manufacturer of "continuous strand" fiberglass. PPG's glass segment accounts for 43 percent of the company's $5.1 billion a year in total revenue.

PPG also makes protective and decorative finishes for automobiles, appliances, industrial equipment and the consumer and industrial products. It has a line of paints marketed to both consumer and commercial customers. The firm's coatings and resins division generates about 35 percent of its total revenue.

In its chemicals division, PPG is not only a world leader in production of chlorine and caustic soda, it also produces chemicals for the optical plastics business, waste treatment, food additives, pharmaceuticals and other manufacturing areas. The chemicals division accounted for about 20 percent of the company's total revenue.

PPG's management has also made several acquisitions in the biomedical systems area, and hopes to expand that area into a fourth major business group.

The company has a strong worldwide market, with foreign business accounting for nearly one-third of its total sales. In total, the company operates about 75 manufacturing facilities and 11 research centers, including operations in Canada, France, Germany, Italy, Mexico, the Netherlands, Spain, Taiwan and the United Kingdom.

EARNINGS GROWTH

PPG's earnings growth has been on a steady upswing since the early 1980s. Prior to that, however, the going was a little rocky. Its earnings per share declined each year from 1979 to 1982. But strong gains since then has helped push the company's total earnings growth over the past ten years to 336 percent.

The company has 40,000 shareholders and 42,000 shareholders of record.

STOCK GROWTH

PPG's stock price has had an excellent run the past decade, with stock price increases eight of ten years from 1977 to 1987. The stock has climbed 471 percent (19 percent per year) from a median of about $7 a share in 1978 to its late 1988 price of $40.

Including reinvested dividends, a $10,000 investment in PPG stock at its median price in 1978 would be worth about $89,000 ten years later. Average annual compounded rate of return: about 24.5 percent.

DIVIDEND YIELD

The company generally pays a good dividend yield, which has averaged about 5 percent over the past ten years. During the three-year rating period from 1985 to 1987, the stock paid an average annual current return of 3.1 percent.

DIVIDEND GROWTH

PPG has raised its dividend 16 consecutive years. The dividend increased 79 percent over the four-year rating period from 1983 to 1987.

SHAREHOLDER PERKS

PPG offers a good dividend reinvestment plan with all fees absorbed by the company. Shareholders may make voluntary cash payments of $10 to $3,000 per quarter.

SUMMARY

Total revenues: $5.2 billion 1987. Earnings per share: $3.19, 1987; $0.73, 1977; 336% increase. Stock price: $40, 11/7/88; $7 (median), 1978; 471% increase (19% per year); price rose 8 of 10 years, 1977–87. Dividend: $1.11, 1987; $0.62, 1983; 4-year increase: 79%. Dividend yield: 3.1% average, 1985–1987. P/E ratio: 10, 1/5/89. Average annual total return to investors, 1978–88: 24.5%.

56

NATIONAL SERVICE INDUSTRIES, INC.

1180 Peachtree Street, NE
Atlanta, GA 30309
(404) 892-2400
Chairman: Erwin Zaban
President and CEO: Sidney Kirschner

EARNINGS GROWTH	★ ★ ★
STOCK GROWTH	★ ★ ★ ★ ★
DIVIDEND YIELD	★ ★ ★
DIVIDEND GROWTH	★ ★ ★
SHAREHOLDER PERKS	★ ★
NYSE—NSI	**16 points**

Diversification has been good to National Service Industries (NSI). This is a company that operates in seven different industry groups. It rents uniforms and linen products, manufactures chemical goods, lighting systems, lamps, envelopes and men's clothing, develops sales aids and installs insulation. And while most of NSI's groups have had their ups and downs over the years, the company, as a whole, has enjoyed earnings increases 24 of the past 25 years.

The Atlanta-based conglomerate, once known primarily as a linen and uniform rental service, has grown to revenues of $1.3 billion a year through an aggressive policy of acquisitions. In 1987 alone, the company acquired 14 smaller companies in its core business segments.

NSI's largest subsidiary is Lithonia Lighting (41 percent of total revenue), the largest lighting fixture manufacturer in the U.S. The company makes fluorescent and high-intensity discharge fixture and architectural downlighting fixtures. In addition to its Lithonia line, NSI also owns Hi-Tek Lighting, Major Reflector Products, National Lighting Standards and RE-LOC Wiring Systems.

The company's other key divisions include:

• Textile rental. Rents table linen, bed linens, towels, uniforms, operating room packs and dust control materials under four subsidiaries: National

Linen Service, National Uniform Service, National Healthcare Linen Service and National Dust Control Service. Accounts for 22 percent of total revenue.

- Chemical. Manufactures chemical products—including soaps, detergents, waxes and disinfectants—primarily for the maintenance, sanitation and water treatment industries. NSI's chemical-related subsidiaries include Zep Manufacturing, Selig Chemical, National Chemical and Canadian Industrial Chemical. Accounts for 14 percent of NSI's total revenue.
- Envelopes. Makes business and specialty envelopes through its Atlantic Envelope Company, and record filing systems through its ATENCO subsidiary.
- Marketing services. Provides sales aids—including binders, booklets, sales kits and display racks—for the carpet, upholstery, tile and wallpaper industries.
- Insulation. Fabricates, installs, maintains and sells commercial, industrial and institutional insulation products.
- Men's apparel. Sells men's dress and sports shirts, jackets, sweaters and sportswear through Block Sportswear, PM Company of New York, Shepherd Sportswear and Kudos.
- Consumer lighting equipment. Makes and markets fluorescent work lamps and decorative fluorescent fixtures through its Home-Vue and Light Concepts subsidiaries.

EARNINGS GROWTH

National Service Industries has had very steady earnings growth over the past two decades, including earnings increases for the past 12 consecutive years. Over the past ten years, earnings per share have increased 221 percent (12 percent per year).

The company, which was first incorporated in 1928, has total annual revenues of $1.33 billion. It has 19,500 employees and 9,000 shareholders of record.

STOCK GROWTH

The company's stock price growth has also been exceptionally consistent, with 13 consecutive years of price increases through 1987. The stock has had three 4-for-3 splits and one 3-for-2 split since 1983. Over the past ten years the stock has increased 487 percent (19 percent per year), from its median of $3.75 in 1978 to its late 1988 price of $22 a share.

Including reinvested dividends, a $10,000 investment in NSI stock at its median price in 1978 would have grown to about $89,000 ten years later. Average annual compounded rate of return (including stock growth and reinvested dividends): about 24.5 percent.

DIVIDEND YIELD

NSI tends to pay good dividend yield, which has averaged about 5 percent over the past decade. During the most recent three-year period, the stock paid an average annual current return of 2.9 percent.

DIVIDEND GROWTH

NSI has increased its dividend each year for the past 25 consecutive years (through 1987) and has paid a dividend each year without a decrease for 51 consecutive years. The dividend payout increased 59 percent during the four-year rating period from 1983 to 1987.

SHAREHOLDER PERKS

The company offers a dividend reinvestment and voluntary stock purchase plan. Participants are assessed a small fee for service and commission expenses. Shareholders of record may buy $10 to $4,000 per month in additional shares through the voluntary cash purchase plan.

SUMMARY

Total revenues: $1.3 billion, 1987. Earnings per share: $1.54, 1987; $0.48, 1977; 221% increase. Stock price: $22, 10/24/88; $3.75 (median), 1978 (487% total increase; 19% annual increase); price rose 10 of 10 years, 1977–87. Dividend: $0.62, 1987; $0.39, 1983; 4-year increase: 59%. Dividend yield: 2.9%, 1985–1987. P/E ratio: 12, 1/3/89. Average annual total return to investor, 1978–88: about 24.5%.

57

NEW YORK TIMES COMPANY

229 West 43rd St.
New York, NY 10036
(212) 556-1234
Chairman, CEO and Publisher of the *New York Times*:
Arthur Ochs Sulzberger
President: Walter E. Mattson
Executive Editor of the *Times:* Max Frankel

EARNINGS GROWTH	★ ★ ★ ★
STOCK GROWTH	★ ★ ★ ★ ★
DIVIDEND YIELD	★ ★
DIVIDEND GROWTH	★ ★ ★
SHAREHOLDER PERKS	★ ★
ASE—NYT.A	**16 points**

Nowhere in America has the decline of the daily newspaper been more evident than in New York. The *Daily Mirror* is gone. The *World-Telegram* is gone. The *New York Sun* is gone. Even the *New York Herald*—which merged with the *Tribune,* then merged again with the *Journal American*—has been off the racks for years.

But Gotham's most distinguished daily is still thriving, and still reporting its version of "all the news that's fit to print," just as it has since 1851.

Newspaper aficionados regard the *New York Times* as the pinnacle of print journalism; the paper received its first Pulitzer Prize in 1917—the year the awards were instituted—and has been winning them regularly ever since. Not everyone, however, has such a keen appreciation for the *Times.* Its more conservative readers may consider its editorial views something less than "fit to print"—the *Times* leans decidedly left. Humor lovers may also feel slighted by the *Times*—the paper carries no comics page. But adore it or deplore it, there's no disputing that the *New York Times* is one of the most influential publications in the world.

The *Times* is circulated in all 50 states and 77 foreign countries. Of its 1.1 million daily subscribers and 1.6 million Sunday readers, more than 30 percent live outside the greater New York City area. The paper's national edition has eight U.S. production sites that print the paper from satellite-transmitted page images created in New York.

The newspaper also serves as the hub of a worldwide news service that reaches 85 million readers in the U.S. and abroad.

In addition to its flagship paper, the New York Times organization owns a number of other publications and several television and radio stations.

The company owns 26 daily and nine nondaily smaller-city newspapers in California, Florida, Alabama, Georgia, Kentucky, Louisiana, Maine, Mississippi, North Carolina, South Carolina and Tennessee. It also owns *Family Circle* (six million circulation), the largest-selling women's magazine in the world, *Decorating Remodeling* magazine, *Child, Southern Travel* and a group of sports magazines, including *Golf Digest, Golf World, Tennis* and *Cruising World*.

The company owns four TV stations (in Tennessee, Pennsylvania, Illinois and Alabama), two radio stations in New York City and a cable television system in southern New Jersey.

Newspapers account for about 81 percent of the company's total revenue, magazines account for about 13 percent and its TV holdings for about 6 percent.

EARNINGS GROWTH

The New York Times Company has annual revenues of $1.7 billion. It has about 10,000 employees and 14,000 shareholders of record of Class A stock. The Ochs family, with about 80 percent of the Class B stock, has voting control of the company.

The company has enjoyed excellent earnings growth over the past decade with increases in earnings per share eight of the past ten years and a total increase in earnings of 416 percent during the period.

STOCK GROWTH

The company's stock price has climbed steadily through the past decade with one 2-for-1 stock split and one 3-for-2 split since 1983. Over the past ten years the stock has increased 559 percent (21 percent per year), from its median of $4.25 in 1978 to its late 1988 price of $28 a share.

Including reinvested dividends, a $10,000 investment in New York Times stock at its median price in 1978 would have grown to about $82,000 ten years later. Average annual compounded rate of return (including stock growth and reinvested dividends): about 23.5 percent.

DIVIDEND YIELD

The Times has traditionally paid a fairly low dividend yield, which has dropped even lower in recent years. Over the past three years the stock has paid an annual average current return of 1.1 percent.

DIVIDEND GROWTH

The Times normally increases its dividend each year. The dividend climbed 82 percent over the four-year rating period from 1983 to 1987.

SHAREHOLDER PERKS

The company does provide a reinvestment and voluntary stock purchase plan for its shareholders, but participants must pay a small fee for service and commission expenses. Shareholders may contribute $10 to $3,000 per quarter to the stock purchase plan.

The company offers no other perks.

SUMMARY

Total revenues: $1.7 billion, 1987. Earnings per share: $1.96, 1987; $0.38, 1977; 416% increase. Stock price: $28, 9/21/88; $4.25 (median), 1978 (559% total increase; 21% annual increase); price rose 9 of 10 years, 1977–87. Dividend: $0.40, 1987; $0.22, 1983; 4-year increase: 82%. Dividend yield: 1.1%, 1985–1987. P/E ratio: 14, 1/4/89. Average annual total return to investor, 1978–88: about 23.5%.

58

MCGRAW-HILL, INC.

1221 Avenue of the Americas
New York, NY 10020
(212) 512-2000
Chairman, President and CEO: Joseph L. Dionne

EARNINGS GROWTH	★ ★ ★
STOCK GROWTH	★ ★ ★ ★ ★
DIVIDEND YIELD	★ ★ ★
DIVIDEND GROWTH	★ ★ ★
SHAREHOLDER PERKS	★ ★
NYSE—MHP	**16 points**

James H. McGraw and John A. Hill started separately, as editors of competing railroad journals in the late 1880s. Not until 20 years later—when both owned fledgling technical publishing operations in New York City—did the two decide to merge. As the story goes, they flipped a coin to see whose name would go first on the company door. Eighty years later, that same name arches across the entrance of a 50-story glass and granite office tower in New York's Rockefeller Center.

As one of the nation's largest publishing concerns (seventh among Fortune 500 publishers in 1988), McGraw-Hill has more than 50 subsidiaries in 20 countries and is involved in an expanding range of publishing ventures, from books, magazines and newsletters to software and database information systems. While the company puts out a few mainstream publications (*Business Week* is its best-known consumer journal), its real strength remains in the technical publishing field. McGraw-Hill has published 12 editions (dating back to 1907) of the *Standard Handbook for Electrical Engineers,* six editions and 450,000 copies of *Perry's Chemical Engineers Handbook,* 11 editions of *Principles of Internal Medicine.* It publishes nearly a dozen magazines and newsletters on aerospace and defense and a number of other publications on energy, transportation and process industries.

The company also publishes hundreds of textbooks from elementary through college levels, produces the Standard & Poors Economic and

Financial reports, develops instructional software and owns a handful of television stations.

McGraw-Hill divides its business into five segments:

- Books. The McGraw-Hill Book Company (32 percent of total revenue; 15 percent of earnings) boasts more than 20,000 books, magazines, newsletters, pamphlets, special publications computer software programs, online computer information services, audio and video cassettes and multi-media packages. Of the company's domestic operations (which accounts for about 82 percent of revenue), higher education and training materials accounted for about a third of sales, elementary and vocational education made up about a fourth of sales, and professional and general publishing comprised about 40 percent of total sales.
- Publications. McGraw-Hill Publications Company (22 percent of revenue, 17 percent of profit), produces more than 60 magazines, newsletters and news services, plus eight business and professional magazines in Japan with Nikkei/McGraw-Hill, a joint venture. Most of the publications in this group are of a highly technical nature, except *Business Week,* which has been a perennial leader in both revenue and circulation among all business magazines.
- Broadcasting. McGraw-Hill Broadcasting Company (5 percent of revenue, 9 percent of profit), owns television stations in Indianapolis (WRTV), Denver (KMGH), San Diego (KGTV) and Bakersfield, California (KERO).
- Information Systems. The McGraw-Hill Information Systems Company (22 percent of revenue; 33 percent of profit) specializes in construction information (F.W. Dodge Regional and National Information Services, *Sweet's, Black's Guide,* and several architectural and electrical magazines), and computers and communications (Osborne computer book publishing, Datapro computer information publishing, and *BYTE, Data Communications* and *Electronics* magazines).
- Standard & Poor's Corporation. (19 percent of revenue; 26 percent of profit) Standard & Poor's provides a debt rating service on more than 15,000 corporations, state and municipal governments and international entities. It also publishes a variety of information services such as CreditWeek and Securities Information Services, and furnishes software, information and processing services for financial institutions, government agencies and businesses.

EARNINGS GROWTH

McGraw-Hill has been a citadel of stability, with more than 15 consecutive years of record earnings. Over the past ten years, the company has increased its earnings per share 214 percent (12 percent per year).

The company's total annual revenue is $1.75 billion. McGraw-Hill has about 16,000 employees and 8,500 shareholders.

STOCK GROWTH

The company's stock price has climbed steadily through the past decade with stock price gains nine of ten years from 1977 to 1987. Over the past ten years the stock has increased 500 percent (20 percent per year) from its median of $11 in 1978 to its late 1988 price of $66 a share.

Including reinvested dividends, a $10,000 investment in McGraw-Hill stock at its median price in 1978 would have grown to about $80,000 ten years later. Average annual compounded rate of return (including stock growth and reinvested dividends): about 23 percent.

DIVIDEND YIELD

McGraw-Hill normally pays a fairly good dividend yield. Over the past three years the stock has paid an average annual current return of 2.8 percent.

DIVIDEND GROWTH

McGraw-Hill has increased its dividend each year since 1974. The dividend has increased 56 percent over the four-year rating period from 1983 to 1987.

SHAREHOLDER PERKS

The company offers a dividend reinvestment and voluntary stock purchase plan. There are no fees or commissions, and shareholders of record may buy $10 to $1,000 per quarter in additional shares through the voluntary stock purchase plan.

SUMMARY

Total revenues: $1.75 billion, 1987. Earnings per share: $3.27, 1987; $1.04, 1977; 214% increase. Stock price: $66, 11/10/88; $11 (median), 1978 (500% total increase; 20% annual increase); price rose 9 of 10 years, 1977–87. Dividend: $1.68, 1987; $1.08, 1983; 4-year increase: 56%. Dividend yield: 2.8%, 1985–1987. P/E ratio: 17, 1/3/89. Average annual total return to investor, 1978–88: about 23%.

MNC FINANCIAL, INC.

10 Light St.
Baltimore, MD 21203
(301) 244-1940
Chairman and CEO: Alan P. Hoblitzell, Jr.
President: Daniel J. Callahan III

EARNINGS GROWTH	★ ★ ★
STOCK GROWTH	★ ★ ★ ★
DIVIDEND YIELD	★ ★ ★
DIVIDEND GROWTH	★ ★ ★ ★
SHAREHOLDER PERKS	★ ★
OTC—MNCF	**16 points**

Banks have discovered a hot new way to enhance their earnings. It's called "fee generation." And MNC Financial, Inc., parent company of Maryland National Bank, has taken the lead in one of the most lucrative fee-generating sidelines in the banking business.

MNC's new game is magic plastic—credit cards. The company, through its MBNA subsidiary, has targeted the nation's most affluent customer base—doctors, lawyers, educators, airline pilots and other well-healed professionals who are most likely to pay their debts. The company has enrolled more than three million cardholders to date, including more MasterCard Gold holders than any other issuer. So far, MNC's strategy is paying off well: Its loan delinquency and loss ratios are about half the national average.

MNC's primary business, however, continues to be the operation of its flagship bank, Baltimore-based Maryland National, the state's largest bank. It has 160 branches statewide and $9.2 billion in total assets. In addition to its retail focus, Maryland National's primary market consists of regional and local businesses with annual sales of $2 million to $50 million.

MNC's other key subsidiaries include:

- American Security Bank, the second largest full-service bank in Washington, D.C., with total assets in excess of $5 billion. American Security, which MNC acquired in 1987, has the most extensive branch network in the District of Columbia, with 30 branch offices. The bank also claims to be the dominant commercial and real estate lender in the D.C. marketplace.

- ASB Capital Management, Inc., an investment advisory and management service for institutional clients. The company manages about $6 billion in assets.

- MNC Affiliates Group, the holding company for MNC's nonbank subsidiaries ($1 billion in total assets). Its holdings include MNC Leasing Corporation, MNC Commercial Corporation, Maryland National Mortgage Corporation, MNC American Corporation and MNC Consumer Discount Company. Its services, which are marketed nationally through 50 offices in 20 states, include equipment leasing, corporate finance activities, asset-based lending, mortgage banking, direct mail consumer lending, industrial banking, vendor leasing, venture capital and credit life insurance.

EARNINGS GROWTH

With total assets of $16.7 billion, MNC ranks among the 40 largest bank holding companies in the U.S. The company has 8,500 employees and about 21,000 shareholders.

MNC Financial, Inc. has had increases in earnings per share nine of the past ten years. During that period earnings have increased a total of 279 percent. Most of that growth occurred in the past five years.

STOCK GROWTH

Like its earnings growth, the company's stock price has increased rapidly the past five years, following some rocky years through the 1970s and early 1980s. Over the past ten years the stock has increased 437 percent (18 percent per year), from its median of $8.75 in 1978 to its late 1988 price of $47 a share.

Including reinvested dividends, a $10,000 investment in MNC stock at its median price in 1978 would have grown to about $79,000 ten years later. Average annual compounded rate of return (including stock growth and reinvested dividends): about 23 percent.

DIVIDEND YIELD

MNC tends to pay a good dividend yield, averaging about 4.5 percent over the past ten years. During the three-year rating period from 1985 to 1987, the stock paid an average annual current return of 3.1 percent.

DIVIDEND GROWTH

MNC has increased its dividend every year since the corporation was re-organized as a bank holding company in 1968. The dividend jumped 117 percent during the four-year rating period from 1983 to 1987.

SHAREHOLDER PERKS

The company offers an outstanding dividend reinvestment and voluntary stock purchase plan. There are no fees or commissions, and shareholders of record may buy $50 to $5,000 per quarter in additional shares through the voluntary cash purchase plan. All cash dividends allocated to the plan are invested in stock at 5 percent discount to the market. (The discount does not apply to voluntary cash payments.)

SUMMARY

Total assets: $16.7 billion, 1987; loans outstanding: $11.6 billion; total net profit: $149 million. Earnings per share: $5, 1987; $1.32, 1977; 279% increase. Stock price: $47, 10/4/88; $8.75 (median), 1978 (437% total increase; 18.5% annual increase); price rose 8 of 10 years, 1977–87. Dividend: $1.43, 1987; $0.66, 1983; 4-year increase: 117%. Dividend yield: 3.1%, 1985–1987. P/E ratio: 7, 1/4/89. Average annual total return to investor, 1978–88: about 23%.

60 Rockwell International

ROCKWELL INTERNATIONAL CORPORATION

2230 East Imperial Highway
El Segundo, CA 90245
(213) 647-5000
Chairman and CEO: Donald R. Beall

EARNINGS GROWTH	★ ★ ★ ★
STOCK GROWTH	★ ★ ★ ★
DIVIDEND YIELD	★ ★ ★
DIVIDEND GROWTH	★ ★ ★
SHAREHOLDER PERKS	★ ★
NYSE—ROK	**16 points**

Rockwell International has sailed through two decades of prosperity on the wings of the B-1 bomber. The venerable war bird has lifted the company to years of rising profits and revenues and helped Rockwell maintain its position as the largest aerospace contractor in the free world.

But storms brew on the horizon for the Pittsburgh conglomerate. Production of the B-1 (and B-1B) bomber, known for its high performance, its sleek design and ability to slip undetected through Soviet radar screens, and its exorbitant price tag ($283 million per unit), has been jettisoned by the Defense Department after 18 years of intermittent production. And Rockwell's bid to replace the lost work could suffer due to recent scrapes the company has had with its biggest customer. The U.S. government, which accounts for about 58 percent of Rockwell's revenue, has leveled double-billing charges against two former Rockwell managers—the third time since 1981 that Rockwell has been charged with defrauding the government. In the most recent case, which involves about $400,000 in satellite repair charges that were allegedly double-billed to the government, Rockwell could face a stiff fine and be temporarily barred from bidding on new aerospace and defense projects.

But Rockwell may still survive the turbulence relatively unimpaired. Although its B-1B work generated nearly 30 percent of its total revenue the past few years, Rockwell's management predicts that by cutting costs and moving ahead with other projects, the company can continue to increase its earnings per share in the years ahead. One cost-cutting measure the firm recently announced was the layoff of some 12,000 workers who had been involved in B-1B production.

Even with the halt in B-1B production, Rockwell anticipates about $500 million a year in B-1B modifications and spare parts production "into the next century." The company is also involved in a handful of other aircraft design and modification projects that could add several hundred million dollars to the company's coffers over the next few years.

Rockwell has a major presence in the U.S. space program and has been contracted to build a $1.6 billion solar power plant for the proposed space station. The company is also at work on a new $1.3 billion replacement shuttle for the Space Shuttle Challenger, which is due to join the fleet in 1991. Rockwell's shuttle operations subsidiary in Houston is managing the space shuttle flight preparation, training and sustaining engineering under a long-term contract with NASA that could bring in an additional $4 billion over the next few years.

The company's space systems division accounts for about 16 percent of its total revenue.

Rockwell is also heavily involved in defense and industrial electronics, which account for about 36 percent of its total revenue. The company makes guidance and control systems for the Peacekeeper and Minuteman missiles, and navigation systems for the Polaris and Trident submarines. It also manufactures air-launched, antiarmor Hellfire missiles for the U.S. Army and Marine Corps.

The company's largest non-military venture is industrial automation equipment, which it manufactures primarily through its Allen-Bradley subsidiary. The company is a leading manufacturer of factory automation equipment for a variety of industries.

Rockwell is also a major manufacturer of telecommunications equipment, automotive products (brakes, axles, springs, joints), and graphics systems (printing presses, mailroom systems, braiding and winding machines). Its automotive products segment accounts for about 14 percent of total revenue, and its general industries segment (graphics, energy products) accounts for about 8 percent of revenues.

EARNINGS GROWTH

Rockwell has had earnings increases for 12 consecutive years. Its earnings per share have climbed 365 percent over the past decade.

The company has 116,000 employees and 95,000 shareholders of record.

STOCK GROWTH

The company's stock price has moved up fairly steadily the past decade, with three 2-for-1 stock splits since 1980. Over the past ten years the stock has increased 395 percent (17 percent per year), from its median of $4.25 in 1978 to its recent 1988 price of $21 a share.

Including reinvested dividends, a $10,000 investment in Rockwell stock at its median price in 1978 would have grown to about $75,000 ten years later. Average annual compounded rate of return (including stock growth and reinvested dividends): about 22 percent.

DIVIDEND YIELD

The company generally pays a good dividend yield, which has averaged about 4 percent over the past ten years. During the three-year rating period from 1985 to 1987, the stock paid an average annual current return of 2.8 percent.

DIVIDEND GROWTH

The company has increased its dividend for more than 15 consecutive years. The dividend increased 55 percent over the four-year rating period from 1983 to 1987.

SHAREHOLDER PERKS

The company offers its shareholders of record a good dividend reinvestment and voluntary stock purchase plan. There are no fees or commissions, and shareholders of record may purchase $10 to $1,000 per month in additional shares through the voluntary stock purchase plan.

SUMMARY

Total revenues: $12.1 billion, 1987. Earnings per share: $2.23, 1987; $0.48, 1977; 365% increase. Stock price: $21, 10/30/88; $4.25 (median), 1978; 395% increase (17% per year); price rose 8 of 10 years, 1977–87. Dividend: $0.65, 1987; $0.42, 1983; 4-year increase: 55%. Dividend yield: 2.8% average, 1985–1987. P/E ratio: 7, 1/3/89. Average annual total return to investors, 1978–88: about 22%.

61

NATIONAL MEDICAL ENTERPRISES, INC.

11620 Wilshire Blvd.
Los Angeles, CA 90025
(213) 479-5526
Chairman and CEO: Richard K. Eamer

EARNINGS GROWTH	★ ★ ★ ★ ★
STOCK GROWTH	★ ★ ★ ★
DIVIDEND YIELD	★ ★ ★
DIVIDEND GROWTH	★ ★
SHAREHOLDER PERKS	★ ★
NYSE—NME	**16 points**

It's no Club Med, but each day National Medical Enterprises (NME) hosts about 50,000 overnight guests. If you have a problem, NME has a bed for you.

The Los Angeles-based health care provider owns 37 general (acute care) hospitals, 49 psychiatric facilities, 13 substance abuse centers, 21 rehabilitation hospitals and 377 long-term care facilities in 40 states. The company also owns one hospital in Singapore and three in England. In all, it owns about 500 facilities with a total of 60,000 beds.

NME's biggest growth segment has been in substance abuse and psychiatric treatment, an area that has become more accessible to patients in recent years because of improvements in insurance coverage. The firm has doubled its capacity in its specialty care centers over the past five years.

NME breaks its business into three health care areas: general hospitals (41 percent of its $3.2 billion in total revenue), specialty hospitals (27 percent of total revenue) and long-term care facilities (32 percent).

- General hospitals. Nearly half of the company's 37 U.S. hospitals are located in California. The company also owns hospitals in Florida, Louisiana, Missouri, Tennessee and Texas. Hospital occupancy has been declining in recent years because of improved technology and stricter insurance policies that require shorter stays by patients. The occupancy rate in NME's general hospitals has averaged only about 50 percent the past five years. In many of its hospitals, NME is addressing the shrinking occupancy problem by adding specialty wings. Fourteen of its hospitals have added psychiatric services and 14 have added substance abuse treatment. The company currently has two new hospitals under construction in Southern California.

- Specialty hospitals. The company's specialty facilities—psychiatric, substance abuse and rehabilitation—are operated by three of its subsidiaries, Psychiatric Institutes of America, Recovery Centers of America and Rehab Hospital Services Corporation. NME adds several new specialty centers each year and had about 15 centers under construction in 1988.
- Long-term care. NME's major long-term care group subsidiary is Hillhaven Corporation, which operates about 360 long term care facilities with 45,000 beds. Its other subsidiaries include Medical Ambulatory Care, which operates 20 kidney dialysis testing centers and four mobile dialysis units in five states, and Medi-$ave Pharmacies, a chain of 130 specialty pharmacies.

EARNINGS GROWTH

NME has had excellent earnings growth in recent years, with earnings per share increases 14 of the past 15 years. Earnings have increased 473 percent over the past 10 years.

The company has annual revenues of $3.2 billion. It employs 80,000 people and has 19,000 shareholders of record.

STOCK GROWTH

NME's stock price has increased 441 percent (18.5 percent per year) over the past ten years, although most of that growth occurred from 1978 (when the median price was $4.25) to 1983 when the stock hit a (split-adjusted) high of about $32.50 per share. Since then, the stock has traded primarily in the $20-to-$30 range. Its late 1988 price was $23 per share.

Including reinvested dividends, a $10,000 investment in NME stock at its median price in 1978 would have grown to about $67,000 ten years later. Average annual compounded rate of return (including stock growth and reinvested dividends): about 21 percent.

DIVIDEND YIELD

The company normally pays a fairly low dividend yield, averaging a little over 2 percent during the past ten years. During the most recent three-year period, the stock has paid an average annual current return of 2.5 percent.

DIVIDEND GROWTH

NME traditionally increases its dividend each year. The dividend climbed 47 percent over the four-year rating period from 1984 to 1988.

SHAREHOLDER PERKS

The company offers a good dividend reinvestment and voluntary stock purchase plan. There are no fees or commissions, and shareholders of record may buy $10 to $1,000 per month in additional shares.

SUMMARY

Total revenues: $3.2 billion, fiscal 1988 (ended 5/31/88). Earnings per share: $2.29, 1988; $0.40, 1978; 473% increase. Stock price: $23, 10/19/88; $4.25 (median), 1978 (441% total increase; 18.5% annual increase); price rose 8 of 10 years, 1977–87. Dividend: $0.63, 1988; $0.43, 1984; 4-year increase: 47%. Dividend yield: 2.5%, 1986–1988. P/E ratio: 11, 1/4/89. Average annual total return to investor, 1978–88: about 21%.

KAMAN

KAMAN CORPORATION

P.O. Box 1
Bloomfield, CT 06002
(203) 243-8311
Chairman, President and CEO: Charles H. Kaman

EARNINGS GROWTH	★ ★ ★
STOCK GROWTH	★ ★ ★ ★
DIVIDEND YIELD	★ ★ ★
DIVIDEND GROWTH	★ ★ ★ ★
SHAREHOLDER PERKS	★ ★
OTC—KAMNA	**16 points**

Kaman Corp, is a defense contractor that not only manufactures the usual line of military hardware—helicopters, missile components, wing flaps, thrust-reversal cowlings and engine parts for military aircraft—it also conducts research designed to provide hypothetical answers to what the world hopes will forever remain hypothetical questions.

Its primary research emphasis: to determine the effects and results of modern warfare, including "nuclear effects research," "electronic warfare simulation," and "testing, development and assessment of strategic and tactical weapons for vulnerability and survivability in hostile environments; countermeasure analysis and signal intelligence." The company also studies "various aspects of the U.S. Strategic Defense Initiative (Star Wars), including wavefront control experiments."

Kaman, founded in 1945 by Charles H. Kaman who remains the company's chairman, president and chief executive, has had one of the most consistent records of growth in the defense industry, with 19 consecutive years of increased earnings.

The Bloomfield, Connecticut, company's main claim to fame is probably its SH-2 Seasprite helicopter, which has been standard equipment aboard U.S. Navy frigates for more than two decades. The copters can carry up to nine passengers plus two crew members. The newer versions of the Seasprite, the SH-2Fs, have been upgraded for use in antisubmarine and antimissile defense. The company reports that the Seasprite has been used extensively in the Persian Gulf for antiterrorist and surveillance missions.

The company's defense segment accounts for 55 percent of its $706 million per year in total revenue and 75 percent of its operating profit.

Through its bearing and supply subsidiary, the company distributes more than 500,000 industrial replacement parts and products—such as bearings, chains, motors, gears, couplings, sprockets, belts, lubricants and seals—to manufacturing plants, mines, mills and farms.

Kaman music produces and markets acoustical and electric guitars and a wide range of other musical instruments and accessories. Ovation guitars is the company's leading line.

EARNINGS GROWTH

Kaman's earnings growth has been unfaltering, with increases in its earnings per share 19 consecutive years. Its earnings per share have climbed 253 percent over the past ten years.

The company reports annual revenues of $708 million. It has 6,500 employees and 6,000 shareholders of record.

STOCK GROWTH

The company's stock price has moved up steadily, with increases nine of ten years through 1987. Since 1981 the company has had one 2-for-1 stock split, two 3-for-1 stock splits and one 8-for-5 stock split. Over the past ten years the stock has increased 373 percent (17 percent per year), from its median of $2.75 in 1978 to its recent 1988 price of $13 a share.

Including reinvested dividends, a $10,000 investment in Kaman stock at its median price in 1978 would have grown to about $62,000 ten years later. Average annual compounded rate of return (including stock growth and reinvested dividends): about 20 percent.

DIVIDEND YIELD

The company generally pays a fairly good yield, which has averaged about 3 percent over the past ten years. During the three-year rating period from 1985 to 1987, the stock paid an average annual current return of 2 percent.

DIVIDEND GROWTH

Kaman has raised its dividend every year since 1971. The dividend was increased 100 percent, from 18 cents to 36 cents, over the four-year rating period from 1983 to 1987.

SHAREHOLDER PERKS

The company offers its shareholders of record an excellent dividend reinvestment and voluntary stock purchase plan. There are no fees and commissions, and shareholders of record may purchase $25 to $5,000 per quarter in additional shares through the voluntary stock purchase plan.

SUMMARY

Total revenues: $708 million, 1987. Earnings per share: $1.27, 1987; $0.36, 1977; 253% increase. Stock price: $13, 11/7/88; $2.75 (median), 1978; 373% increase (17% per year); price rose 9 of 10 years, 1977–87. Dividend $0.36, 1987; $0.18, 1983; 4-year increase: 100%. Dividend yield: 2.0% average, 1985–1987. P/E ratio: 8, 1/5/89. Average annual total return to investors, 1978–88: about 20%.

LOCKHEED CORPORATION

4500 Park Granada Blvd.
Calabasas, CA 91399
818-712-2000
Chairman and CEO: Daniel Tellep

EARNINGS GROWTH	★ ★ ★ ★
STOCK GROWTH	★ ★ ★ ★
DIVIDEND YIELD	★ ★ ★
DIVIDEND GROWTH	★ ★ ★ ★ ★
SHAREHOLDER PERKS	(no points)
NYSE—LK	**16 points**

When you think of the heavens, think of Lockheed.

Lockheed is the lead contractor in the nation's proposed space-based missile defense system. The project, known formally as the U.S. Strategic Defense Initiative and informally as Star Wars, would have the ability to track down attacking enemy nuclear missiles and pluck them—undetonated—from the heavens. Lockheed reports that it is already at work on several phases of the project, including ERIS (Exoatmospheric Reentry-vehicle Interceptor Subsystem), a "kinetic-energy kill vehicle so precisely guided that it can intercept an incoming ballistic warhead traveling at 23,000 miles per hour and destroy it through collision rather than by setting off a nuclear blast." So far, the project is still in the experimental stage.

Lockheed is also helping to develop a laser missile defense system that would use an earth-based "large segmented mirror array that would redirect a high-energy laser beam from the ground to a battle mirror in earth orbit. The battle mirror would then focus the beam to destroy attacking ballistic missiles." The laser beam interceptor system is also in the experimental stage.

The Star Wars system is just one of hundreds of projects the Calabasas, California-based defense contractor is involved in. With annual revenues of more than $11 billion, Lockheed is one of the largest defense contractors in the U.S. and among the 30 largest publicly traded corporations.

One of Lockheed's other space-based pursuits is development of the computer software system for NASA's proposed space station. The station, which is scheduled to be ready for orbit by the mid-1990s, will also have some other Lockheed touches, including the station's thermal control, power, mechanical equipment and crew systems.

Lockheed divides its operations into four segments:

- Missiles and space systems. Involved in military and civilian space systems, strategic fleet ballistic missiles, and tactical defense and communications systems. Lockheed produced the Trident I submarine-launched ballistic missile and is completing development of the new, improved Trident II missile. Missiles and space systems account for about 45 percent of Lockheed's $11.3 billion in total annual revenue.
- Aeronautical systems. Designs and produces special-mission and high-performance aircraft and systems for antisubmarine warfare, for reconnaissance and surveillance and other military and civilian purposes. Lockheed has been working with Boeing and General Dynamics to develop a new fighter jet for the U.S. Air Force (dubbed "ATF," advanced tactical fighter), and was the lead company in the production of the C5-B aircraft. Aeronautical systems account for about 40 percent of Lockheed's revenue.
- Electronic systems. Develops and manufactures radio frequency, infrared, electro-optic, and command, control and communications countermeasures systems; radar; airspace management systems; surveillance systems; automatic test equipment; antisubmarine warfare systems; microwave systems; and fire control systems. This segment accounts for less than 10 percent of Lockheed's total revenue.
- Information systems. Produces computer software and computer graphics equipment. Subsidiaries include CalComp, Dialog Information Services, Metier and Datacom. Information systems represent just over 5 percent of Lockheed's revenue.

EARNINGS GROWTH

Lockheed's earnings have been rising consistently over the past five years. Earnings were a little erratic prior to that, with a major glitch—a $6.48 per share loss—in 1978. The company has had earnings increases seven of the past ten years, with a total increase in earnings per share from 1977 to 1987 of 435 percent.

Lockheed has 100,000 employees and 15,000 shareholders.

Nearly 90 percent of Lockheed's sales are to the U.S. government, a situation that could create volatility in the company's stock. Policy changes in government aerospace and defense spending could have a significant impact on Lockheed's bottom line. Congress has already indicated an intention to cut back on the Star Wars program, which could directly affect Lockheed's future profitability. A major scandal that emerged in 1988 involving bribery, bid-rigging and the passing of inside information among Pentagon officials, industry consultants and defense contractors could hurt the industry. Although Lockheed was not linked to the scandal, it could suffer by association. Congress has already been under pressure to cut back the Pentagon budget, and the recent scandal could provide further incentive. Cutbacks in defense spending would probably lead to a reduction in Lockheed's annual revenues.

An investor's risk with Lockheed's stock, however, is diminished greatly by the stock's favorable stock price-to-earnings ratio. Its stock trades at about four times its earnings-per-share, which is among the lowest of the "Best 100" companies.

STOCK GROWTH

Lockheed's stock price has climbed steadily through the past decade, with a 3-for-1 stock split in 1983. Over the past ten years, the stock has increased 394 percent (17.5 percent per year), from its median of about $8.50 a share in 1978 to its late 1988 price of $42 a share.

Including reinvested dividends, a $10,000 investment in Lockheed's stock at its median price in 1978 would have grown to about $52,000 ten years later. Average annual compounded rate of return (including stock growth and reinvested dividends): about 18 percent.

DIVIDEND YIELD

The company did not pay a dividend until 1983. During the three-year rating period from 1985 to 1987, the stock paid an average annual current return of 2 percent.

DIVIDEND GROWTH

Lockheed's dividend has grown dramatically since 1983, rising 188 percent over the four-year rating period through 1987.

SHAREHOLDER PERKS   (no points)

Lockheed offers no dividend reinvestment plan for its shareholders, nor does it provide any other perks.

SUMMARY

Total revenues: $11.3 billion, fiscal 1987. Earnings per share: $6.64 1987; $1.24, 1977; 435% increase. Stock price: $42, 8/17/88; $8.50 (median), 1978 (394% total increase; 17.5% annual increase); price rose 9 of 10 years, 1977–87. Dividend: $1.30, 1987; $0.45, 1983; 4-year increase: 188%. Dividend yield: 2.0%, 1985–1987. P/E ratio: 4, 1/3/89. Average annual total return to investor, 1978–88: about 18%.

THE DREYFUS CORPORATION

767 Fifth Ave.
New York, NY 10153
(212) 715-6000
Chairman and CEO: Howard Stein
President: Joseph S. DiMartino

EARNINGS GROWTH	★ ★ ★ ★ ★
STOCK GROWTH	★ ★ ★ ★ ★
DIVIDEND YIELD	★ ★
DIVIDEND GROWTH	★ ★ ★
SHAREHOLDER PERKS	(no points)
NYSE—DRY	**15 points**

Dreyfus, the New York-based mutual fund giant, has been one of the few investment companies over the past decade to do as well managing its own money as you would want it to do managing yours.

While most other investment organizations have experienced lackluster growth of late, Dreyfus has had phenomenal returns. Its earnings per share have increased 30-fold over the past ten years, and its stock price has jumped 31-fold during the same period, providing an annual average total return to its stockholders of 47 percent.

Dreyfus handles about 60 different mutual funds totalling $34 billion in assets. Its largest fund is the Dreyfus Liquid Assets fund, a money market fund with about $7.5 billion in assets. Other substantial funds are its Tax-Exempt Bond Fund ($3.1 billion), Tax-Exempt Money Market Fund ($2.6 billion), Dreyfus Fund (stocks) ($2.4 billion), GNMA Fund ($2.0 billion) and Cash Management Fund ($1.9 billion).

About 1.5 million investors own Dreyfus mutual funds.

The company's extraordinary earnings growth can be attributed to a couple of factors. Mutual funds have been the hottest investment vehicle on the market over the past decade, and Dreyfus has been one of the premier mutual fund companies. For many of its funds, the company tacks on a management fee of about half a percent, which translates into tremendous revenue from the billions of dollars in assets the company has under management. On top of that, Dreyfus has only about 1,000 employees, so over-head is minimal.

While mutual funds make up by far the largest share of Dreyfus's in-come, the company does have some other interests. Dreyfus Management is a wholly owned subsidiary that serves as an investment advisor for pension and profit-sharing plans, endowment foundations and employee-benefit funds. Dreyfus also has a smaller Personal Management subsidiary that manages investment portfolios for individual investors.

Dreyfus owns a bank in New Jersey, the Dreyfus Consumer Bank, and operates Dreyfus Precious Metals, which buys and sells precious metals and coins for investors.

EARNINGS GROWTH

Dreyfus has had earnings increases nine of the past ten years (through 1987). During that period, its earnings per share have vaulted 2,750 percent (40 percent per year).

The company has annual revenues of $273 million. It has about 1,000 employees and 3,000 shareholders of record.

STOCK GROWTH

Dreyfus' stock has also experienced tremendous growth over the past ten years. The stock has had two 3-for-1 splits and one 2-for-1 split since 1980. The stock price (adjusting for splits) has increased 3,025 percent (42 percent per year) from its median price of 80 cents a share in 1978 to its recent 1988 price of $25 a share.

Including reinvested dividends, a $10,000 investment in Dreyfus stock at its median price in 1978 would have grown to about $440,000 ten years later. Average annual compounded rate of return (including stock growth and re-invested dividends): about 47 percent.

DIVIDEND YIELD

The company has traditionally paid a good dividend yield—averaging about 4 percent over the past ten years—although it tapered off considerably in the past three years primarily because of the rapid appreciation of the stock. During the three-year rating period from 1985 to 1987, the stock paid an av-erage annual current return of 1.6 percent.

DIVIDEND GROWTH

Dreyfus has had ten consecutive years of increased dividends. The dividend increased 60 percent over the four-year rating period from 1983 to 1987.

SHAREHOLDER PERKS   (no points)

Dreyfus offers no dividend reinvestment plan, nor does it offer any other shareholder perks.

SUMMARY

Total revenues: $273 million, 1987. Assets under management: $34.3 billion, 1987. Earnings per share: $2.28, 1987; $0.08, 1977; 2,750% increase. Stock price: $25, 11/7/88; $0.80 (median), 1978; 3,025% increase (42% per year); price rose 9 of 10 years, 1977–87. Dividend: $0.48, 1987; $0.30, 1983; 4-year increase: 60%. Dividend yield: 1.6% average, 1985–1987. P/E ratio: 11, 1/5/89. Average annual total return to investors, 1978–88: about 47%.

65

The Valspar Corporation

VALSPAR CORPORATION

1101 Third Street South
Minneapolis, MN 55415
(612) 332-7371
Chairman and CEO: C. Angus Wurtele
President: Robert E. Pajor

EARNINGS GROWTH	★ ★ ★ ★ ★
STOCK GROWTH	★ ★ ★ ★ ★
DIVIDEND YIELD	★ ★
DIVIDEND GROWTH	★ ★ ★
SHAREHOLDER PERKS	(no points)
ASE—VAL	**15 points**

Valspar traces its origins to a Boston paint shop called Color and Paint, which opened in 1806. That business eventually became Valentine & Co., which introduced a line of "Valspar" quick-drying varnishes and stains in 1906. Valspar was touted as "the varnish that won't turn white." Its claim to fame was a boiling water test that Valspar-varnished woods could endure with no apparent ill effects.

Through growth, mergers and acquisitions, Valspar has grown to a half-billion dollar company that is still engaged almost exclusively in the manufacture and merchandising of paints, finishes and coatings. The company has experienced tremendous growth over the past ten years, providing its shareholders with an average annual return on investment of about 34 percent.

Valspar is one of the five largest manufacturers of paints and coatings in North America. The company, which is now headquartered in Minneapolis, has 22 manufacturing plants in the U.S. and Canada and licensees throughout the world.

The company's consumer group is the largest of its four product segments, accounting for 34 percent of the firm's annual revenue. Valspar's latex and oil-based paints, wood stains, industrial maintenance coatings and marine coatings are sold primarily to do-it-yourself consumers through home centers, paint and wall covering stores, hardware, farm stores and lumberyards. Valspar's major consumer brands include Colony, Enterprise and Magicolor. It also supplies the paint for private label brands such as Target, Cenex, Courtesy and Lowe's.

Valspar's other three segments include:

- Industrial metal coatings (27 percent of total revenue). The company produces a variety of industrial coatings such as high solids, epoxies, acrylics, electrocoats and powders for use by manufacturers in the appliance, automotive, railcar, farm, industrial, construction and fabricated metal products industries.
- Maintenance and marine (19 percent of revenues). The company produces corrosion-resistant coatings for structures that are subject to extreme environmental conditions such as petrochemical processing plants, ships, waste-treatment and water-treatment facilities, food processing plants and offshore oil rigs.
- Packaging (20 percent of revenues). Valspar makes coatings for food and beverage cans and flexible packaging materials (paper, paperboard, plastic film and aluminum foil).

EARNINGS GROWTH

Valspar has had 13 consecutive years of increased earnings (through 1987). Earnings per share have jumped 747 percent (24 percent per year) over the past decade.

The company has total annual revenues of $448 million. It has about 3,000 employees and 2,000 shareholders of record.

STOCK GROWTH

The company has enjoyed exceptional stock price appreciation the past decade. The stock price has increased 1,289 percent (30 percent per year) over the past ten years, from its median of $1.80 in 1978 to its late 1988 price of $25 a share. The stock has had two 2-for-1 splits since 1984.

Including reinvested dividends, a $10,000 investment in Valspar stock at its median price in 1978 would have grown to about $190,000 ten years later. Average annual compounded rate of return (including stock growth and reinvested dividends): about 34 percent.

DIVIDEND YIELD

The company has paid a fairly good yield in the past, averaging just over 3 percent over the past ten years. During the three-year rating period from 1985 to 1987, the stock paid an average annual current return of only 1.5 percent.

DIVIDEND GROWTH

Valspar has increased its dividend for more than ten consecutive years. The dividend was increased 88 percent over the four-year rating period from 1983 to 1987.

SHAREHOLDER PERKS   (no points)

Valspar provides no dividend reinvestment plan, nor does it offer other special perks for its shareholders.

SUMMARY

Total revenues: $448 million, 1987. Earnings per share: $1.61, 1987; $0.19, 1977; 747% increase. Stock price: $25, 11/9/88; $1.80 (median), 1978; 1,289% increase (30% per year); price rose 8 of 10 years, 1977–87. Dividend: $0.32, 1987; $0.17, 1983; 4-year increase: 88%. Dividend yield: 1.5% average, 1985–1987. P/E ratio: 15, 1/5/89. Average annual total return to investors, 1978–88: about 34%.

66 COMDISCO

COMDISCO, INC.

6111 N. River Rd.
Rosemont, IL 60018
(312) 698-3000
Chairman and President: Kenneth N. Pontikes

EARNINGS GROWTH	★ ★ ★ ★
STOCK GROWTH	★ ★ ★ ★ ★
DIVIDEND YIELD	★ ★
DIVIDEND GROWTH	★ ★ ★ ★
SHAREHOLDER PERKS	(no points)
NYSE—CDO	**15 points**

Comdisco is one of the world's most successful computer companies, but you won't find its research lab in Silicon Valley, and you won't see its brand name in your local computer store. Comdisco dances to a different beat: Rather than building its own equipment, the company leases and resells equipment built by IBM and other manufacturers.

As Comdisco's success attests, computer leasing and remarketing is a classic self-perpetuating market. With the constant advances in computer technology, many companies are reluctant to make a large investment in new equipment that may be out of date a year or two later. So instead of buying, they lease equipment with short-term contract agreements, and when the upgraded models are brought to market, they ship out the old and bring in the new.

How common is computer leasing among the nation's major businesses? Comdisco reports that 94 of the largest 100 computer users in the country lease equipment. Comdisco claims to do business with about 5,000 accounts in total, including about 800 of the *Fortune 1000* companies.

Through its computer remarketing program, Comdisco gets its customers coming and going. When one of its customers outgrows its system, Comdisco will replace the system with a better (and generally more expensive) model—and lease or sell the old system to another company.

Comdisco has been in business since 1969. While it has only about 1,000 full-time employees, Comdisco's total annual revenue is about $1.2 billion.

Leasing services account for about 74 percent of total revenue, and sales account for about 21 percent. The Chicago-area-based firm also does a growing business in disaster recovery services, providing back-up computer systems to companies in case of fire, flood or other disasters.

EARNINGS GROWTH

Comdisco is the world's largest independent leasor of IBM equipment. It has operations throughout the world, with subsidiaries in Canada, France, Germany, Japan, England and about ten other countries. Over the past ten years, the company's earnings growth has not been particularly steady—it has had earnings per share increases only seven of the ten years—but the overall growth has been nothing short of phenomenal. From 1977 to 1987, earnings jumped from 12 cents a share to $1.85, a 1,442 percent increase for the period.

STOCK GROWTH

Comdisco's stock growth has been nearly as impressive as its earnings growth over the past decade. The company has had five 3-for-2 stock splits, one 5-for-4 split and one 2-for-1 split since 1978. Its stock price has climbed 1,100 percent (28% per year) from a (split-adjusted) median of $1.75 per share in 1978 to its late 1988 price of $21.

Including reinvested dividends, a $10,000 investment in Comdisco stock in 1978 would have grown to about $130,000 in 1988. Average annual compounded return (including stock growth and reinvested dividends): about 29 percent.

DIVIDEND YIELD

Comdisco traditionally pays a fairly low dividend yield, averaging well under 2 percent over the past ten years and about 1 percent the past three years.

DIVIDEND GROWTH

The company raises its dividend nearly every year. The dividend doubled from 10 cents in 1983 to 20 cents per share in 1987.

SHAREHOLDER PERKS (no points)

Comdisco offers no perks and no dividend reinvestment plan.

SUMMARY

Total revenues: $1.2 billion, 1987. Earnings per share: $1.85, 1987; $0.12, 1977; 1,442% increase. Stock price: $21, 10/3/88; $1.75 (median), 1978 (1,100% total increase; 28% annual increase); price rose 9 of 10 years, 1977–87. Dividend $0.20, 1987; $0.10, 1983; 4-year increase: 100%. Dividend yield: 1.0%, 1985–1987. P/E ratio: 9*, 1/4/88. Average annual total return to investor, 1978–88: about 29%.

---

*Based on earnings from continuing operations, and does not take into account the $88 million one-time risk arbitrage loss from the October, 1987 stock market crash. Including that loss, the P/E would be 52.

BEMIS COMPANY

625 Marquette Ave.
Minneapolis, MN 55402
(612) 340-6000
Chairman and CEO: Howard Curler
President: John H. Roe

EARNINGS GROWTH	★ ★
STOCK GROWTH	★ ★ ★ ★ ★
DIVIDEND YIELD	★ ★ ★
DIVIDEND GROWTH	★ ★ ★
SHAREHOLDER PERKS	★ ★
NYSE—BMS	**15 points**

Stroll down any grocery store isle, and you'll get a good view of Bemis Company's handiwork. Bemis is a packager that specializes in foods. The company started with grain bags in 1858 and has quietly spread to wraps and packages for virtually every type of product in the grocery business.

The "Peal & Seal" resealable potato chip bags—that's Bemis. Plastic wraps on cheeses, meats and paper towels—that's Bemis. Molded microwavable frozen dinner trays; paper pet food packages; printed labels on canned goods, milk cartons and frozen orange juice containers—that's Bemis. Boxes for crackers, cake mix and breakfast cereals—and the plastic wrappers on the free prizes inside—that's Bemis. The world's fastest hot dog vacuum-packaging machine, the Royal-Vac 400—Bemis again.

Bemis divides its business into two segments, flexible packaging and specialty coated and graphics products.

- Flexible packaging. The Minneapolis-based company has 33 manufacturing plants in 18 states and three foreign countries that specialize in wrapping foods in flexible plastic or paper packages. The flexible packaging segment, which accounts for 69 percent of the company's $930 million in annual revenue, includes several types of business activities:

- Monofilm packaging, such as shrink-wraps and stretch-films, printed roll stock and molded plastic containers.
- Multiwall and small paper bags for seed, feed, fertilizer, flour, cement, chemicals, sugar, rice, pet food.
- Packaging machinery built by Bemis is used to package tissues, candy, frozen vegetables, meats, fertilizer, insulation materials, detergent, pharmaceuticals and other products.

- Specialty coated and graphics products. Bemis has 15 manufacturing plants that produce specially coated and printed products for the packaging industry. This segment accounts for 31 percent of the company's total revenue, and includes adhesive products for mounting and bonding, roll labels, laminates for graphics and photography, specialized padding for furniture and automobiles, vinyl materials and wall coverings.

EARNINGS GROWTH

With total annual revenue of $930 million, Bemis is one of the largest packaging companies in the U.S. The company has about 8,000 employees and 4,000 shareholders of record.

Bemis' earnings growth over the past ten years has been a mediocre 188 percent (11 percent per year), due to a fairly rocky period in the early 1980s. Over the past five years, earnings per share have increased about 250 percent (28 percent per year).

STOCK GROWTH

The company's stock price has grown quickly and consistently over the past ten years, with three 2-for-1 stock splits since 1984. Over the past ten years the stock has increased 736 percent (24 percent per year) from its median of $2.75 in 1978 to its late 1988 price of $23 a share.

Including reinvsted dividends, a $10,000 investment in Bemis stock at its median price in 1978 would have grown to about $125,000 ten years later. Average annual compounded rate of return (including stock growth and reinvested dividends): about 29 percent.

DIVIDEND YIELD

Bemis generally pays a fairly good dividend—it reached as high as 6 percent in the early 1980s. Over the past three years the stock has paid an annual current return of 2.5 percent.

DIVIDEND GROWTH

Bemis increases its dividend most years. Its dividend climbed 80 percent over the four-year rating period from 1983 to 1987.

SHAREHOLDER PERKS

The company offers a good dividend reinvestment and voluntary stock purchase plan with no fees or commissions. Bemis offers no other perks.

SUMMARY

Total revenues: $930 million, 1987. Earnings per share: $1.18, 1987; $0.41, 1977; 188% increase. Stock price: $23, 10/12/88; $2.75 (median), 1978 (736% total increase; 24% annual increase); price rose 9 of 10 years, 1977–87. Dividend $0.36, 1987; $0.20, 1983; 4-year increase: 80%. Dividend yield: 2.5%, 1985–1987. P/E ratio: 17, 1/4/89. Average annual total return to investor, 1978–88: about 29%.

68

GULF + WESTERN INC.

One Gulf + Western Plaza
New York, NY 10023-7780
(212) 373-8000
Chairman and CEO: Martin S. Davis

EARNINGS GROWTH	★ ★
STOCK GROWTH	★ ★ ★ ★ ★
DIVIDEND YIELD	★ ★ ★
DIVIDEND GROWTH	★ ★
SHAREHOLDER PERKS	★ ★ ★
NYSE—GW	**15 points**

Recognized as one of the most prominent entertainment and information enterprises in America, Gulf + Western owns the Hollywood TV and motion picture producer Paramount Pictures, holds a 50 percent stake in the USA cable television network, and owns publishing giants Simon and Schuster and Prentice-Hall. But for all its pomp and prestige, Gulf + Western got its start inauspiciously enough in the automotive spinoff business as a specialty manufacturer of rear bumpers.

In 1956, Charles Bluhdorn and a handful of associates bought up the stock of a company called Michigan Bumper. As Bluhdorn later recalled, he was able to buy the stock at what appeared to be a bargain—about one-third the price of its book value.

"It was only later that I discovered that the only asset the company had was making the rear bumper of the Studebaker," said Bluhdorn. "That was when I realized that sometimes maybe you ought to look at something besides book value."

Bluhdorn tried to sell off the assets but found no takers—even at fire sale prices. Like it or not, Bluhdorn was stuck with Michigan Bumper, so he decided to try to make the best of it. A year later, the company acquired a Houston automotive and electrical products distributor, and changed the corporate name to Gulf + Western. The company first concentrated on the auto parts business, then expanded to other ventures. In 1966, it acquired

Paramount Pictures, the Hollywood movie company, which it still owns today.

Paramount Pictures has been a bright spot for the company in recent years, producing such box-office blockbusters as *Fatal Attraction, The Untouchables, Top Gun, Star Trek IV: The Voyage Home, Crocodile Dundee* and *Beverly Hills Cop.* Paramount also produces some popular TV serials including *Cheers, Family Ties* and *Entertainment Tonight.*

Other Gulf + Western entertainment holdings include New York's Madison Square Gardens, the New York Knicks basketball team and the New York Rangers hockey team. Gulf + Western has also managed to turn beauty into business: It owns Miss Universe, Inc., which organizes, produces and administers the Miss Universe, Miss USA and Miss Teen USA pageants. The company's entertainment segment accounts for about 38 percent of operating income.

In addition to Simon & Schuster and Prentice-Hall, the company has acquired a formidable stable of other publishing houses including Summit, Pocket Books, Linden Press, John Wiley and Sons vocational titles and Poseidon Press. The company has a major stake in the educational publishing market through several of its publishing companies, including Silver Burdett & Ginn, Coronet, Allyn & Bacon and Appleton & Lange.

Some of the firm's recent best sellers include *The Closing of the American Mind, The Great Depression of 1990, Women Who Love Too Much, Dark Angel, Veil: The Secret Wars of the CIA 1981-1987, Hollywood Husbands, A Matter of Honor* and *The Road Less Traveled.* Gulf + Western's publishing operations account for about 21 percent of operating income.

Gulf + Western owns The Associates, the nation's third largest independent finance company (as measured by capital funds). The Associates (which is technically a subsidiary of Associates First Capital Corp.) serves more than one million accounts in 500 offices in 42 states and Puerto Rico. It also has 75 consumer offices in Japan and 45 branches in the United Kingdom. The company deals primarily in real estate-secured loans, installment loans and sales financing. The company also does a business in commercial finance and insurance. Gulf + Western's financial operations account for about 41 percent of its operating income.

EARNINGS GROWTH

Including its financial services division, Gulf + Western has total annual revenues of $4.7 billion. The New York-based company has about 20,000 employees and 35,000 shareholders.

While the firm's publishing and financial services divisions can be expected to provide a fairly stable return, its entertainment division can be quite mercurial, with exploding profits during years when its bigger movies pack the theatres and sagging returns during years when its blockbusters bust.

Over the past 10 years, earnings gains have been moderate, rising 227 percent during the period.

STOCK GROWTH

Despite its moderate earnings growth, Gulf + Western has had excellent stock price growth during the past decade, increasing 660 percent (22.5 percent per year) from its (split-adjusted) median of $5.50 per share in 1978 to its late 1988 price of $42 a share. The stock was split 2-for-1 in 1988 and in 1980, 5-for-4.

Including reinvested dividends, a $10,000 investment in Gulf + Western stock at its median price in 1978 would have grown to about $110,000 ten years later. Average annual compounded rate of return (including stock growth and reinvested dividends): about 27 percent.

DIVIDEND YIELD

The company has paid a fairly good dividend over the years, although the annual yield has dropped recently. During the three-year rating period from 1985 to 1987, the stock paid an average annual current return of 2 percent.

DIVIDEND GROWTH

Gulf + Western has not made a habit of increasing its dividend each year. The company's dividend increased 43 percent over the four-year rating period from 1983 to 1987.

SHAREHOLDER PERKS

At a recent annual meeting, the company gave all of its shareholders in attendance a tax guide published by Simon & Schuster. New shareholders of record also receive a small packet of information on the company along with a personal letter of welcome from Martin S. Davis, the company's chairman and CEO.

Gulf + Western also offers a good dividend reinvestment and voluntary stock purchase plan. There are no fees or commissions, and stockholders may contribute $10 to $1,000 per month to the voluntary stock purchase plan.

SUMMARY

Total revenues: $4.7 billion, 1987 ($2.9 billion not including financial services). Earnings per share: $2.88, 1987; $0.88, 1977; 227% increase. Stock price: $42, 9/9/88; $5.50 (median), 1978; 660% increase (22.5% per year); price rose 8 of 10 years, 1977–87. Dividend: $0.56, 1987; $0.39, 1983; 4-year increase: 43%. Dividend yield: 2.0% average, 1985–1987. P/E ratio: 13, 1/5/89. Average annual total return to investors, 1978–88: about 27%.

69

CoreStates

CORESTATES FINANCIAL CORP

PNB Building P.O. Box 7618
Broad and Chestnut Streets
Philadelphia, PA 19107
(215) 973-3100
Chairman, President and CEO: Terrence A. Larsen

EARNINGS GROWTH	★ ★
STOCK GROWTH	★ ★ ★ ★
DIVIDEND YIELD	★ ★ ★ ★
DIVIDEND GROWTH	★ ★ ★
SHAREHOLDER PERKS	★ ★
OTC—CSFN	**15 points**

Investors in the City of Brotherly Love have been cultivating a growing passion for CoreStates Financial. The Philadelphia-based multibank holding company has been winning their affection the old-fashioned way—by buying them off with years of liberal dividends and excellent stock price growth.

CoreStates' biggest holding is Philadelphia National Bank, the largest savings institution in Philadelphia, with total assets of $9.1 billion. The bank has more than 60 branch offices in four Pennsylvania counties. Philadelphia National has national and regional banking services geared to businesses, financial institutions and government entities; a consumer banking group that offers the normal retail services such as checking, savings, and personal and business loans; a trust group that manages large personal accounts; a pension and profit sharing fund management and investment advisory; and a capital markets group that underwrites municipal bonds and U.S. government bonds.

Philadelphia National also does a good international banking business, with branches in London and Nassau and representative offices in Bangkok, Hamburg, Manila, Sao Paulo, Panama City, Paris, Sydney, Bogota, Tokyo, Singapore and Hong Kong.

CoreStates Financial is also the parent company of two other banks:

- Hamilton Bank ($2.8 billion in total assets). A retail and commercial bank in Lancaster County, Pennsylvania, with more than 60 branches in seven Pennsylvania counties;
- New Jersey National Bank ($2.2 billion in assets). A retail and commercial bank based in Pennington, New Jersey, with more than 80 branch offices in 13 counties of central and southern New Jersey.

Other direct and indirect subsidiaries of CoreStates include: CoreStates Bank of Delaware (credit cards and consumer lending; $1 billion in credit card consumer loans outstanding), Congress Financial Corporation (commercial financing and factoring), Signal Financial Corporation (consumer lending), Philadelphia National Limited (international merchant banking and capital markets services), CoreStates Securities Corporation (discount brokerage service) and CoreStates Investment Advisors (investment advisory, research, trading and fund management).

EARNINGS GROWTH

With total assets of $15 billion, CoreStates is one of the nation's 50 largest bank holding companies. It has 8,000 employees and 25,000 shareholders.

Over the past ten years, the company's earnings have grown quickly, though somewhat inconsistently, with increases only seven of the past ten years. During that span, earnings per share increased 265 percent (about 14 percent per year).

There has been a changing of the guard at CoreStates with the retirement Jan. 1, 1988, of G. Morris Dorrance, Jr., who had served as the CoreStates chairman and chief executive officer since 1970. Replacing him was Terrence A. Larsen, who had served as the firm's president for two years prior to his promotion to chairman and CEO.

STOCK GROWTH

Like its earnings, CoreStates' stock price growth has been somewhat inconsistent over the past decade—with price increases seven of the past ten years—but the long-term growth has been excellent. The stock has had two 2-for-1 splits since 1983 and has increased 433 percent (18 percent per year) from its median of $7.50 in 1978 to its late 1988 price of $40 a share.

Including reinvested dividends, a $10,000 investment in CoreStates stock at its median price in 1978 would have grown to about $97,000 ten years later. Average annual compounded rate of return (including stock growth and reinvested dividends): about 25.5 percent.

DIVIDEND YIELD

CoreStates Financial normally pays an excellent dividend yield that has averaged about 7 percent over the past ten years. During the most recent three-year period, the stock paid an average annual return of 3.8 percent.

DIVIDEND GROWTH

CoreStates traditionally increases its dividend each year. The dividend rose 57 percent over the four-year rating period from 1983 to 1987.

SHAREHOLDER PERKS

CoreStates offers a dividend reinvestment and voluntary stock purchase plan in which shareholders may purchase $25 to $1,000 per month in additional shares. There is a small fee and commission charge for the service.

SUMMARY

Assets: $15 billion, 1987; loans outstanding, $10 billion (total net profit, $162 million). Earnings per share: $3.91, 1987; $1.07, 1977; 265% increase. Stock price: $40, 10/20/88; $7.50 (median), 1978 (433% total increase; 18% annual increase); price rose 7 of 10 years, 1977–87. Dividend: $1.40, 1987; $0.89, 1983; 4-year increase: 57%. Dividend yield: 3.8%, 1985–1987. P/E ratio: 9, 1/3/89. Average annual total return to investor, 1978–88: about 25.5%.

D&B The Dun & Bradstreet Corporation

THE DUN & BRADSTREET CORPORATION

299 Park Ave.
New York, NY 10171
(212) 593-6800
Chairman and CEO: Charles W. Moritz
President and COO: Robert E. Weissman

EARNINGS GROWTH	★ ★ ★ ★
STOCK GROWTH	★ ★ ★ ★ ★
DIVIDEND YIELD	★ ★ ★
DIVIDEND GROWTH	★ ★ ★
SHAREHOLDER PERKS	(no points)
NYSE—DNB	**15 points**

It's a little scary when you think about it. Here's a corporation that knows you *and* your habits, knows what you buy and where you buy it, knows what you watch, what you read and what you do for fun, even better than you know yourself. If Big Brother is indeed out there, his name is Dun & Bradstreet.

Through its expanding family of information-gathering subsidiaries, Dun & Bradstreet is chronicling and categorizing every move of the consuming public. If you've bought a new car recently, changed homes, had a baby, opened a bank account, applied for a charge card, donated to a political cause, joined a health club, subscribed to a magazine or started a business, there's a good chance your act would be duly noted by the cavernous computer database of Donnelly Marketing, a D&B subsidiary. The company keeps tabs on the "demographic and lifestyle data" of more than 80 million U.S. households. The information is used to compile target-marketed lists primarily for use by the direct-marketing industry.

But D&B's probe into the American psyche does not end there. The company also owns Nielsen Media Research, which monitors America's TV viewing habits. Its new Nielsen People Meter, now in a representative sampling of about 4,000 U.S. homes, monitors not only what is being watched but who is watching. By the morning after, Nielsen's clients—made up primarily of companies that advertise on television—can call up the past evenings' results on their own computers.

D&B can also help many of those advertisers see the immediate impact of their commercials. Nielsen's Scantrack is used to track brand sales at more than 2,500 supermarkets throughout the U.S. The company has also initiated plans to probe deeper into individual spending patterns by equipping a nationwide panel of 15,000 households with hand-held scanners to record their every purchase.

Businesses, too, come under the watchful eye of Dun & Bradstreet. D&B Credit Services provides credit ratings and financial information on 9 million U.S. businesses. Moody's Investor Service, another D&B subsidiary, furnishes business and financial information on corporations and issues ratings on corporate and municipal bonds.

D&B's other services include: Donnelly Directory, a publisher of Yellow Pages directories of more than 30 telephone companies; D&B Business Marketing Services, a business-to-business marketing service; and Nielsen Clearing House, a cents-off coupon administration service.

D&B's business information services segment and its marketing services segment each accounts for about 39 percent of the firm's $3.4 billion in total annual revenue. Publishing makes up the remaining 22 percent of revenues.

EARNINGS GROWTH

Dun & Bradstreet has enjoyed excellent, consistent earnings growth. Earnings have increased 23 consecutive years, including a total increase in earnings per share of 387 percent for the most recent ten-year period.

The company has about 60,000 employees and 15,000 shareholders.

STOCK GROWTH

The company's stock price has climbed steadily through the past decade, increasing every year from 1977 to 1987. D&B stock has had two 2-for-1 splits since 1983. Over the past ten years the stock has increased 579 percent (21 percent per year), from its median of $8.25 in 1978 to its late 1988 price of $56 a share.

Including reinvested dividends, a $10,000 investment in Dun & Bradstreet stock at its median price in 1978 would have grown to about $90,000 ten years later. Average annual compounded rate of return (including stock growth and reinvested dividends): about 24.5 percent.

DIVIDEND YIELD

The company has traditionally paid a fairly good dividend, which averaged about 4 percent in the early 1980s. Over the past three years the stock has paid an average annual current return of 2.5 percent.

DIVIDEND GROWTH

Dun & Bradstreet has raised its dividend each year for 36 consecutive years. The dividend climbed 86 percent during the four-year rating period from 1983 to 1987.

SHAREHOLDER PERKS   (no points)

The company offers no dividend reinvestment plan, nor does it offer any other type of shareholder perk.

SUMMARY

Total revenues: $3.4 billion, 1987. Earnings per share: $2.58, 1987; $0.53, 1977; 387% increase. Stock price: $56, 10/11/88; $8.25 (median), 1978; 579% increase (21% per year); price rose 10 of 10 years, 1977–87. Dividend: $1.45, 1987; $0.78, 1983; 4-year increase: 86%. Dividend yield: 2.5%, 1985–1987. P/E ratio: 21, 1/5/89. Average annual total return to investors, 1978–88: 24.5%.

71

BANK ≡ ONE®

BANC ONE CORPORATION
100 East Broad St.
Columbus, OH 43271
(614) 248-5944
Chairman and CEO: John B. McCoy
President: Frank E. McKinney, Jr.

EARNINGS GROWTH	★ ★ ★
STOCK GROWTH	★ ★ ★ ★
DIVIDEND YIELD	★ ★ ★
DIVIDEND GROWTH	★ ★ ★
SHAREHOLDER PERKS	★ ★
NYSE—ONE	**15 points**

Not since the Great Depression has the U.S. banking industry endured such turbulent times. Fraud and unpaid farm loans have toppled dozens of smaller institutions, while defaulting Third World debtors have cost the megabanks billions of dollars. The largest 50 banking organizations, combined, took a $6 billion dive into the red in 1987, and the banking industry as a whole reported a net loss for the first time in half a century.

Against this backdrop, Banc One has been a bastion of stability. The Columbus, Ohio-based holding company of banks in five midwestern states has survived the bank crisis with 19 consecutive years of increased earnings, dating back to the year the company was established. Among the nation's 50 largest banks, Banc One consistently ranks in the top five in return on assets and most recently ranked number one.

Banc One's success is tied in part to its aggressiveness. In the three years since the government eased regulations on interstate banking mergers (1985), the company has acquired twelve banking organizations in Indiana, four in Michigan, two in Ohio and one each in Kentucky and Wisconsin. In all, the Banc One network includes about 314 bank offices in Ohio, 144 in Indiana, 22 in Wisconsin, 15 in Michigan and 10 in Kentucky.

Among its biggest acquisitions were American Fletcher National Bank in Indianapolis, Marine in Milwaukee, Spartan in East Lansing and KYNB Bancshares in Lexington.

The company attributes much of its recent growth to the resurgence of the industrial Midwest. Employment in the bank's five-state region—where 18 percent of the nation's manufacturing value is produced—has been rising steadily since the "rust belt" recession of the early 1980s.

The company's management has vowed to continue its aggressive program of acquisitions throughout the Midwest in the years ahead. To ease the organizational strain created by its rapid expansion, the company has broken its operations into three subsidiary bank holding companies—Banc One Ohio (which includes holdings in Ohio, Kentucky and Michigan), Banc One Indiana and Banc One Wisconsin.

EARNINGS GROWTH

With assets of about $20 billion (excluding its Wisconsin acquisition), Banc One ranks as one of the 35 largest bank holding companies in the U.S. It traditionally ranks near the top in earnings growth and return on assets, and ranks fifth in the U.S. in market value. The company employs 15,000 people and has about 40,000 shareholders.

In an industry that has been reeling, Banc One has enjoyed remarkably consistent earnings growth, increasing its net earnings for 19 consecutive years. Over the past ten years, earnings have increased 205 percent.

STOCK GROWTH

Banc One has experienced good stock growth over the past decade, with three 3-for-2 stock splits since 1982. Over the past ten years the stock has increased 447 percent (18.5 percent per year) from its median of $4.75 in 1978 to its late 1988 price of $26 a share.

Including reinvested dividends, a $10,000 investment in Banc One stock at its median price in 1978 would have grown to about $82,000 ten years later. Average annual compounded rate of return (including stock growth and reinvested dividends): about 23.5 percent.

DIVIDEND YIELD

The company has traditionally paid a good yield, which has averaged about 4.5 percent over the past ten years. During the three-year rating period from 1985 to 1987, the stock paid an average annual current return of 3.3 percent.

DIVIDEND GROWTH

Banc One has increased its dividend for more than 15 consecutive years. The dividend increased 74 percent over the four-year rating period from 1983 to 1987.

SHAREHOLDER PERKS

Banc One offers its shareholders a good dividend reinvestment and voluntary stock purchase plan. There are no fees or service charges, and shareholders may contribute up to $5,000 per quarter to the stock purchase plan.

SUMMARY

Assets: $18.7 billion, 1987; loans outstanding, $12.8 billion (total net profit, $340 million). Earnings per share: $1.98, 1987; $0.65, 1977; 205% increase. Stock price: $26, 9/20/88; $4.75 (median), 1978 (447% total increase; 18.5% annual increase); price rose 8 of 10 years, 1977–87. Dividend: $0.82, 1987; $0.47, 1983; 4-year increase: 74%. Dividend yield: 3.3%, 1985–1987. P/E ratio: 9, 1/4/89. Average annual total return to investor, 1978–88: about 23.5%

RUBBERMAID INCORPORATED

1147 Akron Road
Wooster, OH 44691
(216) 264-6464
Chairman and CEO: Stanley C. Gault
President: Walter W. Williams

EARNINGS GROWTH	★ ★ ★
STOCK GROWTH	★ ★ ★ ★
DIVIDEND YIELD	★ ★
DIVIDEND GROWTH	★ ★ ★
SHAREHOLDER PERKS	★ ★ ★
NYSE—RBD	**15 points**

Rubbermaid got its start in 1920 as a balloon manufacturer called the Wooster Rubber Company. The firm still calls Wooster (Ohio) home, but little else remains the same. Now its goods are made from plastics, and its product line has ballooned to more than a thousand items, including pitchers, mugs and thermos jugs, trash cans, dustpans and computer stands.

Rubbermaid has grown rapidly the past few years, eclipsing the $1 billion mark in sales for the first time in 1987. Its rapid growth is due primarily to a number of key acquisitions, including Little Tikes (toys) in 1984, Gott Corporation (leisure products) in 1985, SECO Industries (floor maintenance products) and MicroComputer Accessories in 1986, and Viking Brush (Canada's leading maker of brushes, brooms and other cleaning aids) in 1987.

The company's products are geared to both consumers (75 percent of sales) and institutional customers (25 percent of sales). In addition to its U.S. sales, Rubbermaid also does a good foreign business—particularly in Canada. Canadian sales account for about 5 percent of total revenue, and all other foreign markets (including Europe, Australia, the Middle East and the Far East) account for about 6 percent.

Rubbermaid breaks its U.S. operations into five divisions:

- Home products. The oldest and largest of Rubbermaid's divisions manufactures such products as sinkware, space organizers, household containers, trash cans, cookware, food storage containers, rubber gloves, casual dinnerware, outdoor furniture and home office products.

- Specialty products. This division makes lawn furniture, planters, bird feeders and a lettering system with peel-off, self-adhesive letters and numbers.
- Commercial products. Products, geared to the commercial, industrial and institutional markets, include brooms, brushes, beverage containers, high chairs, trash cans, pitchers, cups, housekeeping carts and other maintenance, food service and office products.
- SECO Industries. SECO makes floor care products such as mops, buckets, brushes and brooms. It also makes SeBreeze air freshener, which it markets to the maintenance, food service and office segments.
- MicroComputer Accessories. This recent acquisition makes accessories for personal computers, word processors and data terminals, including plastic molded stands for computers and printers, storage racks and disk files.
- Gott Corporation. Gott makes thermos jugs, insulated food chests, canteens and a refreezable ice substitute.
- Little Tikes. Products include toys, pedal cars, children's furniture and other children's recreational equipment.

EARNINGS GROWTH

Rubbermaid has annual revenue of $1 billion. It has about 7,000 employees and 10,000 shareholders. (Insiders own about 15 percent of the common stock.)

The company has had fairly consistent earnings growth over the past decade with earnings increases nine of the past ten years and a total increase in earnings per share of 326 percent during the period.

STOCK GROWTH

The company's stock price has climbed quickly though inconsistently over the past decade, with a stock price increase seven of ten years from 1977 to 1987. The stock has had two 2-for-1 splits since 1983. Over the past ten years the stock has increased 567 percent (21 percent per year) from its median of $3.75 in 1978 to its recent 1988 price of $25 a share.

Including reinvested dividends, a $10,000 investment in Rubbermaid stock at its median price in 1978 would have grown to about $82,000 ten years later. Average annual compounded rate of return (including stock growth and reinvested dividends): about 23.5 percent.

DIVIDEND YIELD

Rubbermaid tends to pay a fairly low dividend yield. Over the past three years the stock has paid an annual current return of 1.4 percent.

DIVIDEND GROWTH

Rubbermaid traditionally raises its dividend each year. The dividend climbed 78 percent over the four-year rating period from 1983–87.

SHAREHOLDER PERKS

Shareholders who attend Rubbermaid's annual meeting are usually rewarded with free Rubbermaid product. One year it was a file case, another year it was a set of food storage containers, and one year it was a dip and snack tray. Shareholders may also shop in the company store where they receive discounts on dozens of Rubbermaid products.

The company also offers a dividend reinvestment and voluntary stock purchase plan. There is a small service fee (not to exceed $3), but the company pays the brokerage commission. Shareholders may buy $10 to $3,000 per quarter in additional shares through the voluntary stock purchase plan.

SUMMARY

Total revenues: $1 billion, 1987. Earnings per share: $1.15, 1987; $0.27, 1977; 326% increase. Stock price: $25, 10/5/88; $3.75 (median), 1978; 567% increase (21% per year); price rose 7 of 10 years, 1977–87. Dividend: $0.32, 1987; $0.18, 1983; 4-year increase: 73%. Dividend yield: 1.4% average, 1985–87. P/E ratio: 19, 1/5/89. Average annual total return to investors, 1978–88: 23.5%.

73

Kimberly-Clark

KIMBERLY-CLARK CORPORATION

P.O. Box 619100
Dallas, TX 75261-9100
(214) 830-1200
Chairman and CEO: Darwin E. Smith

EARNINGS GROWTH	★ ★
STOCK GROWTH	★ ★ ★ ★
DIVIDEND YIELD	★ ★ ★
DIVIDEND GROWTH	★ ★
SHAREHOLDER PERKS	★ ★ ★ ★
NYSE—KMB	**15 points**

Kimberly-Clark has built its business on runny noses, spilt milk and dirty diapers. Capitalizing on life's little calamities has helped push the Dallas-based paper products company to $5 billion a year in total revenues.

Kleenex tissues, Huggies diapers, Hi-Dri paper towels, Delsey toilet paper and Kotex and New Freedom feminine hygiene products are among Kimberly-Clark's better-known brands. The company is also a major manufacturer of napkins, baby wipes and surgical gowns.

The rekindled baby boom has been a boon to Kimberly-Clark's recent success. Its disposal Huggies diapers have been the major growth area of the company over the past few years. Huggies controls about a 30 percent share of the U.S. diaper market. While growth in the U.S. market is expected to plateau soon, the company anticipates increasing sales in foreign markets.

In addition to its consumer products, Kimberly-Clark manufactures a wide range of papers, including newsprint, text papers, lightweight Bible pages, cigarette papers, stationery, envelopes, labels, films and foils.

The company also owns Midwest Express Airlines, a small commercial airline based in Appleton, Wisconsin. Kimberly-Clark's aircraft division (which also includes a small airplane maintenance and refurbishing company) accounts for only about 2 percent of the firm's total profit—but that may change. The company plans to inject about $120 million into Midwest over the next few years to increase the airline's fleet of DC-9s from five to seventeen, and to move its base from Appleton to Milwaukee.

Kimberly-Clark has a worldwide presence, with production facilities in 18 states and about 20 foreign countries. About 12 percent of its total revenues come from Canadian sales, and about 18 percent come from Europe and other foreign markets. (The company does business in South Africa through its Carlton Paper Corporation affiliate, according to the Investor Responsibility Research Center.)

EARNINGS GROWTH

Kimberly-Clark's earnings growth over the past decade has been fairly steady, with earnings per share gains eight of the past ten years. During the ten-year period, its earnings per share increased 166 percent.

The company has 40,000 employees and 20,000 shareholders of record.

Disposable diapers, while a great convenience for new parents, have become one of the biggest problems for landfill operations. The diapers are not biodegradable. There is some speculation that disposable diaper manufacturers like Kimberly-Clark may be asked to either redesign their diapers or help defray the rising costs of their disposal.

STOCK GROWTH

The company's stock price has climbed quickly during the past decade, with three 2-for-1 stock splits since 1984. Over the past ten years the stock has increased 407 percent (17.5 percent per year), from its median of $11.75 in 1978 to its late 1988 price of $57 a share.

Including reinvested dividends, a $10,000 investment in Kimberly-Clark stock at its median price in 1978 would have grown to about $80,000 ten years later. Average annual compounded rate of return (including stock growth and reinvested dividends): about 23 percent.

DIVIDEND YIELD

The company traditionally pays a good dividend yield, which has averaged about 5 percent over the past ten years. During the three-year rating period from 1985 to 1987, the stock paid an average annual current return of 3.3 percent.

DIVIDEND GROWTH

Kimberly-Clark has raised its dividend for more than 15 consecutive years. The dividend was increased 37 percent over the four-year rating period from 1983 to 1987.

SHAREHOLDER PERKS

Kimberly-Clark shareholders can do their Christmas shopping through the company. Each year, the company assembles a Christmas gift box of about a dozen of its products (tissues, paper towels, napkins, stationery, baby wipes and other consumer items) that shareholders may order for themselves or their friends and business associates. The cost is about $10, which includes mailing the packages directly to the recipients. The service has been extremely popular with Kimberly-Clark shareholders, who order about 70,000 gift packages a year.

The company also gives away a nice sample package of its products to shareholders who attend the annual meeting.

Kimberly-Clark offers a dividend reinvestment and voluntary stock purchase plan in which shareholders may purchase up to $3,000 per quarter in additional stock. Participants are subject to a small fee and commission.

SUMMARY

Total revenues: $4.9 billion, 1987. Earnings per share: $3.73, 1987; $1.40, 1977; 166% increase. Stock price: $57, 9/6/88; $11.25 (median), 1978 (407% total increase; 17.5% annual increase); price rose 8 of 10 years, 1977–87. Dividend: $1.44, 1987; $1.05, 1983; 4-year increase: 37%. Dividend yield: 3.3%, 1985–87. P/E ratio: 13, 1/4/89. Average annual total return to investor, 1978–88: 23%.

MERCK & COMPANY, INC.

P.O. Box 2000
126 East Lincoln Ave.
Rahway, NJ 07065
(201) 574-4000
Chairman, President and CEO: P. Roy Vagelos

EARNINGS GROWTH	★ ★
STOCK GROWTH	★ ★ ★ ★ ★
DIVIDEND YIELD	★ ★ ★
DIVIDEND GROWTH	★ ★ ★
SHAREHOLDER PERKS	★ ★
NYSE—MRK	**15 points**

Pssst. I've got a hot one for you: Merck.

And remember, you saw it here first—unless, by chance, you read it in *Fortune* magazine ("America's most admired company," 1987 and 1988), or *Forbes* ("most innovative pharmaceutical company," 1988), or *Business Week* (one of the "best in public service," 1988), or *Business Month* (one of the five "best-managed companies," 1987).

Merck is a major pharmaceuticals company that develops and markets both human and animal health products.

Although the New Jersey-based firm has annual revenues of more than $5 billion, its products are not widely known by the general public. Merck concentrates on specialty medications rather than general over-the-counter potions geared to consumers.

Its most heralded new product is Mevacor, a cholesterol-reducing medicine introduced in 1987. A single daily dose of Mevacor reportedly helps normalize cholesterol levels even among patients with extremely high levels. The company says the development of Mevacor came after 35 years of study and testing. The drug was named one of *Fortune* magazine's "products of the year" in 1987.

The company also recently developed a preventative medicine for onchocerciasis, or "river blindness," a malady that affects about 18 million people in Africa. After developing the medication, however, Merck faced another hurdle—getting it to the poverty-stricken people in the regions where the disease is endemic. The company finally concluded that the only effective way to get it to the people was to offer it free. That act of generosity was applauded by newspapers and politicians, including U.S. Senator Edward Kennedy, who termed Merck's gift "a triumph of the human spirit." (Not everyone is applauding Merck's interational endeavors, however. Some of its shareholders have pressured the company to sever its ties with South Africa. The company did sell its South African subisidary, MSD, in 1988, but Merck continues to market its products there.)

The key to Merck's success is probably its outstanding research and development program. The company employs about 4,900 people in its research activities and spends about $650 million in a year in R&D.

Merck produces pharmaceuticals for the treatment of hypertension and cardiovascular ailments (Vasotec and Aldomet), as well as anti-inflammatory and analgesic medications (Clinoril, Indocin and Dolobid), antibiotics (Mefoxin), ophthalmologicals (Timoptic) and vaccines and biological medicines.

The company also produces some medications for the treatment of animals (which accounts for about 8 percent of Merck's total revenues), and produces specialty chemical products for water treatment, oil field drilling, food processing, cleaning, disinfecting and skin care (9 percent of revenues).

EARNINGS GROWTH

With annual revenues of $5.1 billion, Merck is one of the nation's largest phamaceutical companies. The firm has about 30,000 employees and does business worldwide, with international sales accounting for about 50 percent of its revenue.

If Merck stock has one weakness, it might be that, as the old Wall Street saying goes, "What everyone knows isn't worth knowing." All of the favorable publicity surrounding Merck has helped push its stock price-to-earnings ratio to among the highest in the industry (20). That won't be a problem if the company continues its strong profitability, but the downside risk is slightly greater should Merck come upon hard times.

Merck has had earnings increases nine of the past ten years (from 1977 to 1987). During that period its earnings per share increased a total of 248 percent.

STOCK GROWTH

Merck's stock growth was flat from 1972 to 1984, but it has increased dramatically since. The stock split 2-for-1 in 1986 and 3-for-1 in 1984 to a high of $74 in 1987 (prior to the October 19 crash) and was selling for $57 a share in late 1988.

Over the past ten years the stock has increased 470 percent (19 percent per year), from its median of $10 in 1978 to its recent 1988 price of $57 a share.

Including reinvested dividends, a $10,000 investment in Merck stock at its median price in 1978 would have grown to about $73,000 ten years later. Average annual compounded rate of return (including stock growth and reinvested dividends): about 22 percent.

DIVIDEND YIELD

The company traditionally pays a fairly good dividend yield, which has averaged about 3 percent over the past ten years. During the three-year rating period from 1985 to 1987, the stock paid an average annual current return of 2.1 percent.

DIVIDEND GROWTH

Merck has raised its dividend for more than ten consecutive years. It increased its dividend 74 percent over the four-year rating period from 1983 to 1987 (from 47 cents to 82 cents per share).

SHAREHOLDER PERKS

Merck provides a good dividend reinvestment and voluntary stock purchase plan for its shareholders of record. There are no fees or service charges, and shareholders may contribute $25 to $5,000 per quarter to the stock purchase plan.

SUMMARY

Total revenues: $5.1 billion, 1987. Earnings per share: $2.23, 1987; $0.64, 1977; 248% increase. Stock price: $57, 11/7/88; $10 (median), 1978; 470% increase (19% per year); price rose 8 of 10 years, 1977–87. Dividend: $0.82, 1987; $0.47, 1983; 4-year increase: 74%. Dividend yield: 2.1% average, 1985–87. P/E ratio: 20, 1/3/89. Average annual total return to investors, 1978–88: 22%.

75

The **WALT DISNEY** Company©

THE WALT DISNEY COMPANY

500 South Buena Vista St.
Burbank, CA 91521
(818) 560-1000
Chairman and CEO: Michael D. Eisner
President: Frank G. Wells

EARNINGS GROWTH	★ ★ ★
STOCK GROWTH	★ ★ ★ ★ ★
DIVIDEND YIELD	★ ★
DIVIDEND GROWTH	(no points)
SHAREHOLDER PERKS	★ ★ ★ ★ ★
NYSE—DIS	**15 points**

The sun is finally shining again on the Magic Kingdom. Through the early 1980s, profits were down, investor confidence was waning and gloom and doom reigned throughout the kingdom that Walt built. But like all Disney fairy tales, this one has a happy ending (at least for now). Earnings have been soaring, investor confidence is restored and—except for the evil crash of 1987—Disney's stock price has been climbing faster than Mary Poppins in a whirlwind.

Disney's recent revival at the movie box office has been one of the key contributors to the company's renewed growth. Through its Touchstone Pictures movie label, Disney has added many of Hollywood's top stars to its marquee, including Robin Williams, Bette Midler, Lily Tomlin, Dennis Quaid, Richard Dreyfuss, Emilio Estevez, Tom Selleck, Paul Newman, Tom Cruise, Danny DeVito and the latest kindred spirit of Mickey Mouse and Disney's other animated favorites, Roger Rabbit.

Some of Disney's biggest winners have included *Good Morning, Vietnam, Three Men and a Baby, Big Business, Tin Men, Cocktail* and *The Color of Money.*

The new line-up of stars has helped Disney triple its movie-generated revenues over the past three years. The company has also had some success with its Disney Channel on cable television and in network program offerings such as *Golden Girls, DuckTales* and the *Disney Sunday Movie.* Disney's

225

film entertainment division accounts for about 30 percent of the company's $3 billion in total annual revenue.

The heart and soul of the Magic Kingdom, however, continues to be its theme parks and resorts operations (64 percent of revenues). In addition to its Disney World and Epcot Center attractions in Orlando, Florida, and the original Disneyland Park in Anaheim, California, the company also collects substantial royalties on an independently owned Disneyland in Tokyo and is helping build a "Euro Disneyland" 30 miles east of Paris.

Disney also has a consumer products division that accounts for about 6 percent of revenues. The company sells Disney-related merchandise (such as Mickey Mouse dolls, watches, T-shirts, sunglasses, coffee mugs and related items), and collects licensing fees from other distributors who sell Disney products. Disney has opened several retail stores that carry a selection of Disney merchandise.

Mickey Mouse's show business debut came in 1928 when he starred in *Steamboat Willie,* the movie industry's first talking cartoon. More than 60 years later, Mickey is a little older, a little wiser and still the most popular cartoon character on the planet. Whether the effervescent mouse can carry the company on his shoulders for another 60 years remains to be seen, but Disney's current management team—which is a lot younger than Mickey— seems to have the company headed in the right direction.

EARNINGS GROWTH

Disney's earnings have soared during the past five years (through 1987) after some disappointing results in the early 1980s. Earnings per share have climbed 352 percent over the past ten years, with increases seven of those ten years.

The company reports total annual revenues of $2.9 billion. Disney has 32,000 employees and 77,000 shareholders of record.

STOCK GROWTH

In 1973, Disney stock reached a (split-adjusted) high of $27.75 a share. It started falling immediately thereafter, hit a low of $3.90 in 1974, and didn't reach the $27 level again until 1985. Over the past ten years, the stock has increased 540 percent (20.5 percent per year), rising from a 1978 median of $10 a share to its recent 1988 price of $64 a share.

In 1986, the stock was split 4-for-1.

Including reinvested dividends, a $10,000 investment in Disney stock at its median price in 1978 would have grown to about $73,000 ten years later. Average annual compounded rate of return (including stock growth and reinvested dividends): about 22 percent.

DIVIDEND YIELD

Disney has traditionally paid a fairly modest dividend yield, which has averaged under 2 percent per year over the past ten years. During the three-year rating period from 1985 to 1987, the stock paid an average annual current return of 1 percent.

DIVIDEND GROWTH   (no points)

Disney raised its dividend from 30 cents to 32 cents, from 1983 to 1987. That represents a meager 7 percent increase over the four-year rating period.

SHAREHOLDER PERKS

If you plan to visit one of the Disney amusement parks in the near future, it would pay you to pick up a few shares of Disney stock. Shareholders are eligible for membership in the Magic Kingdom Club, which entitles them to 10 percent off admission to the amusements parks, 5 to 20 percent off the price of accommodations, 10 percent off purchases at Disney Village, access to special cruise and travel packages exclusively for Magic Kingdom members and discounts on Delta flights to Disney areas.

Disney also offers a good dividend reinvestment and voluntary stock purchase plan for its shareholders of record. Shareholders may make cash contributions at any time and in varying amounts of at least $20 per contribution. Participating shareholders pay no fees or commissions.

SUMMARY

Total revenues: $2.9 billion, 1987. Earnings per share: $2.85, 1987; $0.63, 1977; 352% increase. Stock price: $64, 11/7/88; $10 (median), 1978; 540% increase (20.5% per year); price rose 8 of 10 years, 1977–87. Dividend: $0.32, 1987; $0.30, 1983; 4-year increase: 7%. Dividend yield: 1.0% average, 1985–87. P/E ratio: 18, 1/5/89. Average annual total return to investors, 1978–88: about 22%.

76
DOW JONES & COMPANY, INC.

DOW JONES & COMPANY, INC.
200 Liberty Street
New York, NY 10281
(212) 416-2000
Chairman and CEO: Warren H. Phillips
President: Ray Shaw

EARNINGS GROWTH	★ ★ ★
STOCK GROWTH	★ ★ ★ ★ ★
DIVIDEND YIELD	★ ★
DIVIDEND GROWTH	★ ★ ★
SHAREHOLDER PERKS	★ ★
NYSE—DJ	**15 points**

He lived only 51 years, but that was time enough for Charles Henry Dow to cast an indelible impression on Wall Street. In 1884, he compiled the first average of U.S. stock prices, now known as the Dow Jones average. His "Dow theory," a method of stock market analysis still in vogue today, maintains that the market moves like waves of the ocean, punctuated both by main tides and less significant intermediate ripples.

But certainly Mr. Dow's most prominent legacy is a business he started by dispatching business-related news bulletins by messenger to brokers on Wall Street. On July 8, 1889, the 38-year-old Mr. Dow collected all the bulletins he had circulated over the course of the day, bound them together into a small publication, and called it the *Wall Street Journal*.

Today, the *Wall Street Journal* is not only the bible of American business, it is the nation's largest circulation daily newspaper. Each weekday morning, the *Journal* lands on the doorsteps and desktops of about two million subscribers. The *Journal* has four U.S. editions. It is produced in New York and transmitted via satellite to 18 printing plants across the country. The *Journal* also puts out a European edition with 43,000 circulation and an Asian edition with 36,000 circulation.

The *Journal* is the central force of Dow Jones & Company and the major contributor to the firm's $1.3 billion in total annual revenue. While other business publications (such as Los Angeles-based *Investor's Daily*) have tried to nibble away at the *Journal's* dominance in the financial news arena, none has posed a significant threat. As a result, the *Journal* represents a virtual monopoly—an exclusive franchise with enormous pricing power, which translates into highly lucrative profit margins. The *Journal* has been particularly profitable in recent years as the country has become increasingly business oriented. Its advertising sales did, however, slip after October 1987, as some of the *Journal's* biggest institutional advertisers tried to recover from losses in the crash.

An offshoot of the *Journal* is the *National Business Employment Weekly*, a 30,000 circulation publication with articles on job hunting and careers and a large section of classified employment ads.

Dow also publishes *Barron's*, a 300,000-circulation weekly tabloid that concentrates on economic and financial news, and *American Demographics*, a 25,000-circulation publication that analyzes demographic trends and consumer markets.

In addition to its business publications, Dow Jones owns a group of daily community newspapers in small cities in Arizona, California, Connecticut, Kentucky, Massachusetts, Michigan, Minnesota, Missouri, New York, Oregon and Pennsylvania. The papers range in circulation from about 5,000 to 85,000.

The company also operates an information services group that has had exceptional growth the past few years and seems well positioned for the future. The information services group includes Dow News/Retrieval, a database publisher that supplies up-to-the-minute computerized business and financial news to subscribers around the world, Dow Jones News Service (commonly known as Broadtape), a business and financial newswire service, and *Dow Jones Professional Investor Report*, a news service introduced in 1987 that is geared to professional investment managers and traders.

Dow's business publications division accounts for about 65 percent of revenues, its community newspapers account for about 15 percent and its information services account for about 20 percent.

EARNINGS GROWTH

Dow Jones seems to be a company poised for the future, with its global database network and growing list of publications. The company's earnings growth has been very consistent, with increases for 13 consecutive years (through 1987). Earnings per share have increased a total of 329 percent over the past ten years.

The company has approximately 9,000 employees and 11,000 shareholders.

STOCK GROWTH

Dow's stock has climbed steadily through the past decade with two 2-for-1 stock splits and one 3-for-2 split since 1981. Over the past ten years the stock has increased 491 percent (19.5 percent per year), from its median of $5.75 in 1978 to its late 1988 price of $34 a share.

Including reinvested dividends, a $10,000 investment in Dow Jones stock at its median price in 1978 would have grown to about $73,000 ten years later. Average annual compounded rate of return (including stock growth and reinvested dividends): about 22 percent.

DIVIDEND YIELD

Dow normally pays a fairly low dividend yield, which has averaged under 2 percent the past five years. During the three-year rating period from 1984 to 1987, the stock paid an average annual current return of 1.6 percent.

DIVIDEND GROWTH

Dow Jones has increased its dividend each year for 13 consecutive years. The dividend climbed 60 percent over the four-year rating period from 1983 to 1987.

SHAREHOLDER PERKS

Dow Jones offers its shareholders a good dividend reinvestment and voluntary stock purchase plan. There are no fees or service charges, and shareholders may contribute up to $1,000 per month to the stock purchase plan.

SUMMARY

Total revenues: $1.3 billion, fiscal 1987. Earnings per share: $1.80, 1987; $0.42, 1977; 329% increase. Stock price: $34, 10/28/88; $5.75 (median), 1978 (491% total increase; 19.5% annual increase); price rose 8 of 10 years, 1977–87. Dividend: $0.64, 1987; $0.40, 1983; 4-year increase: 60%. Dividend yield: 1.6%, 1985–87. P/E ratio: 12, 1/5/89. Average annual total return to investor, 1978–88: 22%.

BALL CORPORATION

345 South High St.
P.O. Box 2407
Muncie, IN 47305-2326
(317) 747-6100
Chairman, President and CEO: Richard M. Ringoen

EARNINGS GROWTH	★ ★ ★
STOCK GROWTH	★ ★ ★ ★
DIVIDEND YIELD	★ ★ ★
DIVIDEND GROWTH	★ ★ ★
SHAREHOLDER PERKS	★ ★
NYSE—BLL	**15 points**

It was in an earlier era of American life—when families grew their own vegetables and canned them for the winter—that Ball Corporation first made its name. The modern American family is less inclined to can their own produce, but those who do are still likely to use Ball jars.

Ball, which has been in business since 1880, still does a small trade in canning jars, but the Muncie, Indiana, manufacturer has also graduated to bigger and better containers. The company makes metal beverage containers, ends for brewers and soft-drink fillers, and high-barrier plastic sheet and formed containers for foods and juices.

About 50 percent of Ball's $1.1 billion in annual revenue is generated by its beer and soft-drink can business. (The company's biggest customer is brewer Anheuser-Busch, which accounts for 23 percent of Ball's total sales.) Other types of packaging materials account for nearly 20 percent of Ball's sales.

Ball is also involved in two other manufacturing segments:

- Technical products (23 percent of revenues). The company is manufacturing aerospace antenna systems, ground-base laser systems for the U.S. Strategic Defense Initiative (Star Wars) and a laser nighttime illumination system for Air Force fighter planes. It is also involved in the testing of the space shuttle and other expendable launch vehicles.

- Industrial products (10 percent of revenue). Ball makes zinc battery cans (for alkaline batteries), insulated liners for refrigerator and freezer doors and injection molded plastics for the automotive industry. The company also supplies penny blanks to the U.S. Mint for the minting of new coins.

EARNINGS GROWTH

Ball has rolled to 11 consecutive years of record earnings. Earnings per share have climbed 201 percent over the past decade.

The company has 7,000 employees and about 8,000 shareholders.

STOCK GROWTH

The company's stock price has moved up steadily through the past decade, with two 2-for-1 stock splits since 1983. Over the past ten years the stock has increased 400 percent (17.5 percent per year), from its median of $6 in 1978 to its late 1988 price of $30 a share.

Including reinvested dividends, a $10,000 investment in Ball stock at its median price in 1978 would have grown to about $75,000 ten years later. Average annual compounded rate of return (including stock growth and reinvested dividends): about 22 percent.

DIVIDEND YIELD

The company generally pays a fairly good yield, which has averaged about 4 percent over the past ten years. During the three-year rating period from 1985 to 1987, the stock paid an average annual current return of 2.3 percent.

DIVIDEND GROWTH

Ball has raised its dividend 16 consecutive years. The dividend was increased 62 percent over the four-year rating period from 1983 to 1987.

SHAREHOLDER PERKS

Ball has one of the best dividend reinvestment plans in the business. For participating shareholders, dividends are reinvested in additional shares of stock at a 5 percent discount to the fair market price of the stock. Shareholders of record may also contribute $25 to $3,000 per quarter to the commission-free voluntary stock purchase plan.

SUMMARY

Total revenues: $1.05 billion, 1987. Earnings per share: $2.53, 1987; $0.84, 1977; 201% increase. Stock price: $30, 11/8/88; $6 (median), 1978; 400% increase (17.5% per year); price rose 9 of 10 years, 1977–87. Dividend: $0.89, 1987; $0.55, 1983; 4-year increase: 62%. Dividend yield: 2.3% average, 1985–87. P/E ratio: 11.9, 11/8/88. Average annual total return to investors, 1978–88: about 22%.

SCOTT

SCOTT PAPER COMPANY

Scott Plaza One
Philadelphia, PA 19113
(215) 522-5000
Chairman, President and CEO: Philip E. Lippincott

EARNINGS GROWTH	★ ★
STOCK GROWTH	★ ★ ★ ★
DIVIDEND YIELD	★ ★ ★
DIVIDEND GROWTH	★ ★
SHAREHOLDER PERKS	★ ★ ★ ★
NYSE—SPP	**15 points**

Scott Paper has been turning timber to tissue since 1879. As the world's leading manufacturer of sanitary paper products, Scott owns more than three million acres of woodlands—enough to cover all of Delaware and Rhode Island, plus half of Connecticut.

Bathroom tissue, napkins, facial tissue, paper towels and other personal care and cleaning products account for about 70 percent of Scott's revenues. Printing and publishing papers make up about 25 percent of sales, and pulp, forest products and minerals account for the remaining 5 percent.

After some sluggish years in the early 1980s, Scott has been on a roll recently. The company shed some of its less profitable businesses, upgraded and expanded its plants, added some new products and tightened its operations. Since 1982, when Scott's chief executive, Philip Lippincott, began the restructuring, earnings have grown at a 30 percent annual compounded rate, and return on equity has climbed from about 5 percent to 18 percent.

Scott puts out a line of brand name products under its own label (Scot-Tissue, ScotTowels, Scotties tissues and Scott napkins) as well as a long list of other cleverly targeted brands:

It has its "soft" sell brands—Soft-Weve, Soft Blend and Soft 'n Pretty bathroom tissues, Soft-Cote wipes, Softees napkins, and Sofkins premoistened adult cleansing wipes—and its hard sell brands—Sani-Tuff soap dispensing systems, and Sturdi-Wipes, Dura-Weve and Job Squad towels. Other leading Scott products include Viva paper towels, Expressions napkins,

Escort, Waldorf and Cottonelle bathroom tissue, Sequel and Premiere commercial roll towels, Craftmaster napkins, and Promise wash cream and bladder control pads. The company also makes Wash a-bye Baby and Baby Fresh wipes, Dry-Up and WypAll towels, Eurobath and ProCare soap dispensers, WinCup cups, American doilies and Kachoos children's tissues.

The Philadelphia-based manufacturer does most of its $4 billion in annual sales in the U.S. market, although it has also become a major force in the increasingly competitive European market (20 percent of sales).

EARNINGS GROWTH

While Scott Papers is the world leader in tissue paper production, its $4.1 billion in annual revenues puts it about eighth among U.S. forest products companies. Scott has about 26,000 employees (plus 12,000 employees in affiliated companies) and 45,000 shareholders.

Although the company's earnings growth has been exceptional the past five years, its ten-year total is less impressive. Scott's earnings per share have gone up 283 percent with earnings increases seven of those past ten years.

STOCK GROWTH

After bouncing around in the early 1980s, Scott's stock price has climbed steadily through the past few years (save for the crash of '87). The company has had no recent stock splits, but the price has increased 362 percent (16.5 percent annually) over the past decade, from a median of about $8 a share in 1978 to its late 1988 price of $37.

Including reinvested dividends, a $10,000 investment in Scott Paper stock at its median price in 1978 would have grown to about $70,000 ten years later. Average annual compounded rate of return (including stock growth and reinvested dividends): about 21.5 percent.

DIVIDEND YIELD

Scott generally pays a fairly competitive dividend (around 5 percent in the early 1980s). Over the past three years the stock has paid an annual current return of 2.3 percent.

DIVIDEND GROWTH

Over the four-year rating period from 1983 to 1987, Scott's dividend has increased 36 percent.

SHAREHOLDER PERKS

Scott has an excellent shareholder perks program. The company offers a Christmas gift box that shareholders of record may have mailed to friends, clients or business associates. The box, which costs about $10, contains toilet tissue, paper towels, baby wipes, a variety of napkins (dinner, luncheon and cocktail) and facial tissues. The company receives nearly 20,000 orders from shareholders each Christmas.

The company also hands out a sample box of paper products at its annual meetings.

Scott offers a dividend reinvestment and voluntary stock purchase plan. Shareholders of record may buy $10 to $3,000 per quarter in additional shares through the plan. There is a small service and commission charge.

SUMMARY

Total revenues: $4.1 billion, 1987. Earnings per share: $3.06, 1987; $0.80, 1977; 283% increase. Stock price: $37, 10/4/88; $8 (median), 1978; (362% total increase; 16.5% annual increase); price rose 8 of 10 years, 1977–87. Dividend: $0.68, 1987; $0.50, 1983; 4-year increase: 36%. Dividend yield: 2.3%, 1985–87. P/E ratio: 8, 1/4/89. Average annual total return to investor, 1978–88: about 21.5%.

R.R. DONNELLEY & SONS COMPANY

2223 Martin Luther King Drive
Chicago, IL 60616
(312) 326-8000
Chairman: John B. Schwemm
President and CEO: John R. Walter

EARNINGS GROWTH	★ ★ ★
STOCK GROWTH	★ ★ ★ ★
DIVIDEND YIELD	★ ★ ★
DIVIDEND GROWTH	★ ★ ★
SHAREHOLDER PERKS	★ ★
NYSE—DNY	**15 points**

If you read, then you've undoubtedly read something printed by R. R. Donnelley & Sons. If you read a lot, then you probably spend some time with a Donnelley-printed publication almost every day.

R. R. Donnelley prints everything from books and magazines to catalogs and phone directories. It is the largest commercial printer in the United States, with printing plants in a dozen states and three British cities.

Donnelley prints *Time, Business Week, Newsweek, U.S. News & World Report, Life, People, Sports Illustrated, Family Circle, Ladies Home Journal, Modern Maturity, Mademoiselle, Scientific American, Advertising Age, Glamour, Farm Journal, RedBook, Sesame Street, Crain's Chicago Business* and scores of other periodicals. It also prints Sunday magazines for such newspapers as the *New York Times,* the *Chicago Tribune* and the *Los Angeles Times.* Magazine printing accounts for about 21 percent of Donnelly's $2.5 billion a year in total revenues.

Donnelley, which has been in business since 1912, also claims to be the leading book producer in nearly every category, including textbooks, trade books (soft-cover and hard-cover), Bibles, college and professional books, subscription and mail-order books, and encyclopedias and other reference books. Donnelley prints books for more than 900 publishers. Book printing accounts for about 18 percent of Donnelley's total revenue.

Donnelley's biggest revenue source is catalog printing (34 percent of sales). It prints catalogs for major retailers (such as Sears and J.C. Penney) as well as for smaller specialty merchants. Donnelley also does a good business in preprinted inserts for newspapers for such retailers as K mart, Wal-Mart, Dayton-Hudson, Macy's, Zayre and Radio Shack.

The company is also a leading printer of phone books in the U.S. and the U.K. (20 percent of total revenue). Donnelley prints phone directories for more than 3,000 U.S. communities. The Chicago-based printer also does some printing of financial and software manuals. In 1987, it acquired Metromail, which has been a key competitor in the direct-mail business.

Although Donnelley has operations in England, its foreign sales account for less than 7 percent of its total revenue.

EARNINGS GROWTH

Donnelley has had increases in earnings and revenues for more than ten consecutive years. Earnings per share have climbed 247 percent over the past decade.

The company has annual revenues of $2.5 billion. It has about 22,000 employees and 9,000 shareholders of record.

In 1988, Donnelley became involved in a securities trading scandal. Several of Donnelley's press operators were fired for illegally selling advance copies of *Business Week* to stock brokers. The brokers—several of whom also lost their jobs—allegedly profited from the information by buying stocks recommended in the magazine before the general public had a chance to see the articles.

Whether the scandal will have any long-term effect on Donnelley's stock remains to be seen.

STOCK GROWTH

The company's stock price has risen consistently over the past ten years, increasing 386 percent (17 percent per year), from its median of $7 in 1978 to its late 1988 price of $34 a share.

Including reinvested dividends, a $10,000 investment in Donnelley stock at its median price in 1978 would have grown to about $62,000 ten years later. Average annual compounded rate of return (including stock growth and reinvested dividends): about 20 percent.

DIVIDEND YIELD

The company generally pays a moderately low dividend yield which has averaged about 3 percent over the past ten years. During the three-year rating period from 1985 to 1987, the stock paid an average annual current return of 2 percent.

DIVIDEND GROWTH

Donnelley traditionally raises its dividend every year. The dividend increased 70 percent over the four-year rating period from 1983 to 1987.

SHAREHOLDER PERKS

Donnelley offers a good dividend reinvestment and voluntary stock purchase plan which is free to shareholders of record. Shareholders may contribute as little as $10 a month or as much as $60,000 a year to the stock purchase plan.

SUMMARY

Total revenues: $2.5 billion, 1987. Earnings per share: $2.29, 1987; $0.66, 1977; 247% increase. Stock price: $34, 11/7/88; $7 (median), 1978; 386% increase (17% per year); price rose 9 of 10 years, 1977–87. Dividend: $0.70, 1987; $0.41, 1983; 4-year increase: 70%. Dividend yield: 2% average, 1985–87. P/E ratio: 14, 1/4/89. Average annual total return to investors, 1978–88: about 20%.

RPM, INC.

2628 Pearl Rd.
P.O. Box 777
Medina, OH 44258
(216) 225-3192
Chairman and CEO: Thomas C. Sullivan
President: James A. Karman

EARNINGS GROWTH	★ ★
STOCK GROWTH	★ ★ ★
DIVIDEND YIELD	★ ★ ★
DIVIDEND GROWTH	★ ★ ★ ★ ★
SHAREHOLDER PERKS	★ ★
OTC—RPOW	**15 points**

As one of the world's leading producers of paints and protective coatings, RPM seems to be as impervious to the ravages of time and decay as the solutions it manufactures. The 42-year-old Medina, Ohio, manufacturer has run up record sales and earnings every year since its inception in 1947.

RPM makes coatings for everything from toy boats to offshore oil rigs. The Statue of Liberty and the Eiffel Tower both sport coats of RPM's protectants. The company makes coatings for factories, bridges, machinery, grain bins, office towers, warehouses and scores of other applications. Its products battle the elements in some 75 countries in virtually every corner of the globe.

RPM, which was founded by the late Frank C. Sullivan as Republic Powered Metals, began as a one-product manufacturer. Its product was Alumanation, a heavy-duty protective coating that is still the largest selling liquid aluminum coating in the world.

Through acquisitions and internal expansion, RPM has grown to become a $342 million-a-year operation.

Technically, RPM is a shell—a holding company that specializes in acquiring companies in the coatings industry. The company has made more than 20 acqusitions in the past two decades. Under RPM's system, the acquired companies continue to operate relatively independently as "free-standing subsidiaries."

In every acquisition the company has made in the past 20 years, the principal executives of the acquired companies have stayed on to run their companies. The small executive staff of RPM's parent company helps with planning and budgeting and promotes communication and cross-fertilization of product ideas among its various subsidiaries, but, beyond that, the individual subsidiaries are left alone to run their own shows.

Most of RPM's subsidiaries are involved in the manufacture of corrosion protection, waterproofing and maintenance products. Its key products are paints, sealants, roofing materials and touch-up products for autos and furniture. It also makes fabrics and wall coverings.

RPM divides its business into two market segments:

- Industrial: RPM sells waterproofing and rustproofing products for industrial structures such as manufacturing plants and bridges. This sector accounts for 80 percent of RPM's products.
- Do-it-yourself market. The company sells beautifying, waterproofing and renovating products to homeowners through retail stores such as K mart and Ace Hardware. Among its more popular products are Bondex paint and patch products, Testor hobby products and Zinsser shellac-based products.

Among RPM's more recent acquisitions are the Carboline Company, a manufacturer of high-performance specialty coatings, and American Emulsions, a producer of specialty chemicals for the textile, water-treatment and paper industries.

EARNINGS GROWTH

RPM's earnings growth has not been spectacular the past decade, but its flawless streak of 41 straight years of earnings and sales increases makes it one of the most consistent companies in America. Over the past ten years, the company's earnings per share have increased 188 percent.

RPM has 1,500 employees, 600 sales representatives and about 6,000 shareholders of record. It operates 31 plants in North America and Belgium.

STOCK GROWTH

RPM's stock growth has been steady the past ten years, increasing 327 percent (15.5 percent per year), from a median of about $3.75 a share in 1978 to its late 1988 price of $16 per share. The stock has had one 5-for-4 split and one 3-for-2 split in the past ten years.

Including reinvested dividends, a $10,000 investment in RPM stock at its median price in 1978 would have grown to about $55,000 ten years later. Average annual compounded rate of return (including stock growth and rein-vested dividends): about 18.5 percent.

DIVIDEND YIELD

The company generally pays a fairly good dividend yield. During the three-year rating period from 1986 to 1988 the stock paid an average annual cur-rent return of 3.4 percent.

DIVIDEND GROWTH

RPM has increased its dividend for 14 consecutive years. The dividend has been raised 157 percent over the four-year rating period from 1984 to 1988.

SHAREHOLDER PERKS

RPM provides a good dividend reinvestment and voluntary stock purchase plan for its shareholders of record. There are no fees or service charges, and shareholders may contribute $10 to $2,000 per month to the stock purchase plan.

SUMMARY

Total revenues: $342 million, fiscal 1988 (ended 5/31/88). Earnings per share: $0.95, 1988; $0.33, 1977; 188% increase. Stock price: $16, 9/1/88; $3.75 (me-dian), 1978 (327% total increase; 15.5% annual increase); price rose 8 of 10 years, 1977–87. Dividend: $0.54, 1988; $0.21, 1984; 4-year increase: 157%. Divi-dend yield: 3.4%, 1986–88. P/E ratio: 17, 1/5/89. Average annual total return to investor, 1978–88: about 18.5%.

81

MCDONALD'S CORPORATION

McDonald's Plaza
Oak Brook, IL 60521
(312) 575-3000
Chairman: Fred L. Turner
President and CEO: Michael R. Quinlan

EARNINGS GROWTH	★ ★ ★ ★
STOCK GROWTH	★ ★ ★
DIVIDEND YIELD	★ ★
DIVIDEND GROWTH	★ ★ ★
SHAREHOLDER PERKS	★ ★ ★
NYSE—MCD	**15 points**

Say it fast: "Twoallbeefpattiesspecialsaucelettucecheesepicklesonionsona sesameseedbun." Which, of course, is just another way of saying "Big Mac," a sandwich that might best be described as the burger that swallowed the world. You can grab a Mac and some fries in some 50 countries on five continents. You can wake up to an Egg McMuffin in Mexico City, sample a Quarter Pounder in Panama, and cap off the day with a McDLT in Istanbul.

Since the late Ray Kroc opened his first McDonald's in 1955, more than 65 billion hamburgers have been served under the golden arches. There are more than 120,000 McDonald's restaurants around the world—about one-quarter of which are located outside the U.S. Australia has more than 200 McD's. England and West Germany have nearly 300 each, and Canada and Japan have more than 500.

And every 15 hours, somewhere in the world, a new McDonald's opens its doors for business. The company opens more than 500 new restaurants each year. Each day, 22 million people dine at McDonald's.

The company's success at the grill has translated well to success on the corporate bottom line. McDonald's has had an impeccable record of earnings growth, attaining record earnings for more than 90 consecutive quarters dating back to the year the company went public.

But is there a limit to McDonald's growth? Can the company ever fully McSaturate the world burger market? Some day, perhaps, but not for a few years to come—especially if consumers in Russia, China and the Eastern Bloc countries become as predisposed to the Big Mac attack as the rest of the world. The company has already penetrated the Iron Curtain: In 1988 McDonald's reached an agreement to open several restaurants in Russia.

Most McDonald's restaurants are owned by independent businesspeople who operate them through a franchise agreement with the company. The company usually tries to recruit investors who will be active, on-premise owners rather than outside investors. The conventional franchise arrangement is for a term of 20 years and requires an investment of about half a million dollars, 60 percent of which may be financed. Each outlet is also subject to franchise fees based on a percentage of sales.

Quality assurance is a major point of emphasis at McDonald's. The company goes to great extremes to see that each of its restaurants complies with its company standards. Edward Rensi, the president and chief operating officer of McDonald's U.S. division, personally visits 15 to 20 restaurants a week and about 400 a year to ensure that things are functioning properly out in the field.

EARNINGS GROWTH

McDonald's has turned burgers 'n' fries into a $5 billion a year business ($15 billion if you count all foods sold at all McDonald's outlets). It controls a 36 percent share of the $25 billion-a-year U.S. fast-food hamburger market—roughly the equivalent of Burger King, Wendy's and Hardee's combined.

Over the past ten years, the company's earnings have increased 327 percent (15.5 percent per year).

McDonalds has 140,000 employees and 30,000 shareholders of record. Joan Kroc (Ray's widow) still holds 9 percent of McDonald's stock.

STOCK GROWTH

McDonald's stock has increased steadily through the past decade, with three 3-for-2 stock splits since 1982. Over the past ten years the stock price has climbed 328 percent (16 percent per year), from its median of $10.50 in 1978 to its late 1988 price of $45 a share.

Including reinvested dividends, a $10,000 investment in McDonald's stock at its median price in 1978 would have grown to about $48,000 ten years later. Average annual compounded rate of return (including stock growth and reinvested dividends): about 17 percent.

DIVIDEND YIELD

The company generally pays a low dividend yield, which has averaged just over 1 percent over the past ten years. During the three-year rating period from 1985 to 1987, the stock paid an average annual current return of 1.1 percent.

DIVIDEND GROWTH

McDonald's has upped its dividend every year since it began paying them in 1976. The dividend increased 68 percent over the four-year rating period from 1983 to 1987.

SHAREHOLDER PERKS

The approximately 2,000 shareholders who attend McDonald's annual meeting each year on the campus of Hamburger University in Oak Brook, Illinois, can stay for a tour of the facilities and a free McDonald's meal. McDonald's offers no coupons or special gifts for new shareholders, but it does have an investor hotline (although it is not a toll-free number) that gives the latest company news. A wealth of material on McDonald's, including a directory of McDonald's locations and a listing of ingredients in each McDonald's product, is also available to shareholders (and to anyone else who requests it).

The company offers an outstanding dividend reinvestment and voluntary stock purchase plan. There are no fees or service charges, and shareholders may contribute $50 to $75,000 a year to the stock purchase plan. Charles Ebeling, the company's corporate communications director, says about 40 percent of the company's shareholders of record participate in the plan, one of the highest participation rates in corporate America.

SUMMARY

Total revenues: $4.9 billion, 1987. Earnings per share: $2.86, 1987; $0.67, 1977; 327% increase. Stock price: $45, 11/7/88; $10.50 (median), 1978; 328% increase (16% per year); price rose 8 of 10 years, 1977–87. Dividend: $0.49, 1987; $0.29, 1983; 4-year increase: 68%. Dividend yield: 1.1% average, 1985–87. P/E ratio: 15, 1/4/89. Average annual total return to investors, 1978–88: about 17%.

82

American Brands, Inc.

AMERICAN BRANDS, INC.
1700 East Putnam Ave.
P.O. Box 811
Old Greenwich, CT 06870-0811
(203) 698-5000
Chairman and CEO: William J. Alley
President and COO: Thomas C. Hays

EARNINGS GROWTH	★ ★
STOCK GROWTH	★ ★ ★ ★
DIVIDEND YIELD	★ ★ ★ ★ ★
DIVIDEND GROWTH	★
SHAREHOLDER PERKS	★ ★
NYSE—AMB	**14 points**

It was that special charcoal filter that inspired Tareyton smokers to boast, "I'd rather fight than switch." But American Brands, maker of Tareyton, Pall Mall, Lucky Strike, Carlton and Malibu cigarettes, has been doing some serious switching of its own in recent years as it looks for new sideline ventures to take the pressure off of its wilting domestic tobacco trade.

Through a series of acquisitions, American Brands has assembled a divergent lineup of products from Jim Beam whiskey to Titleist golf balls. The company manufactures sportswear, office products, eyeglasses, hardware, cookware and coatracks. It also operates a major life insurance company.

Cigarettes, however, remain the primary source of income for American Brands. The company is the nation's fifth-largest cigarette manufacturer, with about 7 percent of domestic consumption. Although its operating profits from U.S. tobacco sales are still on the rise, total sales have flattened out in recent years as a growing number of Americans have been kicking the smoking addiction.

But what American Brands has lost in U.S. cigarette sales it has made up for in international sales. In fact, the Old Greenwich, Connecticut-based manufacturer is one of the few U.S. companies with higher European sales ($6.25 billion in total 1987 sales including $4.7 billion in tobacco sales) than U.S. sales ($2.9 billion including $1.4 in tobacco sales). But because of much

246

higher profit margins in the U.S. tobacco market, operating profits from its domestic trade ($430 million) remain considerably higher than its foreign tobacco market ($244 million).

American Brands owns Gallaher Limited, the largest tobacco company in the United Kingdom with a 38.5 percent share of the U.K. cigarette market.

The company's other key segments include:

* Distilled spirits (7 percent of sales). The company acquired the distilled spirits operations of National Distillers and Chemical Corporation in 1987. The company makes Jim Beam whiskey, Old Grand-Dad bourbon, DeKuyper cordials, Gilbey's gin and vodka and Windsor Canadian Supreme whiskey. Jim Beam is the best-selling bourbon in the world and, along with its 20 related brands, is the third-largest liquor company in the U.S.
* Hardware (3 percent of sales). American Brands owns Master Lock, maker of padlocks, door locks, cable locks and built-in locker locks. Other products include Swingline staple guns, glue guns, nail drivers, riveters, W.R. Case & Sons Cutlery, and other products in the tool storage, kitchen cabinet and window covering markets.
* Office products (6 percent of sales). The company makes a wide variety of office products—staplers, paper clips, folders, notebooks, pens, pencils, desk trays, etc.—through several subsidiaries including ACCO World, Swingline, Wilson Jones, Perma Products and Acme Visible.
* Financial services. (16 percent of operating income; revenues from this segment are not included as part of the company's net sales). Franklin Life Insurance Company, a wholly owned subisidiary of American Brands, sells life insurance, annuities, and accident and health insurance. The company has about $35 billion of insurance in force and assets of $5.3 billion. Its operating income in 1987 was $168 million.
* Golf and leisure products (3 percent of sales). The company's Titleist Division makes golf balls, clubs and accessories. Its Foot-Joy subsidiary makes golf shoes and golf gloves.
* Optical goods and services (3 percent of revenues). American Brands' Dollond & Aitchison Group, based in England, is the largest manufacturer of eyeglasses and optical gear in Europe.
* Specialty businesses (11 percent of revenues). The company owns two British newspaper, confectionery and tobacco chains, NSS and Forbuoys. Its TM Group operates 55,000 vending machines in England. Other subsidiaries include Acushnet Rubber, Regal China and Golden Belt packaging.

EARNINGS GROWTH

American Brands has had increased earnings eight of the past ten years. Its earnings per share have climbed 201 percent during that period.

The company has 52,000 employees and 83,000 shareholders of record. The company's earnings from domestic tobacco sales continues to rise, but it faces increasingly difficult market conditions. Cigarette sales in the U.S. have been declining at about 2 percent per year, and legislation designed to restrict smoking in public places is being enacted. New public awareness programs alerting consumers to the hazards of smoking—and its ties to lung cancer and heart disease—have also been initiated. Cigarette packages must now carry warnings such as "Smoking causes lung cancer, heart disease, emphysema, and may complicate pregnancy," and "Quitting smoking now greatly reduces serious risks to your heart." Cigarette advertising, which has been banned from TV and radio since 1971, may be restricted even further in the future. All of these restrictions will probably further reduce U.S. cigarette sales.

On top of that, tobacco companies are now facing a stiffer challenge in the courts to take some of the financial responsibility for the deaths and health problems that their products have caused. Although only one verdict out of about 260 court cases tried, to date, has gone against tobacco companies, many other cases are pending.

By diversifying into other markets, American Brands is attempting to minimize the potential lost revenue from the dwindling U.S. tobacco market.

STOCK GROWTH

American Brands's stock price increased 13 consecutive years through 1987. The stock has had two 2-for-1 splits since 1981. Over the past ten years the stock has increased 360 percent (16.5 percent per year), from its median of $11.75 in 1978 to its late 1988 price of $54 a share.

Including reinvested dividends, a $10,000 investment in American Brands stock at its median price in 1978 would have grown to about $85,000 ten years later. Average annual compounded rate of return (including stock growth and reinvested dividends): about 24 percent.

DIVIDEND YIELD

The company generally pays an excellent dividend yield, which has averaged about 7 percent over the past ten years. During the three-year rating period from 1985 to 1987, the stock paid an average annual current return of 5.1 percent.

DIVIDEND GROWTH

American Brands has raised its dividend for 20 consecutive years, although the increases have not been very substantial of late. The dividend was increased only 19 percent over the four-year rating period from 1983 to 1987.

SHAREHOLDER PERKS

The company offers its shareholders of record an excellent dividend reinvestment and voluntary stock purchase plan. There are no fees or commissions, and shareholders of record may purchase $10 to $10,000 per quarter in additional shares through the voluntary stock purchase plan.

The company also hands out a small packet of product samples at its annual meeting.

SUMMARY

Total revenues: $9.15 billion, 1987. Earnings per share: $4.42, 1987; $1.47, 1977; 201% increase. Stock price: $54, 11/9/88; $11.75 (median), 1978; 360% increase (16.5% per year); price rose 10 of 10 years, 1977–87. Dividend: $2.11, 1987; $1.78, 1983; 4-year increase: 19%. Dividend yield: 5.1% average, 1985–87. P/E ratio: 11, 1/4/89. Average annual total return to investors, 1978–88: about 24%.

83

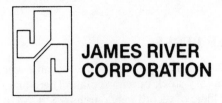

JAMES RIVER CORPORATION

P.O. Box 2218
Tredegar Street
Richmond, VA 23217
(804) 644-5411
Chairman and CEO: Brenton S. Halsey
President: Robert C. Williams

EARNINGS GROWTH	★ ★ ★ ★
STOCK GROWTH	★ ★ ★ ★ ★
DIVIDEND YIELD	★ ★
DIVIDEND GROWTH	★ ★
SHAREHOLDER PERKS	★
NYSE—JR	**14 points**

Maybe money *does* grow on trees. That might explain the phenomenal growth of Richmond, Virginia, papermaker James River Corporation. This is a company that wasn't even in business until 1969, and didn't eclipse the $100-million mark in revenues until 1978. Yet today, James River owns more than 100 manufacturing facilities and ranks among the world's largest paper companies, with total annual sales of more than $5 billion.

James River produces paper and plastic products, including Dixie cups, Northern tissues and Brawny and Gala paper towels. It is the nation's second-largest producer of towel and tissue products (behind Scott Paper) and is the leading manufacturer of specialty industrial and packaging papers. The company's management attributes its spectacular growth over the past two decades to an "aggressive acquisition and internal growth strategy."

Among its recent acquisitions were Crown Zellerbach, a Nevada-based pulp, papermaking and specialty packaging business; Canada Cup, a manufacturer of plastic and paper food and beverage service products; Specialty Papers Company; Amarin Plastics, a manufacturer of plastic disposable cutlery; and Fiberplastics, Inc., maker of Handi-Kup foam cups and containers.

James River divides its business into several basic product lines:

- Sanitary paper products (26 percent of total sales). The company makes Gala, Bolt, Spill Mate and Zee paper towels, Northern, Nice 'n' Soft and Aurora bathroom tissues and a line of other consumer-geared facial tissues and napkins. It also puts out a line of industrial and commercial paper towels and tissues.
- Communication papers (24 percent of sales). James River is one of the world's largest producers of communications papers, including computer and copy papers, writing papers, text paper, newsprint and coated and uncoated printing paper for catalogs, magazines and advertising materials.
- Disposable food and beverage service products (15 percent of sales). The company makes Dixie and Papermaid paper and plastic plates, cups and bowls. It also manufactures trays, cartons, place mats, sandwich wrap, coffee filters, waxed paper, sandwich wrap and plastic utensils.
- Specialty industrial and packaging papers (11 percent of sales). James River is the largest U.S. producer of specialty papers used in the manufacture of automobile, industrial and household filters, sanding belts, gaskets, masking tape base, electrical insulators and medical applications. Its specialty papers are also used for pet food and food packaging.
- Paperboard packaging (8.5 percent of sales). The company makes packages for cereal boxes, ice cream cartons, meat packages and cardboard containers for a variety of products from light bulbs to gelatin.
- Flexible packaging (7.5 percent of sales). The company makes plastic and paper packages for cheese, frozen foods, bread, cookies, Kool Aid, soap, potato chips and other consumer products.

The company's other products include wood pulp (3 percent of sales), imaging and coated film products (2 percent of sales) and non-woven fabrics (3 percent) used for disposable consumer, industrial and medical products such as diapers, baby wipes, surgical masks, nurses' caps and certain types of paper towels.

EARNINGS GROWTH

While the company's revenues have shot up unabated since its inception two decades ago, its growth in earnings per share has come in fits and starts. Three of the past ten years, the earnings per share declined. Two other years it increased by only 2 or 3 percent. Yet, thanks to sizeable gains during the other five years, the company has enjoyed an excellent ten-year increase of 402 percent (18 percent per year average).

James River has annual revenues of $5.1 billion. It has 36,000 employees and 20,000 shareholders of record.

STOCK GROWTH

The company's stock price growth has been a little more consistent than its earnings growth, rising eight of ten years through 1987. The company has had five 3-for-2 stock splits since 1978. Over the past ten years the stock has increased 600 percent (21.5 percent per year), from its median of $4 in 1978 to its late 1988 price of $28 a share.

Including reinvested dividends, a $10,000 investment in James River stock at its median price in 1978 would have grown to about $80,000 ten years later. Average annual compounded rate of return (including stock growth and reinvested dividends): about 23 percent.

DIVIDEND YIELD

The company generally pays a fairly low dividend yield, which has averaged under 2 percent over the past ten years. During the three-year rating period from fiscal 1986 to 1988, the stock paid an average annual current return of 1.4 percent.

DIVIDEND GROWTH

The company increases its dividend most years. The dividend increased 48 percent over the four-year rating period from 1984 to 1988.

SHAREHOLDER PERKS

At its annual meetings, James River passes out a sample box to each shareholder in attendance. The box includes Northern bathroom tissue, Dixie Cups, industrial wipes and table covers. The company sometimes includes a coupon for one of its products in its annual report. The company does not offer a dividend reinvestment plan.

SUMMARY

Total revenues: $5.1 billion, fiscal 1988 (ended 4/24/88). Earnings per share: $2.36, 1987; $0.47, 1978; 402% increase. Stock price: $28, 11/4/88; $4 (median), 1978; 600% increase (21.5% per year); price rose 8 of 10 years, 1977–87. Dividend: $0.40, 1987; $0.27, 1983; 4-year increase: 48%. Dividend yield: 1.4% average, 1985–87. P/E ratio: 11, 1/4/89. Average annual total return to investors, 1978–88: about 23%.

84

CONSOLIDATED EDISON COMPANY
OF NEW YORK, INC.

4 Irving Place
New York, NY 10003
(212) 460-4600
Chairman and CEO: Arthur Hauspurg
President and COO: Eugene R. McGrath

EARNINGS GROWTH	★				
STOCK GROWTH	★ ★				
DIVIDEND YIELD	★ ★ ★ ★ ★				
DIVIDEND GROWTH	★ ★ ★				
SHAREHOLDER PERKS	★ ★ ★				
NYSE—ED	**14 points**				

In the city that never sleeps, it's Consolidated Edison that keeps the bright lights burning, the night spots rocking and the subways rolling.

Con Edison supplies the electrical power for virtually all of New York City and most of Westchester County. It also supplies gas in much of New York, and steam in much of Manhattan.

Keeping the juice flowing through the Big Apple is no small task. On one steamy July day in 1987, Con Edison cranked out more than 9 million kilowatts of electricity.

Con Edison's system includes 85,000 miles of underground cable with 29,000 underground transformers, and 35,000 miles of overhead wires with 44,000 overhead transformers.

The company uses more than a dozen generating stations. About 27 percent of its electricity is produced from nuclear fuel, 25 percent from oil, 22 percent from natural gas and 26 percent from other sources including hydroelectric, refuse and coal power.

Con Ed's electricity sales account for about 82 percent of its total revenue, natural gas sales account for about 12 percent and steam sales account for just over 5 percent.

EARNINGS GROWTH

Consolidated Edison is one of the nation's largest utilities, with annual revenues of about $5 billion. It has 20,000 employees and 180,000 shareholders.

Earnings for Con Ed have grown slowly over the years, which is typical of the tightly regulated utilities industry. In fact, although Con Ed's earnings growth of only 95 percent over the past ten years seems paltry compared to most *Best 100* companies (it ranks dead last), it still ranks at the high end of the utility industry.

The company's earnings growth will never be exceptional because of rate hike restrictions. In fact, the company has not been allowed to raise its electric rates since 1983, nor its gas rates since 1985. But it's hard to beat the company's built-in stability. There is a constant demand for its service, and it has a monopoly in the large and ever-expanding New York area.

Con Ed does, however, face one potentially costly problem. The steam generators in its Indian Point 2 nuclear plant appear to be weakening. The company has already purchased and stored replacement generators at a cost of $36 million. If replacement is required, the company estimates that installation costs would exceed $100 million plus replacement power costs for the six months or so that the system would be out of service.

STOCK GROWTH

Con Ed's stock price growth has been respectable over the past decade, particularly when compared to other utilities. The stock price increased seven of ten years through 1987. Over the past decade the stock has increased 258 percent (13 percent per year), from its median of $12 in 1978 to its late 1988 price of $43 a share.

Including reinvested dividends, a $10,000 investment in Con Ed's stock at its median price in 1978 would have grown to about $73,000 ten years later. Average annual compounded rate of return (including stock growth and reinvested dividends): about 22 percent.

DIVIDEND YIELD

The company has traditionally paid an outstanding dividend yield, averaging about 9 percent over the past ten years. During the three-year rating period from 1985 to 1987, the stock paid an average annual current return of 6.6 percent.

DIVIDEND GROWTH

Con Ed has raised its dividend for 13 consecutive years. The dividend increased 57 percent over the four-year rating period from 1983 to 1987.

SHAREHOLDER PERKS

Con Edison makes a concerted effort to keep its shareholders up-to-date on the company's operations. Since 1980 it has been sponsoring several shareholder forums each year, which it typically conducts at meeting halls in the boroughs where the company offers service. It also conducts at least one forum outside New York each year in a selected city where it has a number of shareholders. In recent years, forums have been conducted in New Orleans, Chicago and near Newark.

"We think it's good to keep our shareholders apprised of what we're doing," says David Templin, manager of Con Ed's investor relations department. "It's the type of thing that helps make them goodwill ambassadors for the company. Most of our shareholders are also customers in our service area. By building their loyalty through these forums, maybe next time one of their neighbors pops off about Con Edison, they'll stick up for us."

The company also offers a good dividend reinvestment and voluntary stock purchase plan. There are no fees or commissions, and shareholders may contribute $20 to $3,000 per quarter to the stock purchase plan.

SUMMARY

Total revenues: $5.1 billion, 1987. Earnings per share: $4.42, 1987; $2.27, 1977; 95% increase. Stock price: $43, 9/9/88; $12 (median), 1978; (258% total increase; 13% annual increase); price rose 7 of 10 years, 1977–87. Dividend: $2.96, 1987; $1.88, 1983; 4-year increase: 57%. Dividend yield: 6.6%, 1985–87. P/E ratio: 10, 1/5/89. Average annual total return to investor, 1978–88: about 22%.

85

PNC FINANCIAL CORP

Fifth Avenue and Wood Street
Pittsburgh, PA 15265
(412) 762-2666
Chairman, President and CEO: Thomas H. O'Brien

EARNINGS GROWTH	★
STOCK GROWTH	★ ★ ★ ★
DIVIDEND YIELD	★ ★ ★ ★
DIVIDEND GROWTH	★ ★ ★
SHAREHOLDER PERKS	★ ★
NYSE—PNC	**14 points**

In the mahogany-paneled board rooms of America's high-powered financial institutions, the talk rarely revolves around merely "making money." The new game in town is "capturing assets," and Pittsburgh-based PNC Financial Corporation has come up with more ways to do that than just about any other player in the financial arena.

PNC operates:

- a money management service that offers financial planning, trust and investment advisory services and manages $79 billion in investments—making it the country's fifth largest investment manager;
- a family of mutual funds (operated through its Provident Bank subsidiary) with $19 billion in assets—more than any other bank mutual fund group in the nation;
- an investment banking division that markets its services to emerging corporations of $10 to $100 million in annual revenue; PNC helps the companies raise capital and implement mergers and acquisitions;
- a wholesale corporate banking service with offices in most U.S. metropolitan areas and about a dozen foreign cities; and
- a chain of bank holding companies with nearly 475 retail branch bank offices.

With total assets of $36.5 billion, PNC Financial—formerly Pittsburgh National Bank—is one of the nation's 15-largest bank holding companies. The company owns 23 commercial banking subsidiaries in Pennsylvania, Kentucky, Ohio and southern Indiana. Among the largest are its flagship bank, Pittsburgh National ($15 billion in total assets), Provident National Bank in Philadelphia ($6.2 billion), Citizens Fidelity Bank in Louisville ($5 billion) and Central Bank in Cincinnati ($3 billion).

PNC's corporate banking division reports total commercial and construction loans outstanding of about $13 billion. The company's strength is most concentrated in the mid-Atlantic and southern states, although it offers services throughout the U.S. and abroad. It claims to do business with 300 of the *Fortune 500* companies.

EARNINGS GROWTH

After more than a decade of increased earnings, PNC Financial slipped in 1987, but still came away better than most of its contemporaries in the financial industry. The October, 1987 stock market crash took its toll on most financial institutions, and foreign debt defaults battered some of the major international lenders. PNC suffered along with the industry, but still ranked first among the nation's 15-largest bank holding companies in both return on assets (0.79 percent) and return on equity (12.21 percent). (Banc One, another *Best 100* selection, had a higher return on assets but is not ranked among the 15 largest banks.

PNC has about 11,000 employees and 25,000 shareholders.

Over the past ten years PNC's earnings per share has grown 117 percent, from $1.35 a share in 1977 to $2.93 per share in 1987 (earnings had reached a record $4.76 cents per share in 1986, and was expected to return to that level—or higher—after 1987).

STOCK GROWTH

Like its earnings growth, PNC's stock also experienced a slight drop-off after 1986, but the company's longer-term growth has been quite good, climbing 360 percent (16.5 percent per year), from its 1978 median of $9.50 to its late 1988 price of $44 a share.

The stock has had two 2-for-1 splits since 1981.

Including reinvested dividends, a $10,000 investment in PNC stock at its median price in 1978 would have grown to about $73,000 in 1988. Average annual compounded return (including stock growth and reinvested dividends): about 22 percent.

DIVIDEND YIELD

PNC has traditionally paid a fairly high dividend yield. Over the past three years the stock has paid an annual average current return of 3.8 percent.

DIVIDEND GROWTH

PNC normally raises its dividend each year. The dividend climbed 58 percent over the four-year rating period from 1983 to 1987.

SHAREHOLDER PERKS

PNC offers shareholders an excellent dividend reinvestment and stock purchase plan. There are no fees or commissions, and stock purchased through reinvested dividends is discounted 5 percent to the market value. Shareholders may also contribute $50 to $1,000 per month to the voluntary cash stock purchase plan.

SUMMARY

Assets: $36.5 billion, 1987; loans outstanding, $20.6 billion (total net income, $256 million). Earnings per share: $2.93, 1987; $1.35, 1977; 117% increase. Stock price: $44, 10/5/88; $9.50 (median), 1978; (360% total increase; 16.5% annual increase); price rose 8 of 10 years, 1977–87. Dividend: $1.60, 1987; 4-year increase: 58%. Dividend yield: 3.8%, 1985–87. P/E ratio: 10, 1/5/89. Average annual total return to investor, 1978–88: about 22%.

86

SUPER VALU STORES, INC.

11840 Valley View Road
Eden Prairie, MN 55344
(612) 828-4000
Chairman, CEO and President: Michael W. Wright

EARNINGS GROWTH	★ ★ ★
STOCK GROWTH	★ ★ ★ ★
DIVIDEND YIELD	★ ★
DIVIDEND GROWTH	★ ★
SHAREHOLDER PERKS	★ ★ ★
NYSE—SVU	**14 points**

In the long journey from farm field to dinner table, foods may pass through many hands. Super Valu makes its business as one of the middlemen in the chain, wringing out the slimmest of margins by buying from producers and selling to grocers. On total annual revenues of nearly $10 billion, the company has after-tax earnings of little more than $100 million—a margin of just over 1 percent.

Super Valu is the nation's largest food wholesaler, serving about 3,000 independent retail grocers in 32 states. But the Minneapolis-based company is more than a wholesaler. It not only stocks its customers shelves, it also provides marketing and advertising support, store management assistance, inventory control and accounting and payroll services. It offers building design and construction services, consumer research, personnel management assistance, trading stamp programs and insurance. Super Valu may even provide direct financial assistance for its customers, including financial loans and the acquisition and subleasing of store buildings.

The company's wholesale business accounts for about 85 percent of total sales and 75 percent of operating income. Super Valu's other businesses include:

- Retail food stores. Super Valu owns about 100 retail grocery stores, which account for about 14 percent of total revenue and only about 2 percent of operating income. The company operates the 53-store Cub

Foods chain, of which it owns 19 stores and franchises 34 stores to independent retailers.

- ShopKo Stores: Super Valu owns a chain of 75 ShopKo department stores. The stores sell housewares, hardware, appliances, paint, toys, sporting goods, photo supplies, clothing, cosmetics, drugs, health aids and other general mechandise. ShopKo stores range in size from 30,000 square feet to 106,000 square feet and are located in medium-sized cities throughout the upper Midwest and Northwest. ShopKo has been very profitable, accounting for about 11 percent of Super Valu's total revenues and 24 percent of its earnings.

EARNINGS GROWTH

Super Valu has had earnings gains 14 of the past 15 years, although earnings growth in recent years has slowed considerably. The slowing growth rate may indicate that Super Valu—which once was considered one of the highest flyers of the food industry—has reached maturity. Still, the company's management is considered competent and its market is still expanding.

The company's earnings per share have increased 257 percent over the past ten years.

The company has annual revenues of $9.4 billion, a deceptively high figure due to the tremendous volume of sales generated in its business. A more representative figure is its annual net earnings of about $112 million, which ranks in the middle of the pack among the *Best 100* list.

Super Valu has about 36,000 employees and 10,000 shareholders.

STOCK GROWTH

Super Valu's stock price has had an excellent ten-year growth rate, although the past five years have not been particularly impressive. The stock has had three 2-for-1 splits since 1978. Over the past decade the stock has increased 411 percent (18 percent per year), from its median of $4.50 in 1978 to its late 1988 price of $23 a share.

Including reinvested dividends, a $10,000 investment in Super Valu stock at its median price in 1978, with all dividends reinvested, would be worth about $62,000 ten years later. Average annual compounded rate of return (including stock growth and reinvested dividends): about 20 percent.

DIVIDEND YIELD

The company generally pays a fairly low dividend yield which has averaged about 2.5 percent over the past ten years. During the three-year rating period from 1985 to 1987, the stock paid an average annual current return of 1.9 percent.

DIVIDEND GROWTH

Super Valu has increased its dividend for more than a dozen consecutive years. Over the four-year rating period from 1983 to 1987, the dividend was raised 47 percent.

SHAREHOLDER PERKS

Shareholders who attend Super Valu's annual meeting receive a complimentary box of the company's private label groceries, including such items as candy, cookies, crackers, toothbrushes and soap dishes.

The company also offers its shareholders an excellent dividend reinvestment and voluntary stock purchase plan. There are no fees or service charges, and shareholders may contribute $10 to $3,000 per month to the stock purchase plan.

SUMMARY

Total revenues: $9.4 billion, 1988 (ended 2/27/88). Earnings per share: $1.50, 1987; $0.42, 1977; 257% increase. Stock price: $23, 9/9/88; $4.50 (median), 1978 (411% total increase; 18% annual increase); price rose 9 of 10 years, 1977–87. Dividend: $0.44, 1988; $0.30, 1984; 4-year increase: 47%. Dividend yield: 1.9%, 1986–88. P/E ratio: 14, 1/5/89. Average annual total return to investor, 1978–88: about 20%.

87

GANNETT CO., INC.

1100 Wilson Blvd.
Arlington, VA 22209
(703) 284-6000
Chairman, President and CEO: John J. Curley

EARNINGS GROWTH	★ ★ ★
STOCK GROWTH	★ ★ ★
DIVIDEND YIELD	★ ★ ★
DIVIDEND GROWTH	★ ★ ★
SHAREHOLDER PERKS	★ ★
NYSE—GCI	**14 points**

Gannett Company has pushed its way through a crowded field of media titans to become USA's largest circulation newspaper chain.

The reason: Aggressive acquisitions and "McPaper."

McPaper? "The Nation's Newspaper," *USA Today,* first in readership, second in USA circulation (to *Wall Street Journal*).

Its lure:

- national prespective;
- color and graphics;
- short, easily digestible articles; and
- lists and bullets.

After five years of losses, *USA Today* had its first profitable quarter in the fourth quarter of 1987. The paper has a daily circulation of 1.6 million and readership of nearly 6 million, according to survey figures.

Although its critics sometimes poke fun at its punchy, upbeat style, *USA Today* has been one of the most imitated newspapers in USA history. The paper—published mornings, five days a week—has ushered in a new renaissance of colors, graphics and capsulized articles among newspapers across the country.

But Gannett is far more than *USA Today.*

Gannett's other interests:

- Newspaper group (accounts for 82 percent of Gannett's $3.1 billion in annual revenue). Gannett owns 90 daily newspaper and 35 non dailies, making it USA's biggest newspaper chain. Total chain circulation of 6.2 million is also nation's biggest. Its largest papers (besides *USA Today*) include: *Detroit News, Louisville Courier-Journal, Cincinnati Enquirer, Des Moines Register.*
- Billboards (7 percent of total revenue). Gannett Outdoor is North America's largest outdoor advertising group.
- Broadcasting (11 percent of revenue). The company owns ten television stations (in Phoenix, Denver, Washington, D.C., Jacksonville, Atlanta, Boston, Minneapolis-St. Paul, Greensboro, Oklahoma City and Austin), nine FM radio stations and seven AM stations.

In its first 20 years as a publicly traded company (through 1987), Gannett has never had a year in which it didn't set new records for revenues and dividends. Even more extraordinary: The Arlington, Virginia publisher has had 80 consecutive quarters of record earnings.

Impressive as those figures may be, Gannett's growth might be even stronger if *USA Today* would finally start to pay its way, or actually turn a profit. Over the years, Gannett has poured close to $500 million into its flagship paper, and it's still waiting for the payoff. While *USA Today's* circulation is approaching two million, its advertising revenues continue to disappoint. After the paper's 1987 fourth-quarter profit—the first in its history—advertising sales in 1988 declined, and the paper appeared headed for another year of losses. But, if success is a state of mind, the perky *USA Today* might already be the market leader.

EARNINGS GROWTH

Gannett has had 20 consecutive years of record sales and earnings. Earnings per share have climbed 241 percent over the past decade.

The company has 36,000 employees and 13,000 shareholders of record.

STOCK GROWTH

Gannett's stock price has climbed steadily if unspectacularly the past ten years, rising 258 percent (14 percent per year), from its 1978 median of $9.50 a share to its late 1988 price of $34. The stock has split 3-for-2 twice and 2-for-1 once since 1980.

Including reinvested dividends, a $10,000 investment in Gannett stock at its median price in 1978 would have grown to about $50,000 ten years later. Average annual compounded rate of return (including stock growth and reinvested dividends): about 17.5 percent.

DIVIDEND YIELD

The company generally pays a fairly good yield, which has averaged about 3.5 percent over the past ten years. During the three-year rating period from 1985 to 1987, the stock paid an average annual current return of 2.4 percent.

DIVIDEND GROWTH

Gannett has raised its dividend 20 consecutive years. The dividend has increased 54 percent over the four-year rating period from 1983 to 1987.

SHAREHOLDER PERKS

Gannett offers an excellent dividend reinvestment and voluntary stock purchase plan for its shareholders of record. There are no fees or service charges, and shareholders may contribute $10 to $5,000 per month to the stock purchase plan.

SUMMARY

Total revenues: $3.1 billion, 1987. Earnings per share: $1.98, 1987; $0.58, 1977; 241% increase. Stock price: $34, 11/9/88; $9.50 (median), 1978; (258% total increase; 14% annual increase); price rose 9 of 10 years, 1977–87. Dividend: $0.94, 1987; $0.61, 1983; 4-year increase: 54%. Dividend yield: 2.4% average, 1985–87. P/E ratio: 16, 1/5/89. Average annual total return to investor, 1978–88: about 17.5%.

AMERICAN HOME PRODUCTS CORPORATION

685 Third Ave.
New York, NY 10017-4085
(212) 878-5000
Chairman, President and CEO: John R. Stafford

EARNINGS GROWTH	★ ★ ★
STOCK GROWTH	★ ★
DIVIDEND YIELD	★ ★ ★ ★
DIVIDEND GROWTH	★ ★
SHAREHOLDER PERKS	★ ★ ★
NYSE—AHP	**14 points**

Whether it's aches in your bones or ants in your home, a smudge on your glass or a pain in the gums, American Home Products has the cure for what ails you. The maker of Advil and Anacin, Anbesol oral pain reliever, Preparation H hemorrhoidal medication, Black Flag insect killer, Easy-Off glass and oven cleaners and a host of other popular health products and household aids has put together 35 consecutive years of record sales, earnings and dividends.

American Home Products divides its operations into five segments: pharmaceuticals (47 percent of total revenue), consumer health care products (17 percent), medical supplies and diagnostic products (11 percent), food products (11 percent) and household products (13 percent).

Among its better-known consumer health care products (in addition to those listed above) are Dristan and Viromed cold formulas, Primatene asthma remedy, Denorex dandruff shampoo, Quiet World and Sleepeze sleeping aids, Medicated Cleansing Pads (for hemorroids), and Bisodol and Ropan antacids. The company also markets condoms and birth control products.

In 1987, the company acquired bankrupt A.H. Robins (maker of the infamous Dalkon Shield intrauterine birth control device that spurred a rash of lawsuits from women who claimed to have been injured by the devices). With Robins came such well-known products as Chap Stick, Robitussin (the largest selling cough syrup in the U.S.) and Dimetapp (the second largest selling over-the-counter cold and allergy medication).

Some of American Home's leading household products include Woolite detergent, Sani-Flush toilet cleaner, Pam cooking sprays, Wizard air freshners, GulfLite and KwikLite charcoal lighters, 3-in-One oils, Easy-On starch, Old English furniture polish and Antrol insect killer.

The New York-based manufacturer also produces a small line of foods, including Chef Boyardee pizzas, Mamma Leone's pasta, Jiffy Pop popcorn and Dennison's chili.

The company's Wyeth-Ayerst subsidiary manufactures prescription medicines, including antibiotics, infant nutritionals, psychotherapeutics, an antiarthritic medicine, an antileukemia drug, an influenza vaccine, an antihistamine and several types of medications to treat hormornal and cardiovascular ailments.

Its Sherwood Medical subsidiary manufactures products for the areas of patient care, nursing care, operating room procedures, dental care and diagnostic procedures. American Home also owns Corometrics Medical Systems, which makes medical monitors and data storage systems, and Fort Dodge Laboratories, which specializes in veterinary medicines.

The company sells its products worldwide. Foreign sales account for about 30 percent of its total revenue. It has subsidiary operations in Europe, Asia, Latin America, Australia and Africa (including South Africa, where it owns Wyeth-Ayerst, Ltd.).

EARNINGS GROWTH

American Home has had a sensational run of 35 consecutive years of earnings increases. But while its growth has been steady, it has also been fairly slow relative to the other companies listed among the *Best 100*. Over the past ten years, its earnings have increased just under 200 percent.

With revenues of $5.03 billion a year, American Home is among the five largest phamaceutical companies in the U.S. The New York-based firm has 45,000 employees and 74,000 shareholders of record.

In acquiring A.H. Robins, American Home Products may have been flirting with trouble. Merely by its association with the beleagured company, American Home could alienate some consumers who are still outraged over Robins' negligence, which allegedly led to the injuries (and a few deaths) to about 195,000 of its female contraceptive users. However, American Home anticipates no direct financial loss from legal actions brought against Robins. As terms of the acquisition, a $2.4 billion trust fund was set up to settle claims from the suit. So far, however, even the Robins trust fund has been ensconced in turmoil amid charges that the trustees are dragging their feet in doling out the money and that they are spending too much of the fund on legal fees, their own expenses—including dinners at the exclusive Hay Adams Hotel in Washington, D.C.—and on the salary of a trust administrator who is reportedly earning $1 million in wages and benefits over five years.

STOCK GROWTH

The company's stock price has climbed steadily though modestly over the past ten years. The stock has increased 181 percent (11 percent per year), from its median of $29.50 in 1983 to its late 1988 price of $83 per share.

Including reinvested dividends, a $10,000 investment in American Home Products stock at its median price in 1978 would have grown to about $44,000 ten years later. Average annual compounded rate of return (including stock growth and reinvested dividends): about 16 percent.

DIVIDEND YIELD

American Home tends to pay a good dividend yield. Over the past three years the stock has paid an average annual current return of 4.3 percent.

DIVIDEND GROWTH

The company has increased its dividend for 35 consecutive years. During the four-year rating period from 1983 to 1987, the dividend increased 39 percent.

SHAREHOLDER PERKS

The company occasionally sends out coupons for some of its food and health care products along with its dividend mailings.

The company also offers a dividend reinvestment and voluntary stock purchase plan. Shareholders may contribute $10 to $3,000 per quarter to the voluntary stock purchase plan.

SUMMARY

Total revenues: $5.03 billion, 1987. Earnings per share: $5.73, 1987; $1.94, 1977; 195% increase. Stock price: $83, 10/12/88; $29.50 (median), 1978 (181% total increase; 11% annual increase); price rose 9 of 10 years, 1977–87. Dividend: $3.34, 1987; $2.40, 1983; 4-year increase: 39%. Dividend yield: 4.3%, 1985–1987. P/E ratio: 13, 1/5/89. Average annual total return to investor, 1978–88: about 16%.

FUQUA INDUSTRIES, INC.

4900 Georgia-Pacific Center
Atlanta, GA 30303
(404) 658-9000
Chairman: J.B. Fuqua
President and CEO: Lawrence Klamon

EARNINGS GROWTH	★ ★ ★ ★
STOCK GROWTH	★ ★ ★ ★ ★
DIVIDEND YIELD	★ ★
DIVIDEND GROWTH	★ ★
SHAREHOLDER PERKS	(no points)
NYSE—FQA	**13 points**

Fuqua Industries' balance sheet has been a picture of health over the past two decades, thanks to America's growing legion of shutterbugs. Since Fuqua acquired Colorcraft Corporation in 1967, the photo processing company has increased sales more than a hundred-fold, from $3 million a year in 1967 to $304 million a year in 1987.

Colorcraft develops more than two billion photos a year—one out of every eight color prints in America.

And Colorcraft, which is already the most profitable photoprocessing business in the U.S., can look for an even greater market share in the future. Fuqua reached an agreement with Eastman Kodak in 1988 to combine Colorcraft with Kodak's U.S. photofinishing operations, giving the new company a total of more than 90 processing plants around the country and revenues of nearly $650 million. Under the agreement, Fuqua holds 51 percent interest in the combined company (called "Qualex,") and Eastman Kodak holds 49 percent.

In addition to its color processing division, Fuqua is a leading manufacturer of lawn mowers and sporting goods.

Fuqua owns Snapper Power Equipment, manufacturers of Snapper lawn mowers, snowblowers, power trimmers and garden tillers. The Snapper subsidiary, with annual sales of about $300 million, accounts for about 37 percent of Fuqua's total revenues.

Fuqua's sporting goods division is one of the largest suppliers of sporting goods and recreational equipment in the world. The company manufactures equipment for golf, physical fitness, camping, fishing, baseball, basketball, football and racquet and water sports. Its annual sales of about $180 million account for about 23 percent of Fuqua's total revenue.

Fuqua also owns Georgia Federal Bank, which it acquired in 1986, but it was reportedly hoping to sell the institution as soon as it could find a suitable buyer.

EARNINGS GROWTH

The Atlanta-based company has annual revenues of $772 million. It has 11,000 employees and 9,000 shareholders. The company remains very much a family operation, with J.B. Fuqua serving as chairman of the board and CEO and J. Rex Fuqua serving as president. Insiders own about 10 percent of the company's stock.

Over the past decade, Fuqua's earnings growth has been somewhat erratic, including a 57-cent-per-share loss in 1981 and earnings declines three of the past ten years. But overall, the earnings growth has been excellent, increasing 579 percent over the past ten years.

STOCK GROWTH

Fuqua's stock has experienced outstanding growth through the past decade with two 2-for-1 splits. Over the past ten years the stock has increased 886 percent (265 percent per year), from its median of $2.75 in 1978 to its late 1988 price of $27 a share.

Including reinvested dividends, a $10,000 investment in Fuqua stock at its median price in 1978 would have grown to about $130,000 ten years later. Average annual compounded rate of return (including stock growth and dividends): about 29 percent.

DIVIDEND YIELD

Fuqua pays a fairly low dividend, with an average annual yield of about 1 percent over the past three years.

DIVIDEND GROWTH

Fuqua traditionally raises its dividend each year. Its dividend increased 33 percent in the four-year rating period from 1983 to 1987.

SHAREHOLDER PERKS   (no points)

Fuqua offers no dividend reinvestment plan, nor does the company provide any other perks for its shareholders.

SUMMARY

Total revenues: $772 million, 1987. Earnings per share: $2.92, 1987; $0.43, 1977; 579% increase. Stock price: $27, 9/1/88; $2.75 (median), 1978 (881% total increase; 26% annual increase); price rose 9 of 10 years, 1977–87. Dividend: $0.24, 1987; $0.18, 1983; 4-year increase: 33%. Dividend yield: 1.0%, 1985–1987. P/E ratio: 6, 1/5/89. Average annual total return to investor, 1978–88: about 29%.

Melville

MELVILLE CORPORATION

3000 Westchester Ave.
Harrison, NY 10528
(914) 253-8000
Chairman, President and CEO: Stanley P. Goldstein

EARNINGS GROWTH	★ ★ ★
STOCK GROWTH	★ ★ ★ ★
DIVIDEND YIELD	★ ★ ★
DIVIDEND GROWTH	★ ★ ★
SHAREHOLDER PERKS	(no points)
NYSE—MES	**13 points**

Once a fledgling footware retailer, Melville Corporation has stepped up its operation by establishing a growing toehold in a broad range of other specialty retail markets. Its diversification strategy has helped keep the company's growth in step: Melville has had increased sales for 33 consecutive years and increased earnings 23 out of the past 24 years.

But in spite of its success—and its $5.9 billion in total sales—there's a good chance you've never heard of Melville. The Harrison, New York, holding company maintains a low profile. But you've probably browsed through some of its stores. The company owns more than 6,000 retail outlets throughout the U.S., including Thom McAn (shoes) and Marshalls (discount clothing).

Melville has relied on a steady diet of acquisitions to keep its revenues growing. In 1987, for instance, the company acquired a chain of 25 pharmacies, 33 Accessory Lady fashion stores and 36 Leather Loft leather goods stores. In 1988, it acquired the 190-store Berman leather goods chain. Melville has also grown from within, building 200 to 300 new stores a year.

While rapid expansion has been one of its keys to success, knowing when to pull the plug has also helped Melville's management maintain a healthy balance sheet. The company closed 127 of its less profitable outlets in 1987 and anticipated closing another 100 stores in 1988.

The company breaks its operations into four divisions:

- Apparel (34 percent of sales). Marshalls, with 286 stores and $1.6 billion in net sales, is its leading division. The company also owns Chess King (553 apparel stores) and Wilsons (227 leather fashion stores).
- Footwear (26 percent of sales). The company operates 2112 Meldico shoe shops in K mart stores throughout the U.S. It also operates Thom McAn (1,000 stores) and Fan Club (90 athletic-shoe stores).
- Drug, health and beauty aids (25 percent of sales). Melville operates 700 CVS drug stores and 14 Freddy's stores.
- Toys and household furnishings (15 percent of sales). The company owns the nationwide chain of Kay-Bee toy stores (676 outlets), Linens 'n' Things (144 stores), This End Up (196 furniture stores) and Prints Plus (74 prints and posters stores).

EARNINGS GROWTH

Melville has had record earnings 14 consecutive years, 23 of the past 24 years. Earnings per share have climbed 254 percent over the past decade.

The company has 90,000 employees and 10,500 shareholders of record. Directors control about 24 percent of the stock.

STOCK GROWTH

The company's stock price increased nine of ten years through 1987. Over the past ten years the stock has increased 390 percent (17 percent per year), from its median of $14.50 in 1978 to its late 1988 price of $71 a share.

Including reinvested dividends, a $10,000 investment in Melville stock at its median price in 1978 would have grown to about $67,000 ten years later. Average annual compounded rate of return (including stock growth and reinvested dividends): about 21 percent.

DIVIDEND YIELD

The company generally pays a moderate yield, which has averaged about 3.5 percent over the past ten years. During the three-year period from 1985 to 1987, the stock paid an average annual current return of 2.8 percent.

DIVIDEND GROWTH

Melville has raised its dividend 24 consecutive years. The dividend was increased 61 percent over the four-year rating period from 1983 to 1987.

SHAREHOLDER PERKS (no points)

Melville provides no dividend reinvestment plan, nor does it offer any other special perks for its shareholders.

SUMMARY

Total revenues: $5.9 billion, 1987. Earnings per share: $5.25, 1987; $1.48, 1977; 254% increase. Stock price: $71, 11/9/88; $14.50 (median), 1978; 390% increase (17% per year); price rose 9 of 10 years, 1977–87. Dividend: $1.76, 1987; $1.09, 1983; 4-year increase: 61%. Dividend yield: 2.8% average, 1985–1987. Trailing P/E ratio: 13.5, 11/9/88. Average annual total return to investors, 1978–88: about 21%.

91
JOSTENS

JOSTENS, INC.
5501 Norman Center Drive
Minneapolis, MN 55437
(612) 830-3300
Chairman and CEO: H. William Lurton
President: Don Lein

EARNINGS GROWTH	★ ★		
STOCK GROWTH	★ ★ ★		
DIVIDEND YIELD	★ ★ ★		
DIVIDEND GROWTH	★ ★ ★		
SHAREHOLDER PERKS	★ ★		
NYSE—JOS	**13 points**		

Jostens might not be categorized as a "fine" jeweler in the traditional sense, but its rings adorn the fingers of many of nation's most celebrated stars. U.S. Olympic team members from both the 1988 winter and summer games received Josten-made Olympic rings, and many of the top college and professional athletes—including the 1987 major league baseball All-Stars, the World Series Champions, the Rose Bowl champions and the NCAA national basketball champions—were awarded Josten-made championship rings. Jostens also produced the gold medals for the 1988 Winter Olympics and donated about 6,000 gold medals for the 1987 Special Olympics.

But Jostens is not just the "jeweler of champions." In fact, the company bills itself as "America's class ring company." It produces the class rings for thousands of high schools and colleges throughout the country.

The company has compiled one of the most consistent records of growth of any corporation in America, with 31 consecutive years of increased sales and earnings.

Jostens, which was founded in 1897 as a small jewelry and watch shop in Owatonna, Minnesota, is also a leading publisher of school yearbooks and a producer of graduation products, plaques and trophies, custom-printed apparel and computer-based educational products. The firm, which moved its headquarters to Minneapolis in 1969, provides the graduation announcements, diplomas and related graphic products for more than 10,000 U.S. high schools and colleges.

The company's Artex division is a leading producer of "imprinted garments." The company holds licensing agreements to print and sell T-shirts and other apparel with pictures of Snoopy, Walt Disney characters and "Far Side" characters, and logos from the National Football League.

Jostens's scholastic division (rings and memorabilia) is its largest segment, accounting for about 35 percent of the company's $560 million in annual revenue. Printing and publishing accounts for about 20 percent, its Artex and "recognition" segments (plaques, trophies, etc.) make up about 10 percent each, and its education and Canadian divisions each accounts for about 5 percent of total revenue. Jostens sold its business products division in late 1987 for $110 million. Business products had accounted for 15 percent of the company's annual revenue.

EARNINGS GROWTH

Jostens has had 31 consecutive years of earnings growth. The company's earnings per share have increased 188 percent over the past ten years.

With total annual revenues of $560 million, Jostens's has 8,000 employees and 1,500 independent sales representatives. The company has about 7,500 shareholders of record.

STOCK GROWTH

The company's stock price growth has also been very consistent, with price gains 12 of 13 years through 1987. Over the past ten years, the company has had two 3-for-2 stock splits, one 5-for-4 split and one 2-for-1 split. Adjusting for splits, the stock price has increased 300 percent (15 percent per year) during that period, from a median of $4.25 a share in 1978 to its recent 1988 price of $17.

Including reinvested dividends, a $10,000 investment in Jostens stock at its median price in 1978, with all dividends reinvested, would be worth about $60,000 ten years later. Average annual compounded rate of return including stock growth and reinvested dividends: about 19.5 percent.

DIVIDEND YIELD

The company generally pays a good dividend yield. Over the past three years the stock paid an average annual current return of 2.8 percent.

DIVIDEND GROWTH

Jostens has increased its dividend 21 consecutive years. The dividend was raised 60 percent over the four-year rating period from 1984 to 1988.

SHAREHOLDER PERKS

Jostens offers a good dividend reinvestment and voluntary stock purchase plan for its shareholders of record. Shareholders may contribute $25 to $1,000 to the stock purchase plan each month and are assessed no fees or commissions.

SUMMARY

Total revenues: $560 million, fiscal 1988 (ended 6/30/88). Earnings per share: $1.24, 1988; $0.43, 1978; 188% increase. Stock price: $17, 9/6/88; $4.25 (median), 1978; 300% increase (15% per year); price rose 9 of 10 years, 1977-87. Dividend: $0.56, 1987; $0.35, 1984; 4-year increase: 60%. Dividend yield: 2.8% average, 1985-87. P/E ratio: 14, 1/4/89. Average annual total return to investors, 1978-88: 19.5%.

AUTOMATIC DATA PROCESSING, INC.

One ADP Blvd.
Roseland, NJ 07068
(201) 994-5000
Chairman and CEO: Josh S. Weston
President: William J. Turner

EARNINGS GROWTH	★ ★ ★ ★
STOCK GROWTH	★ ★ ★ ★
DIVIDEND YIELD	★ ★
DIVIDEND GROWTH	★ ★ ★
SHAREHOLDER PERKS	(no points)
NYSE—AUD	**13 points**

Every payday, Automatic Data Processing (ADP) doles out the payroll checks for some nine million employees—pretty formidable numbers for a company that, for all practical purposes, does no manufacturing and sells no products.

What ADP does sell is a broad range of computer processing services. The Roseland, New Jersey, company bills itself as "the largest independent company in the U.S. dedicated exclusively to providing computerized record-keeping and information services."

Among those services is a payroll processing service that ADP provides for 160,000 businesses in the U.S. and abroad. ADP is the market leader in payroll processing. (The nine million checks the company turns out every pay period are payroll checks for the companies it serves. ADP itself has 21,000 employees.)

ADP began operations in 1949, slipping in on the ground floor of the burgeoning computer processing industry. The company has been reaping the rewards ever since. From the year of its inception, ADP has run up a phenomenal string of 39 consecutive years of record earnings and revenues, including double-digit growth for the past 108 consecutive quarters.

ADP's oldest and largest sector is "employer services," which accounts for nearly half of the firm's $1.4 billion in total annual revenue. In addition to its payroll processing, the division handles payroll tax filing, management reports, labor distribution, job costing, personnel and human resource information and unemployment compensation management. The company serves employers throughout the U.S. and Canada, plus Holland, the United Kingdom and Brazil.

The firm is also involved in a number of other areas of data processing including accounting services, insurance estimating, banking services and computer network services. Its brokerage business segment—which accounts for about 25 percent of ADP's revenues—performs the back-office order entry and recordkeeping for more than 350 brokerage clients. On peak days, the company handles more than 200,000 securities trades.

The company recently reached an agreement to install stock quote service systems, for Merrill Lynch and Shearson Lehman, which should propel ADP to the leading market-share vendor of stock quote monitors.

The company is also the nation's largest independent provider of automated teller machine (ATM) services for financial institutions.

EARNINGS GROWTH

ADP has had 41 consecutive years of record sales and earnings. Earnings per share have climbed 378 percent over the past decade.

ADP has 21,000 employees and 14,000 shareholders of record.

STOCK GROWTH

The company's stock price has moved up steadily through the past decade with two 2-for-1 stock splits since 1981. Over the past ten years the stock has increased 407 percent (17.5 percent per year), from its median of $7.50 in 1978 to its recent 1988 price of $38 a share.

Including reinvested dividends, a $10,000 investment in ADC stock at its median price in 1978 would have grown to about $57,000 ten years later. Average annual compounded rate of return (including stock growth and reinvested dividends): about 19 percent.

DIVIDEND YIELD

The company generally pays a fairly low yield, which has averaged about 1.5 percent over the past ten years. During the three-year rating period from 1985 to 1987, the stock paid an average annual current return of 1.1 percent.

DIVIDEND GROWTH

ADP has raised its dividend 14 consecutive years. The dividend was increased 59 percent over the four-year rating period from 1984 to 1988.

SHAREHOLDER PERKS   (no points)

The company provides no dividend reinvestment plan, nor does it offer any other perks for its shareholders.

SUMMARY

Total revenues: $1.55 billion, fiscal 1988 (ended 6/30/88). Earnings per share: $2.20, 1988; $0.46, 1977; 479% increase. Stock price: $38, 11/8/88; $7.50 (median), 1978; 407% increase (17.5% per year); price rose 9 of 10 years, 1977–87. Dividend: $0.46, 1988; $0.29, 1984; 4-year increase: 59%. Dividend yield: 1.1% average, 1986–88. P/E ratio: 17, 1/4/89. Average annual total return to investors, 1978–88: about 19%.

93

GENUINE PARTS COMPANY

2999 Circle 75 Parkway
Atlanta, GA 30339
(404) 953-1700
Chairman and CEO: Wilton Looney
President: Larry L. Prince

EARNINGS GROWTH	★ ★
STOCK GROWTH	★ ★ ★
DIVIDEND YIELD	★ ★ ★
DIVIDEND GROWTH	★ ★ ★
SHAREHOLDER PERKS	★ ★
NYSE—GPC	**13 points**

Genuine Parts has been a lifeline the past 60 years to all the jalopies and beaters and lemons that have limped along the nation's highways. And vice versa. By catering to the "automotive after-market," the Atlanta-based auto parts distributor has built a business that seems immune to recession. In fact, it's depression-tested. The company, which began operations in 1928, posted record sales every year of the 1930s. More recent results have been just as steady. The firm has had increases in total profits for 27 consecutive years and in total sales for 38 straight years.

Genuine Parts owns about 500 automotive parts stores in 34 states and three Canadian provinces (most under the NAPA Auto Parts name) and serves about 5,500 independently owned jobbing stores. The stores are served by 65 distribution centers that each carry about 100,000 different parts for domestic and foreign automobiles.

Genuine does no manufacturing itself. The firm is strictly a wholesale distributor. It buys parts from more than 170 domestic suppliers. The company does, however, operate six plants that rebuild small automotive parts. Genuine's automotive parts group accounts for about 68 percent of its $2.6 billion in annual revenue.

The company also owns Motion Industries, a distributor of industrial parts, including bearings and fluid transmission equipment, and agricultural and irrigation equipment. Motion operates 160 outlets in 20 states and sells about 100,000 different items. Genuine's Canadian subsidiary, Oliver Industrial Supply, operates eight distribution centers.

The industrial parts segment accounts for about 18 percent of the company's revenue.

Genuine's other business is its office products group (14 percent of revenues), which distributes a broad line of computer supplies, office furniture, office machines and general office supplies through its S.P. Richards Company subsidiary. The company distributes more than 16,000 items to 8,000 office supply dealers in 20 states.

EARNINGS GROWTH

Genuine Parts' earnings growth has been very steady the past few years. The company has had increases in total profits for 27 consecutive years and increases in earnings per share 14 of the past 15 years. Its earnings per share have increased 165 percent over the past ten years.

With total revenues of $2.6 billion, the company has 14,000 employees and about 7,000 shareholders of record.

STOCK GROWTH

The company's stock price has also climbed steadily through the past decade with three 3-for-2 stock splits since 1979. The stock price has increased 9 of the past ten years, with a total increase of 253 percent (14 percent per year) from its median of $10.75 in 1978 to its recent 1988 price of $38 a share.

Including reinvested dividends, a $10,000 investment in Genuine parts stock at its median price in 1978 would have grown to about $48,000 ten years later. Average annual compounded rate of return (including stock growth and reinvested dividends): about 17 percent.

DIVIDEND YIELD

The company has traditionally paid a fairly good dividend, averaging about 3.5 percent over the past ten years. During the past three years, the stock has paid an average annual current return of 3.2 percent.

DIVIDEND GROWTH

Genuine Parts increases its dividend almost every year, although it did decline in 1987 for the first time in many years. The dividend climbed 51 percent during the four-year rating period from 1983 to 1987.

SHAREHOLDER PERKS

The company offers a good dividend reinvestment and voluntary stock purchase plan. There are no fees or commissions, and shareholders of record may buy $10 to $3,000 per quarter in additional shares.

SUMMARY

Total revenues: $2.6 billion, 1987. Earnings per share: $1.88, 1987; $0.71, 1977; 165% increase. Stock price: $38, 10/19/88; $10.75 (median), 1978 (253% total increase; 13% annual increase); price rose 9 of 10 years, 1977–87. Dividend: $0.92, 1987; $0.61, 1983; 4-year increase: 51%. Dividend yield: 3.2%, 1985–87. P/E ratio: 16, 1/5/89. Average annual total return to investor, 1978–88: about 17%.

EXXON CORPORATION

1251 Avenue of the Americas
New York, NY 10020
(212) 333-1000
Chairman and CEO: L.G. Rawl
President: L.R. Raymond.

EARNINGS GROWTH	★ ★
STOCK GROWTH	★ ★
DIVIDEND YIELD	★ ★ ★ ★ ★
DIVIDEND GROWTH	★
SHAREHOLDER PERKS	★ ★
NYSE—XON	**12 points**

If you had to characterize Exxon in just one word, "big" would be the obvious choice.

With total annual revenues of about $80 billion, Exxon is the largest petroleum enterprise in the world, and the second largest corporation in America (behind General Motors). (It is also the largest company on the *Best 100* list.) Formerly known as Standard Oil of New Jersey, Exxon employs about 100,000 people and has more than 700,000 shareholders. It has operations in 80 countries, operates about 16,000 oil wells, and owns or holds mineral and oil rights to more than 100 million acres of property throughout the world. Each day, the company produces about 1.8 million barrels of oil and 5.2 billion cubic feet of natural gas.

Despite its cumbersome size and a subpar performance the past decade by the oil industry, Exxon still managed to provide its shareholders with an excellent average annual return of more than 20 percent over the past ten years.

You might think that a company the size of Exxon would have a diversity of corporate interests outside its principal business. But nearly every phase of Exxon's operation deals in some way with oil and gas. This is a company that sticks to its knitting. Almost 90 percent of the company's revenue comes directly from its petroleum and natural gas business. Exxon explores for gas and oil, extracts it, refines it and distributes it. The company owns thousands of service stations in the U.S. and abroad (including both Exxon and Esso stations). About 39 percent of its total revenues come from domestic sales and 61 percent from foreign sales.

Its refined petroleum is used not only for fuel and lubricants, but also for the production of plastics, synthetic rubber, solvents and chemicals. Exxon's chemicals segment generates nearly 10 percent of its annual revenue. Some of its key chemical products include polyethylene and polypropylene film, fabrics and cordage, and phosphate fertilizers.

Exxon also does a small business in coal and mineral production (less than 1 percent of total revenues).

EARNINGS GROWTH

The petroleum market has been on unstable footing in recent years, and Exxon's earnings record reflects that. Its earnings have increased only six of the last ten years. But the overall increase has been respectable, with earnings per share rising 154 percent during that period.

While the oil and energy market remains volatile, there is at least one clear plus in owning Exxon stock. This is a company that has turned in a respectable performance during a time when oil was in a slump. When the energy industry takes a turn for the better—and that will happen sooner or later—Exxon should be in a position to profit handsomely from that recovery.

STOCK GROWTH

Like its earnings growth, Exxon's stock price growth has been a bit inconsistent over the past decade, improving only seven of the past ten years. The stock has had two 2-for-1 splits since 1981. In all, Exxon stock has increased 267 percent (14 percent per year) from its median of $12.25 in 1978 to its late 1988 price of $45 per share.

Including reinvested dividends, a $10,000 investment in Exxon stock at its median price in 1978 would have grown to about $73,000 ten years later. Average annual compounded rate of return (including stock growth and reinvested dividends): about 22 percent.

DIVIDEND YIELD

Exxon has traditionally paid an outstanding dividend yield. During the high interest days of the early 1980s, Exxon's annual dividend reached a peak of more than 10 percent. Over the past three years, the stock has paid an average annual return of 5.7 percent.

DIVIDEND GROWTH

Exxon usually increases its dividend each year, although the increases are often minimal. During the four-year rating period from 1983 to 1987, the dividend increased 23 percent.

SHAREHOLDER PERKS

The company offers an excellent dividend reinvestment and voluntary stock purchase plan. There are no fees or commissions, and shareholders of record may buy up to $60,000 per year in additional shares through the voluntary stock purchase plan.

SUMMARY

Total revenues: $76.4 billion, 1987. Earnings per share: $3.43, 1987; $1.35, 1977; 154% increase. Stock price: $45, 10/12/88; $12.25 (median), 1978 (267% total increase; 14% annual increase); price rose 7 of 10 years, 1977–87. Dividend: $1.90, 1987; $1.55, 1983. 4-year increase: 23%. Dividend yield: 5.7%, 1985–87. P/E ratio: 11, 1/5/89. Average annual total return to investor, 1978–88: about 22%.

Westinghouse

WESTINGHOUSE ELECTRIC CORPORATION

Westinghouse Building
Gateway Center
11 Stanwix Street
Pittsburgh, PA 15222
(412) 244-2000
Chairman and CEO: John C. Marous
President and COO: Paul E. Lego

EARNINGS GROWTH	★ ★
STOCK GROWTH	★ ★ ★ ★
DIVIDEND YIELD	★ ★ ★
DIVIDEND GROWTH	★ ★ ★
SHAREHOLDER PERKS	(no points)
NYSE—WX	**12 points**

George Westinghouse was a tinkerer, but a prolific one. Before his death in 1914, he was credited with nearly 400 inventions ranging from railroad car air brakes to electric turbines, from air compressors to distribution systems for natural gas.

Versatile visionary that he was, however, Westinghouse would still have had a hard time foreseeing the vast conglomeration of divergent concerns that his company would someday become. Westinghouse Electric, the company George founded in 1886, has stretched the limits of corporate diversity to unparalleled proportions.

Westinghouse owns radio stations and Group W TV stations throughout the U.S.; it builds radar, communications and missile launching systems for the military; runs a large financial services operation; makes wristwatches; builds furniture; manages toxic and hazardous waste sites; installs elevators, escalators and people movers; supplies fuel and components for nuclear power generators; develops residential housing subdivisions; manufactures refrigeration compartments, and bottles more 7-Up than any other company in America.

The Pittsburg-based corporation divides its operations into six market areas:

- Broadcasting. In addition to its TV and radio stations, Westinghouse produces programs such as *Hour Magazine* for television syndication and provides satellite access for cable networks.
- Defense electronics. Westinghouse installed the radar systems for all of the U.S. Air Force's F-16 fighter planes, and anticipates billions of dollars in sales over the next few years for its work on the Air Force's newest fighter plane, the Advanced Tactical Fighter (ATF). Westinghouse will provide the radar systems, electrical generators and other integrated electronic systems for the ATFs.

  Westinghouse also manufacturers infrared detection systems, torpedoes, missile-launching systems, airborne surveillance equipment, aerospace electronic control systems and marine propulsion and launching apparatus.
- Energy and utility systems. Westinghouse manufactures nuclear reactor systems and components, steam turbine generators, combustion turbine generators and combined cycle plants. It sells nuclear fuel to plants, transports radioactive wastes, and makes fuel assemblies and zirconium tubing for nuclear fuel rods used in reactors.

  The company also constructs waste-to-energy plants that generate electricity through the burning of solid wastes.
- Industrial and construction. Westinghouse is becoming a market leader in the treatment of toxic and hazardous wastes. The company also produces a wide variety of electronic components and systems such as starter motors, circuit devices, transformers, safety switches, panel boards, switchboards and wiring systems, factory automation systems, environmental control equipment and power transfers for utility companies.
- Diversified markets. Westinghouse is one of the largest elevator and escalator installers in the U.S., and is involved in the manufacture of airport people mover systems and propulsion equipment for trolleybuses. Westinghouse owns Longines-Wittnauer Watch Company (the official time keeper of the 1988 Summer and Winter Olympics), sells office furnishings and modular furniture systems, and manufactures Thermo King refrigeration compartments for trucks, ships and railroad cars. (Thermo King equipment is used in more than 80 countries). The company is a leading soft drink bottler (7-Up, A&W, Hawaiian Punch, Schweppes, among others), and a developer of exclusive housing communities in Florida.
- Financial services. About 15 percent of Westinghouse's net income comes from its financial services subsidiary. The company specializes in lending to expanding businesses and commercial and residential real es-

tate developers. It also runs a leasing business that deals in capital equipment such as commercial aircraft and power generation facilities.

EARNINGS GROWTH

With revenues of nearly $11 billion, Westinghouse is one of the nation's 35 largest publicly-traded corporations. It has operations and subsidiaries worldwide (foreign sales account for about 20 percent of sales). The company has about 112,000 employees and 120,000 shareholders of record.

Westinghouse has had earnings increases 12 of the past 13 years. Over the past 10 years, its earnings per share climbed 230 percent.

Westinghouse is involved in a couple of issues that could prove troublesome, although neither is expected to have a significant impact on the company's bottom line. One is a series of lawsuits filed against the company alleging defects in Westinghouse generators installed in nuclear power plants in the 1960s (one case has been largely dismissed, another settled out of court, and a couple of others are still pending). The company also anticipates additional expenses to comply with new hazardous waste disposal regulations, and to cover litigation expenses "associated with polychlorinated biphenyls, asbestos and other materials."

STOCK GROWTH

Westinghouse has had excellent stock price growth over the past decade, with increases nine of ten years from 1977 to 1987. The stock price has climbed 378 percent (17 percent per year), from its median of $10.25 a share in 1978 to its late 1988 price of $49.

Including reinvested dividends, a $10,000 investment in Westinghouse stock at its median price in 1978, with all dividends reinvested, would be worth about $75,000 ten years later. Average annual compounded rate of return (including stock growth and reinvested dividends): about 22 percent.

DIVIDEND YIELD

The company generally pays a good dividend yield, which has averaged about 5 percent over the past ten years. During the three-year rating period from 1985 to 1987, the stock paid an average annual current return of 2.8 percent.

DIVIDEND GROWTH

Westinghouse increased its dividend 82 percent over the four-year rating period from 1983 to 1987.

SHAREHOLDER PERKS (no points)

Westinghouse does not offer a dividend reinvestment plan for its shareholders nor does it offer any other type of shareholder perk.

SUMMARY

Total revenues: $10.7 billion, 1987. Earnings per share: $5.12, 1987; $1.55, 1977; 230% increase. Stock price: $49, 8/23/88; $10.25 (median), 1978; 378% increase (17% per year); price rose 9 of 10 years, 1977–87. Dividend: $1.64, 1987; $0.90, 1983; 4-year increase: 82%. Dividend yield: 2.8% average, 1985–87. P/E ratio: 9, 1/5/89. Average annual total return to investors, 1978–88: about 22%.

96

MARTIN MARIETTA

MARTIN MARIETTA CORPORATION

6801 Rockledge Drive
Bethesda, MD 20817
(301) 897-6000
Chairman and CEO: Norman R. Augustine
President: Caleb B. Hurtt

EARNINGS GROWTH	★ ★
STOCK GROWTH	★ ★ ★ ★
DIVIDEND YIELD	★ ★ ★
DIVIDEND GROWTH	★
SHAREHOLDER PERKS	★ ★
NYSE—ML	**12 points**

Martin Marietta is a defense and aerospace contractor noted most for its Pershing, Peacekeeper and Titan missiles.

The Pershing II, deployed in Europe beginning in 1983 under considerable controversy, already appears destined for the scrapyards as a result of the recently negotiated INF treaty. The treaty calls for the removal and disposal of all 108 missiles within three years of ratification, although Martin Marietta still anticipates a "continuation of spares and services work" for several more years. The strength of the Pershing II, known as a "surface-to-surface ballistic missile" is its mid-range speed and accuracy. Within six minutes of launch, the European-based Pershings could be striking targeted cities inside the Soviet Union.

When first introduced, the Peacekeeper intercontinental ballistic missile drew a mild furor less for its destructive force than for its name—which could well have come straight from the "Newspeak" language of George Orwell's *1984* (where "war is peace, freedom is slavery, ignorance is strength"). The Peacekeepers are larger and more powerful than the Pershing IIs and have a much greater range (6,900 miles), but are being deployed far from their presumed targets in silos at F.E. Warren Air Force Base in Wyoming. The missiles are 70 feet long and weigh 195,000 pounds. They carry MIRV warheads ("multiple independently targeted reentry vehicles"), which include a cluster of bombs that, when the missile nears its destination, splits up and heads to separate targets. One MIRV warhead is capable of leveling an entire city. A single explosion can create a giant fireball with temperatures of about 100 million degrees Kelvin—roughly five times hotter than the center of the sun—and winds of 500 to 550 miles an hour. Martin Marietta reports that the Peacekeeper has completed 17 consecutive successful test flights.

The Titan missilies are the largest and oldest of the country's surviving strategic missiles. Many of the older Titan missiles are now being converted for use as space launch vehicles to propel commercial and military payloads and satellites into space. The company also manufacturers new Titans for that purpose.

Martin Marietta is also at work on a number of other sophisticated military projects. Since 1981, the company has produced more than 16,000 Copperheads, a cannon-launched guided projectile, and is currently involved in the manufacture of the Hellfire Laser Seeker, a component of the Hellfire air-to-ground missiles (being built by Rockwell), which seek out their targets by laser. The U.S. Army has ordered 13,963 Hellfire missiles, of which about 4,000 have been delivered.

The Bethesda, Maryland-based manufacturer is producing the Army's Patriot missile and launcher for the air defense of field armies. Some of the missiles have been deployed with air defense units in Germany and The Netherlands. Martin Marietta is also under contract to the U.S. Navy to build vertical missile launching systems for some of its ships.

The company's space systems division works closely with NASA on a number of projects including the Magellan spacecraft, which is scheduled to be launched in 1989 on a mission to map the surface of Venus.

Among the other ventures Martin Marietta is involved in are information and communication systems, data systems, energy systems and "materials" (the company is the second largest producer of crushed stone in the U.S.; it also supplies refractory materials for steelmaking).

The company divides its business into four primary segments, astronautics (38 percent of total revenue), electronics (37 percent), information systems (17 percent) and materials (7 percent).

Martin Marietta's $5.17 billion in annual revenues places it tenth among all U.S. defense contractors.

EARNINGS GROWTH

Martin Marietta has had steady earnings growth the past 10 years—with earnings per share increases nine of those years. Over the 10-year period, earnings per share have increased 240 percent.

The company, which was formed in 1961 by the consolidation of Martin Company (originally founded in 1909) and American-Marietta Company (1913), has 70,000 employees and 41,000 shareholders.

STOCK GROWTH

The company has enjoyed excellent, consistent stock price growth throughout the past decade, increasing nine of ten years from 1977 to 1987. The stock has had three 3-for-2 splits since 1981. Over the past ten years the stock has increased 353 percent (16 percent per year) from its median of $9.50 in 1978 to its late 1988 price of $43 a share.

Including reinvested dividends, a $10,000 investment in Martin Marietta stock at its median price in 1978 would have grown to about $67,000 ten years later. Average annual compounded rate of return (including stock growth and reinvested dividends): about 21 percent.

DIVIDEND YIELD

The company tends to pay a pretty good dividend yield, which has averaged about 5 percent over the past ten years. During the most recent three-year period, the stock has paid an annual current return of 2.5 percent.

DIVIDEND GROWTH

Martin Marietta traditionally increases its dividend yield each year, but often in increments as small as two to three cents per share. The dividend edged up 21 percent during the four-year rating period from 1983 to 1987.

SHAREHOLDER PERKS

The company offers an excellent dividend reinvestment and voluntary stock purchase plan. There are no fees or commissions, and shareholders of record may buy $50 to $100,000 per year in additional shares through the voluntary stock purchase plan.

SUMMARY

Total revenues: $5.2 billion, 1987. Earnings per share: $4.31, 1987; $1.27, 1977; 240% increase. Stock price: $43, 10/20/88; $9.50 (median), 1978 (353% total increase; 16% annual increase); price rose 9 of 10 years, 1977–87. Dividend: $1.05, 1987; $0.86, 1983; 4-year increase: 21%. Dividend yield: 2.5%, 1985–87. P/E ratio: 8*, 1/5/89. Average annual total return to investor, 1978–88: about 21%.

*Based on earnings from continuing operations.

PEPSICO, INC.
Purchase, NY
10577
(914) 253-2000
Chairman and CEO: D. Wayne Calloway

EARNINGS GROWTH	★ ★
STOCK GROWTH	★ ★ ★
DIVIDEND YIELD	★ ★ ★
DIVIDEND GROWTH	★
SHAREHOLDER PERKS	★ ★ ★
NYSE—PEP	**12 points**

The debate lingers on: Which taste do drinkers really prefer? Is it the real taste(s) of Coke, or is it that other brand? Although both have "winning" taste tests to their credit, Coca-Cola outsells its rival two to one worldwide. But where the *real* corporate cola war is waged—the battle of the balance sheet—who should emerge as the choice of a new generation? Just say Pepsi, please.

Over the past decade, PepsiCo has enjoyed a better return on investment for its shareholders than Coke (19.5 percent per year compared to 17 percent) and faster earnings growth. Pepsi is also the larger of the two companies, with annual revenues of $11.5 billion compared to $7.7 billion for Coca-Cola.

While Coca-Cola has stayed primarily with its strength—selling soft drinks (524 million times a day), Pepsi has spilled over into new areas. It owns Kentucky Fried Chicken, Pizza Hut, Taco Bell and Frito-Lay.

Soft drinks make up 36 percent of Pepsi's total revenue and 32 percent of its operating profit. (Soft drink sales account for 82 percent of Coca-Cola's revenues and 95 percent of its operating income; Coke also owns Minute Maid and other food lines and holds a 49 percent share of Columbia Pictures.)

In addition to its cola, Pepsi also produces Mountain Dew and Slice soft drinks, and recently acquired 7-Up International.

293

The soft drink business has been on a steady incline for many years. On average, each American consumer drinks about 43 gallons of soft drinks each year—about twice the per-capita average of 20 years ago. Total soft drink sales in the U.S. have reached about $40 billion a year, of which Pepsi holds a 33 percent share. Pepsi is also available in 150 other countries (including the Soviet Union) and holds a 15 percent share of the 12 billion-case international market.

It's snack foods operation is Pepsi's most profitable division. Although it accounts for only 28 percent of total revenue, the snack foods segment makes up 41 percent of the company's operating profits. Fritos, Doritos, Chee-tos, Ruffles and GrandMa's cookies are its leading products.

Restaurants account for 36 percent of Pepsi's revenue and 27 percent of its operating profit. Its total of 16,500 Pizza Hut, Kentucky Fried Chicken and Taco Bell restaurants gives PepsiCo the largest restaurant system in the world.

EARNINGS GROWTH

PepsiCo has had earnings per share increases only seven of the past ten years. During that period, earnings increased 214 percent.

As the world's second largest soft drink producer, PepsiCo has 215,000 employees and 90,000 shareholders.

STOCK GROWTH

The company has had good stock price appreciation through the past decade, although its growth has been a little erratic, with increases only seven of ten years through 1987. Over the past ten years the stock has increased 321 percent (15.5 percent per year), from its median of $9.50 in 1978 to its late 1988 price of $40 a share.

Including reinvested dividends, a $10,000 investment in PepsiCo stock at its median price in 1978 would have grown to about $60,000 ten years later. Average annual compounded rate of return (including stock growth and reinvested dividends): about 19.5 percent.

DIVIDEND YIELD

The company generally pays a fairly good yield, which has averaged about 4 percent over the past ten years. During the three-year rating period from 1985 to 1987, the stock paid an average annual current return of 2.4 percent.

DIVIDEND GROWTH

Pepsi has raised its dividend for more than 15 consecutive years, but not by much. The dividend was raised 24 percent over the four-year rating period from 1983 to 1987.

SHAREHOLDER PERKS

At its annual meeting, PepsiCo shareholders are treated to a variety of freebies, including some cans of the company's new or improved soft drinks, a couple of packages of Frito-Lay snacks, and coupons for Kentucky Fried Chicken and Pizza Hut. The company also hands out special gifts, such as a Pepsico umbrella with all the company's logos on it, or a Taco Bell clock.

The company offers its shareholders of record a good dividend reinvestent and voluntary stock purchase plan. There are no fees or commissions, and shareholders of record may contribute as little as $10 per month or as much as $60,000 per year to purchase additional shares through the voluntary stock purchase plan.

SUMMARY

Total revenues: $11.5 billion, 1987. Earnings per share: $2.26, 1987; $0.72, 1977; 214% increase. Stock price: $40, 11/10/88; $9.50 (median), 1978; 321% increase (15.5% per year); price rose 9 of 10 years, 1977–87. Dividend: $0.67, 1987; $0.54, 1983; 4-year increase: 24%. Dividend yield: 2.4% average, 1985–87. P/E ratio: 14, 1/4/89. Average annual total return to investors, 1978–88: 19.5%.

ELI LILLY AND COMPANY

Lilly Corporate Center
Indianapolis, IN 46285
(317) 276-2000
Chairman, President and CEO: Richard D. Wood

EARNINGS GROWTH	★ ★
STOCK GROWTH	★ ★ ★
DIVIDEND YIELD	★ ★ ★
DIVIDEND GROWTH	★ ★
SHAREHOLDER PERKS	★ ★
NYSE—LLY	**12 points**

They invade the respiratory passage, inhabit the intestinal track and penetrate the circulatory system. For Eli Lilly and Company, finding new ways to battle the micro-organisms that cause disease has become a mission and a business. As one of the world's leading manufacturers of antibiotics, the company draws more than $1 billion a year—about 35 percent of its $3.6 billion in total revenues—from its line of oral and injectable antibiotic medicines.

For most of its 112 years, Eli Lilly has been viewed primarily as a family business, domimated by the heirs of the late Col. Eli Lilly. But over the past two decades, the Indianapolis-based manufacturer has emerged as a growing force in the pharmaceuticals market. It is one of the 10 largest publicly-traded pharmaceuticals companies in the U.S.

While none of Lilly's medicines would be considered household names, some of its prescription pharmaceuticals dominate their fields. For instance, Ceclor, an oral antibiotic drug for the treatment of respiratory tract infections in children and adults, is the top selling product in its class.

The company's other leading antibiotic medications include Mandol, Nebcin and Vancocin injectables and Keflex and Keftab oral medications.

Several of Lilly's newer medicines have begun to make an impact in their particular areas. The company says Prozac, an antidepressant introduced in the U.S. in 1988, has been well-accepted by psychiatrists because its side effects tend to be less severe than those of other antidepressants. Humatrope, a new drug used to treat children who are unusually small because of deficient pituitary glands, is now selling both in the U.S. and abroad. Axid, an ulcer medication, was introduced with great fanfare in 1988.

In addition to its medications, Lilly does a good business in medical instruments. Two of its strongest subsidiaries are Advanced Cardiovascular Systems, a leading developer of coronary angioplasty catheters used to open blood vessels, and Cardiac Pacemakers, a manufacturer of heart pacemakers and implantable heart defibrillators. Lilly (and its subsidiaries) also manufacture monitoring systems, intravenous fluid-delivery and control systems and a number of diagnostic products. Lilly's medical instruments segment accounts for about 18 percent of its total revenue.

Through its Elanco Products subsidiary, Eli Lilly also has a major stake in the livestock and agricultural segment. The company manufactures livestock feed additives designed to help hogs and cattle bulk up more efficiently, and herbicides (including Treflan) and pesticides to help farmers keep down the weeds and keep out the bugs.

Lilly does business in about 130 countries (including a fully owned subsidiary in South Africa). Foreign operations account for about 31 percent of the company's total revenue.

EARNINGS GROWTH

Lilly's earnings growth has not been dramatic, but it has been very consistent, with earnings increases for more than 15 consecutive years. Over the past ten years, earnings per share have increased 177 percent.

The company has 26,000 employees and 32,000 shareholders of record. Nearly 20 percent of Lilly's stock is closely held by Lilly Endowment, Inc.

STOCK GROWTH

The company's stock price has experienced good growth over the past decade, increasing 300 percent (15 percent per year) from its median of $22.50 in 1978 to its late 1988 price of $90 a share. The stock's growth has, however, been a little bit erratic, with stock price increases only seven of ten years from 1977 to 1987.

Including reinvested dividends, a $10,000 investment in Eli Lilly stock at its median price in 1978 would have grown to about $57,000 ten years later. Average annual compounded rate of return (including stock growth and reinvested dividends): about 19 percent.

DIVIDEND YIELD

Lilly generally pays a fairly good dividend, which has averaged around 4 percent over past ten years. During the most recent three-year period, the stock paid an average annual current return of 2.9 percent.

DIVIDEND GROWTH

Lilly has raised its dividend every year for many years. The dividend rose 45 percent over the four-year rating period from 1983 to 1987.

SHAREHOLDER PERKS

The company offers a good dividend reinvestment and voluntary stock purchase plan. There are no fees or commissions, and shareholders of record may buy $25 to $12,000 per year in additional shares through the voluntary stock purchase plan.

SUMMARY

Total revenues: $3.6 billion, 1987. Earnings per share: $4.29, 1987; $1.55, 1977; 177% increase. Stock price: $90, 10/20/88; $22.50 (median), 1978 (300% total increase; 15% annual increase); price rose 7 of 10 years, 1977–87. Dividend: $2.00, 1987; $1.38, 1983; 4-year increase: 45%. Dividend yield: 2.9% average, 1985–87. P/E ratio: 17, 1/5/89. Average annual total return to investor, 1978–88: about 19%.

MASCO CORPORATION

21001 Van Born Road
Taylor, MI 48180
(313) 274-7400
Chairman and CEO: Richard A. Manoogian
President: Wayne B. Lyon

EARNINGS GROWTH	★ ★ ★
STOCK GROWTH	★ ★ ★ ★
DIVIDEND YIELD	★ ★
DIVIDEND GROWTH	★ ★ ★
SHAREHOLDER PERKS	(no points)
NYSE—MAS	**12 points**

You could have a house full of Masco furnishings and never know it. Masco specializes in the mundane—it makes faucets, door knobs and locks, plumbing supplies, kitchen cabinets and other household items. But while Masco has become a big name in the household industry—with $2 billion a year in annual sales—it is by no means a household name. Its anonymity is aided by the fact that, of all its products, not one carries the Masco name.

The Michigan manufacturer's lack of renown, however, has done little to dampen its market success. Masco has posted 31 consecutive years of increased earnings, and has raised its dividend 29 straight years.

Acquisitions have been the key to Masco's recent growth. Two of its most significant recent acquisitions were Drexel Heritage and Henredon (1986) and Lexington Furniture (1987) which, combined, helped propel Masco to become the second largest U.S. manufacturer of furniture. Home furnishings account for 28 percent of Masco's $2 billion a year in total revenue.

Masco is also the world's leading faucet manufacturer. Its brands include Delta, Peerless, Delex, Artistic Brass, Epic, Damixa, American Bath, Mariani and Mixet. Its other kitchen and bathroom product lines include cabinet-makers Merillat and Fieldstone, plumbing supplies manufacturers Brass-Craft and Plumb Shop, and high-end kitchen appliance makers Thermador and Waste King. The company also owns several lines of bathtub, shower, spa and whirlpool manufacturers.

Kitchen and bathroom products account for 54 percent of Masco's $2 billion a year in total revenue.

The company draws 18 percent of its revenues from specialty building producers, including Baldwin, Weiser, Falcon and Winfield, which manufacture residential and commercial locks and related hardware.

EARNINGS GROWTH

Masco has had 31 consecutive years of increased earnings. Earnings per share have increased 244 percent over the past decade.

Masco has 27,000 employees and 8,000 shareholders of record.

STOCK GROWTH

The company has had good stock price appreciation over the past decade with two 2-for-1 stock splits since 1983. Over the past ten years the stock has increased 376 percent (17 percent per year) from its median of $5.25 in 1978 to its late 1988 price of $25 a share.

Including reinvested dividends, a $10,000 investment in Masco stock at its median price in 1978 would have grown to about $57,000 ten years later. Average annual compounded rate of return (including stock growth and reinvested dividends): about 19 percent.

DIVIDEND YIELD

The company generally pays a fairly low yield, which has averaged about 2 percent over the past ten years. During the three-year rating period from 1985 to 1987, the stock paid an average annual current return of 1.4 percent.

DIVIDEND GROWTH

Masco has raised its dividend 29 consecutive years. The dividend was raised 73 percent over the four-year rating period from 1983 to 1987.

SHAREHOLDER PERKS   (no points)

The company provides no dividend reinvestment plan, nor does it offer any other perks for its shareholders.

SUMMARY

Total revenues: $2.0 billion, 1987. Earnings per share: $1.65, 1987; $0.48, 1977; 244% increase. Stock price: $25, 11/9/88; $5.25 (median), 1978; 376% increase (17% per year); price rose 8 of 10 years, 1977–87. Dividend: $0.38, 1987; $0.22, 1983; 4-year increase: 73%. Dividend yield: 1.4% average, 1985–87. P/E ratio: 13, 1/5/89. Average annual total return to investors, 1978–88: about 19%.

100

HEWLETT PACKARD

HEWLETT-PACKARD COMPANY

3000 Hanover St.
Palo Alto, CA 94304
(415) 857-1501
Chairman: David Packard
President and CEO: John Young

EARNINGS GROWTH	★ ★ ★ ★
STOCK GROWTH	★ ★ ★ ★
DIVIDEND YIELD	★
DIVIDEND GROWTH	★ ★
SHAREHOLDER PERKS	(no points)
NYSE—HWP	**11 points**

What if...two young electronics wizards fresh from Stanford University decided to convert their small garage into a workshop to design and build electronic equipment?

What if...those two Californians spent the next 50 years, side by side, toying with their ideas, building their company and pioneering the computer revolution?

Over the past half century, William Hewlett and David Packard have answered all the "What if's" in their business with resounding "Can do's." Their company has grown to $8 billion in annual revenue, and they've assembled a product list of more than 10,000 computer and electronics-related items—laser printers, three-dimensional software programs, diagnostic ultrasonic imagers, logic analyzers, and powerful, scientific and financial calculators the size of a postcard.

Hewlett-Packard has attracted a loyal following not only in this country, but throughout the world. Foreign customers account for about half of the company's annual income. Queen Elizabeth was so impressed with Hewlett-Packard that she once paid a visit to its Palo Alto, California, headquarters. And in 1987, she presented "the Queen's Award for Export Achievement" to Hewlett-Packard's British subsidiary.

(Not everyone, however, is equally impressed with the company's international trade record. Hewlett-Packard has a wholly-owned subsidiary in South Africa with 261 employees and $36 million a year in annual sales.)

Packard, 76, and Hewlett, 75, began their partnership building electronic test equipment in Packard's garage in 1939. They first incorporated their company eight years later.

Packard, who took a leave from the company from 1969 to 1971 to become Deputy Secretary of Defense in the Nixon administration, still serves as the company's chairman of the board. Hewlett retired as the company's vice chairman in 1987.

The company's broad line of electronics and computer gear includes:

* Computer products. Business, scientific and architectural computer systems, portable and desktop computers, advanced software, laser disc drives, laser printers, handheld calculators.
* Medical equipment. Monitoring systems for critical care patients, fetal monitors, electrocardiographs, cardiac catheterization systems, blood gas measuring systems.
* Test equipment. Oscilloscopes, voltmeters, gas and liquid chromatographs, communications test instruments.
* Electronic components. Microwave semiconductors, fiber-optic devices, light-emitting diodes.

EARNINGS GROWTH

With $8.1 billion in annual revenue, Hewlett-Packard is one of the nation's 50 largest manufacturers, and the fourth largest computer company (behind IBM, Unisys and Digital Equipment). The company has sales and service offices in 103 U.S. cities and 37 foreign countries. It also markets its products through distributorships in 65 other countries. Hewlett-Packard's sales organization includes about 30,000 individuals. In total, the company employs about 82,000 people and has 74,000 shareholders.

The company has had consistent growth over the past decade, with earnings increases nine of the past ten years. Earnings per share have increased 372 percent during the period.

STOCK GROWTH

Hewlett-Packard has had solid stock growth over the past ten years with three 2-for-1 stock splits since 1979. Over the past ten years the stock has increased 392 percent (177.5 percent per year) from its median of $9.75 in 1978 to its late 1988 price of $48 a share.

Including all reinvested dividends, a $10,000 investment in Hewlett-Packard stock at its median price in 1978 would be worth about $52,000 ten years later. Average annual compounded rate of return (including stock growth and reinvested dividends): about 18 percent.

DIVIDEND YIELD

The company has traditionally paid a very low dividend, averaging less than 1 percent per year. Over the past three years the stock has paid an average annual current return of 0.5 percent.

DIVIDEND GROWTH

Hewlett-Packard usually increases its dividends annually. Over the four-year rating period from 1983 to 1987, the company raised its dividends a total of 44 percent.

SHAREHOLDER PERKS (no points)

Hewlett-Packard does not provide a dividend reinvestment plan for its shareholders, nor does it offer any other perks.

SUMMARY

Total revenues: $8.1 billion, 1987. Earnings per share: $2.50, 1987; $0.53, 1977; 372% increase. Stock price: $48, 9/20/88; $9.75 (median), 1978 (392% total increase; 17% annual increase); price rose 8 of 10 years, 1977–87. Dividend: $0.23, 1987; $0.16, 1983; 4-year increase: 44%. Dividend yield: 0.5%, 1985–87. P/E ratio: 16, 1/5/89. Average annual total return to investor, 1978–88: about 18%.

HONORABLE MENTION

All revenue figures are from 1987 unless otherwise noted.

AMP, Inc. World's largest producer of electrical and electronic connection devices. Produces more than 100,000 types or sizes of terminals, splices, connectors, cable assemblies, switches and related products. Has had a 15 percent compounded rate of growth since the company went public in 1956. Revenues: $2.3 billion. Friendship Road, Harrisburg, PA 17105. (717) 564-0100.

Alberto Culver Co. Manufactures beauty products such as Alberto VO5 shampoos, hair sprays and conditioners. Revenues: $514 million.2525 Armitage Ave., Melrose Park, IL 60160. (312) 450-3000.

Alco Standard Corp. Involved in paper distribution and conversion, office products distribution and the manufacture of food service equipment and specialty food products. Also owns specialty manufacturing and service companies in the aerospace and steel converting industries. Revenues: $3.6 billion. P.O. Box 834, Valley Forge, PA 19482-0834. (215) 296-8000.

Ames Department Stores, Inc. Operates 350 department stores in 18 states. Concentrates on smaller population areas. Also owns G.C. Murphy Department Stores, operating about 150 stores in 15 states, and Mathews and Boucher, a wholesale sporting goods business. Revenues: $2.1 billion. 2418 Main St., Rocky Hill, CT 06067. (203) 563-8234.

American International Group, Inc. One of the world's leading insurance companies, providing property, casualty, marine, life and financial services insurance to clients in more than 130 countries and jurisdictions. Revenues: $11.3 billion. 70 Pine St., New York, NY 10270. (212) 770-5963.

American Stores Co. Operates 1,460 retail stores in 39 states, including Acme Markets, Jewel Food, Star Markets, Alpha Beta, Skaggs Alpha Beta and Osco Drug. Revenues: $14.3 billion. 444 E. First South, Salt Lake City, UT 84127-0447. (801) 539-0112.

Angelica Corp. Rents, sells and launders uniforms and other on-the-job apparel. Major market is health care services. Revenues: $307 million. 10176 Corporate Square Drive, St. Louis, MO 63132. (314) 991-4150.

Apogee Enterprises, Inc. The nation's leading installer of curtainwall and window systems. Owns Harmon Glass, Viracon and other glass fabrication subsidiaries. Has had a compounded annual growth rate of 26 percent over the past 38 years. Revenues: $312 million (fiscal 1988, ended 2/28/88). 7900 Xerxes Ave. S., Minneapolis, MN 55431. (612) 835-1874.

Apple Computer, Inc. Manufactures microprocessor-based personal computers, including the Apple II and Macintosh. Has had erratic stock price and earnings growth since going public in 1980. Revenues: $2.7 billion. 10260 Bandley Drive, Cupertino, CA 95014. (408) 996-1010.

Atlanta Gas Light Co. The largest natural gas distribution company in the southeastern U.S. Serves 215 Georgia communities. Excellent dividends.

Revenues: $983 million. 235 Peachtree St. N.E., P.O. Box 4569, Atlanta, GA 30302. (404) 770-4994.

Avery International Corp. Produces self-adhesive base materials primarily for industrial applications, self-adhesive labels, tags, indexing and tabbing guides and other product lines for industrial and consumer use. Has a strong international business. Revenues: $1.5 billion. 150 North Orange Grove Blvd., Pasadena, CA 91103. (818) 304-2000.

Bairnco Corp. Parent company of several manufacturing firms: Genlyte Group—lighting fixtures and controls; Keene Corp.—electronic products for aerospace, military, communications and other applications; Shielding Systems Corp.— anechoic chambers and electromagnetic shielding for security, defense and health care applications; and Kasco Corp.— knives and other cutting products. Revenues: $360 million. 200 Park Ave., New York, NY 10166. (212) 490-8722.

Bandag, Inc. World's leading manufacturer of tread rubber. Also manufactures equipment and supplies for retreading tires by a "cold" bonding reaction. Has more than 1,000 franchised dealers in 100 countries. Outstanding stock price and earnings growth over the past decade. Revenues: $423 million. Bandag Center, Muscatine, IA 52761-5886. (319) 262-1400.

George Banta Co. One of the larger printing companies in the U.S. Prints books, magazines, catalogs and multimedia kits. Also prints flexible packaging for consumer products and is involved in graphic and video production. Has 17 U.S. production facilities. Revenues: $302 million. 100 Main St., Menasha, WI 54952. (414) 722-7777.

Barnett Banks, Inc. Florida's leading banking organization. Also has operations in Georgia. Has a total of 502 banking offices, 33 banking affiliates and 11 non-banking affiliates. Assets: $23.5 billion. Net income: $198 million. 100 Laura St., Jacksonville, FL 32203-0789. (904) 791-7720.

Beckton, Dickinson and Co. Manufactures a broad line of medical products for health care professionals, medical research institutions, industry and the general public. Has extensive foreign sales. Revenues: $1.6 billion. One Becton Drive, Franklin Lakes, NJ 07417-1880. (201) 848-7178.

Bergen Brunswig Corp. Distributes pharmaceuticals and health care products, medical and surgical supplies, consumer electronics products and prerecorded videocassettes. Revenues: $3.4 billion. 4000 Metropolitan Drive, Orange, CA 92668. (714) 385-4000.

Bruno's, Inc. Operates 111 supermarkets and combination food and drug stores, most of which are in Alabama. Stores include Food World, Bruno's Food & Pharmacy, FoodMax and Consumer Warehouse. Revenues: $1.1 billion. 300 Research Pkwy., Birmingham, AL 35211. (205) 940-9400.

Burlington Northern, Inc. Operates one of the largest railroad systems in the U.S., with 25,639 miles of track through the western and northwestern U.S. Also involved in the production of oil, gas, coal and other minerals.

Revenues: $6.6 billion. 999 Third Ave., Seattle, WA 98104-4097. (206) 467-3838.

California Water Service Co. One of the largest investor-owned water companies in the U.S. As a public utility water company, it owns and operates 21 water systems serving 38 cities and communities in California with a population of 1.4 million. Revenue: $112 million. 1720 N. First St., San Jose, CA 95112. (408) 298-1414.

Campbell Soup Co. Leading U.S. producer of canned soups. Also makes LeMenu frozen dinners, Pepperidge Farm desserts and bakery goods, V8 juice, Prego pastas, Mrs. Paul's fish, Vlasic pickles, Franco-American Spaghettios, Swanson frozen dinners and pot pies and Godiva chocolates. Good shareholder perks. Revenues: $4.5 billion. Campbell Place, Camden, NJ 08103-1799. (609) 342-4800.

Capital Cities/ABC, Inc. Owns the American Broadcasting Company and a number of local television and radio stations and daily and weekly newspapers. Has had excellent earnings growth, with more than 15 consecutive years of record earnings. Revenues: $4.4 billion. 24 E. 51st St., New York, NY 10022. (212) 421-9595.

Charming Shoppes, Inc. Operates a chain of 840 women's specialty stores under the name Fashion Bug and Fashion Bug Plus in 33 states. Revenues: $638 million. 450 Winks Lane, Bensalem, PA 19020. (215) 245-9100.

Chrysler Corp. Third largest U.S. auto manufacturer. Makes Plymouth, Dodge and Chrysler cars. Excellent growth since 1982. Revenues: $26.3 billion. 12000 Chrysler Drive, Highland Park, MI 48203. (313) 956-5252.

Cincinnati Financial Corp. Sells a full range of insurance through several subsidiaries. Revenues: $883 million. 6200 S. Gilmore Road, Cincinnati, OH 45250-5496. (513) 870-2000.

Coca-Cola Co. World's leading soft drink producer. Makes Coca-Cola, Tab, Sprite, Fresca, Fanta, Minute Maid fruit juice and Hi-C. Revenues: $7.7 billion. 310 North Ave. N.W., Atlanta, GA 30301. (800) GET COKE (438-2653).

Consolidated Natural Gas Co. Produces, transmits and distributes natural gas in Ohio, Pennsylvania and the Northeast. Revenues: $2.3 billion. CNG Tower, Pittsburgh, PA 15222-3199. (412) 227-1000.

Cray Research, Inc. World's leading supercomputer manufacturer. Founded in 1972, it has been one of the fastest growing companies in America. Has had phenomenal earnings growth and a 43 percent average annual return for shareholders over the past ten years through 1988 (although its growth has moderated recently). Pays no dividend. Revenues: $687 million. 608 Second Ave. South, Minneapolis, MN 55402. (612) 333-5889.

Crestar Financial Corp. (formerly United Virginia Bankshares). Holding company for several banks, including Crestar Bank of Virginia. Assets: $9.7 billion. Crestar Center, 919 E. Main St., Richmond, VA 23261. (804) 782-5000.

Dayton Hudson Corp. Operates 577 stores in 36 states, including Dayton's, Hudson's and Mervyn's department stores, Target discount stores and Lechmere consumer electronics and appliance stores. Revenues: $10.7 billion. 777 Nicollet Mall, Minneapolis, MN 55402. (612) 370-6948.

Diebold, Inc. Manufactures a variety of "transaction delivery systems" such as automatic teller machines, interactive touch-screen terminals, payment and credit card authorization terminals, automated fuel terminals and videocassette dispensing machines. Revenues: $439 million. 818 Mulberry Road S.E., Canton, OH 44711. (216) 489-4000.

Digital Equipment Corp. World's leading manufacturer of networked computer systems and associated peripheral equipment. It is also the leader in systems integration with its networks, communications, services and software products. Excellent earnings growth; pays no dividend. Revenues: $9.4 billion. 111 Powdermill Road, Maynard, MA 01754. (617) 493-5350 (investor inquiries); (617) 351-4401 (annual report).

Dillard Department Stores, Inc. Operates 135 department stores in mid-U.S. Revenues: $2.2 billion. 900 W. Capitol Ave., P.O. Box 486, Little Rock, AK 72203. (501) 376-5200.

Dover Corp. Builds elevators, electronics products, parts and equipment for various manufacturing industries, including petroleum and aerospace. Revenues: $1.6 billion. 277 Park Ave., New York, NY 10172. (212) 826-7160.

Dow Chemical Co. Manufactures industrial chemicals, agricultural chemicals, plastics and consumer products including Fantastik cleaner, Handi-Wrap, Saran Wrap, Spray 'n' Wash, Yes laundry detergent, Vivid bleach, Ziploc bags and Glass Plus cleaner. Revenues: $13.4 billion. 2030 Williard H. Dow Center, Midland, MI 48674. (517) 636-3216.

A.G. Edwards, Inc. Nation's sixth-largest stock brokerage firm (and largest outside of New York). Has 350 offices in 46 states. Provides a full range of financial services and products for individual and institutional investors. Revenues: $504 million (fiscal 1988, ended 2/28/88). One N. Jefferson Ave., St. Louis, MO 63103. (314) 289-3000.

EG&G Inc. Manufactures scientific and technical products for commercial and government clients. Specializes in sensitive measuring instruments. Makes components for military and industrial markets and conducts automotive testing, biomedical research and site-management programs in the military, energy and aerospace industries. Revenues: $1.2 billion. 45 William St., Wellesley, MA 02181. (617) 237-5100.

Emerson Electric Co. Involved in engineering and development of consumer, industrial and military parts and equipment. Involved in factory automation and antisubmarine warfare production. Thirty consecutive years of record earnings per share. Revenues: $6.2 billion. 8000 W. Florissant, P.O. Box 4100, St. Louis, MO 63136. (314) 553-2000.

Family Dollar Stores. Operates 1,500 discount department stores in East, South and Midwest. Revenues: $560 million. 10401 Old Monroe Road, P.O. Box 25800, Charlotte, NC 28212. (704) 847-6961.

Flowers Industries, Inc. Makes fresh and frozen breads, buns, specialty rolls, sweet and salted snacks, frozen specialty vegetables, fruits, cakes and pies. Revenues: $797 million. U.S. Highway 19, Thomasville, GA 31799. (912) 226-9110.

GTE Corp. Comprises one of the largest telephone systems in the U.S., with 13 million lines in more than 30 states. Also manufactures communications and electrical products. Pays excellent dividends. Revenues: $15.5 billion. 1 Stamford Forum, Stamford, CT 06904. (203) 965-3797.

The Gap, Inc. Operates a chain of 815 apparel stores, including 681 Gap stores, 92 Banana Republics, 39 GapKids, and 3 Hemisphere stores. Revenues: $1.1 billion. 900 Cherry Ave., P.O. Box 60, San Bruno, CA 94066. (415) 952-4400.

Geico Corp. Sells insurance as Government Employees Insurance Co. Specializes in multiple-line property and casualty insurance for government employees and others. Premiums: $1.4 billion. Geico Plaza, Washington, D.C. 20076. (201) 986-3000.

General Cinema Corp. Operates movie theatres in about 300 suburban shopping malls in 33 states. Also owns a 59 percent share of Nieman Marcus department stores. Recently sold its pop bottling operation to PepsiCo (in early 1989). This operation had accounted for about 85 percent of General Cinema's operating earnings. Has had a 27 percent average annual return to investors over the past ten years. Revenues: $1 billion. 27 Boylston St., Chestnut Hill, MA 02167. (617) 232-8200.

General Dynamics Corp. Manufactures military aircraft (F-16), submarines, tanks, missiles (Redeye, Sparrow, Stinger, Tomahawk), guns and other weapons. Also manufactures space systems and electronic products. Revenues: $9.3 billion. Pierre Laclede Center, St. Louis, MO 63105. (314) 889-8200.

General Electric Co. One of the world's largest and most diversified industrial corporations. Manufactures products for the generation, transmission, distribution, control and utilization of electricity. Makes lamps, appliances, motors, electrical construction equipment, locomotives, power generators, nuclear power fuel assemblies, commercial and military jet engines, engineered plastics, and products for aerospace, military and medical diagnostic applications. Owns RCA Corp., parent company of the National Broadcasting Co. (NBC-TV). Revenues: $40.5 billion. 3135 Easton Turnpike, Fairfield, CT 06431. (203) 373-2431.

General Mills, Inc. Produces a variety of food products, including Cheerios, Trix and Total cereals; Betty Crocker foods; Bisquick; Yoplait; Pop Secret. Also owns Red Lobster Restaurants, Eddie Bauer sportswear stores and Talbot's women's apparel stores. Revenues: $5.2 billion. 9200 Wayzata Blvd., Minneapolis, MN 55440. (612) 540-2311.

General Re Corp. Parent company of General Reinsurance Co., the nation's largest property-casualty reinsurer. Revenues: $3.4 billion. 695 E. Main St., Stamford, Ct. 06904-2351. (203) 328-5000.

Gerber Scientific, Inc. Manufactures factory automation systems for a variety of industries. Also makes computer-aided design and computer-aided manufacturing (CAD/CAM) products in computer-controlled drafting and photoplotting, interactive design and other applications. Revenues: $269 million. 83 Gerber Road West, South Windsor, CT 06074. (203) 644-1551.

Gillette Co. Leading manufacturer of razors in North America. Also manufactures toiletries (Right Guard) and cosmetics, writing instruments and office products. Good shareholder perks. Revenues: $3.2 billion. Prudential Tower Building, Boston, MA 02199. (617) 421-7000.

P. H. Glatfelter Co. Manufactures printing, writing and specialty papers. Excellent earnings growth past five years. Revenues. $423 million. 228 South Main St., Spring Grove, PA 17362. (717) 225-4711.

Great Northern Nekoosa Corp. Manufactures paper products, including newsprint, business papers and containerboard. Revenues: $2.6 billion. 75 Prospect St., Stamford, CT 06904. (203) 359-4000.

Guilford Mills, Inc. Makes fabrics for apparel and industrial and home furnishing products. Designs, dyes, prints and finishes knit, woven and elastomeric fabrics for sale to swimwear and sportswear manufacturers. Shareholder return on investment has averaged 30 percent the past ten years (through 1988). Revenues: $578 million. 4925 West Market St., Greensboro, NC 27407. (919) 292-7550.

Hasbro, Inc. Largest toy manufacturer in U.S. Manufactures about 300 toys and 200 games. Has had phenomenal but erratic earnings and stock price growth over the past ten years. Revenues: $1.3 billion. 1027 Newport Ave., Pawtucket, RI 02862. (401) 727-5000.

IC Industries, Inc. Produces specialty foods, manufactures aerospace and refrigeration equipment and operates 2,144 Midas car repair shops worldwide. Excellent earnings growth and stock price appreciation recently. One Illinois Center, 111 E. Wacker Drive, Chicago IL 60601. (312) 565-3000.

Jacobson Stores, Inc. Operates a chain of department stores primarily in Michigan and Florida. Revenues: $327 million. 1200 N. West Ave., Jackson, MI 49202. (517) 787-3600.

Johnson & Johnson. Manufactures health-related consumer and pharmaceutical products (Band Aids, Tylenol, Playtex, Stayfree, Sure & Natural and Carefree panty shields, baby products). Revenues: $8 billion. One Johnson & Johnson Plaza, New Brunswick, NJ 08933. (201) 524-0400.

Kinder-Care, Inc. Leading operator of day care centers in U.S. Operates about 1,100 centers. Also owns Sylvan Learning Centers and has a financial services division and a specialty retail division. Revenues: $507 million. 2400 Presidents Drive, Montgomery, AL 36116. (205) 277-5090.

John Labatt Ltd. Large Canadian beer brewer and food processing company. Revenue: $5.1 billion (fiscal 1988, ended 4/30/88). 451 Ridout St. North, London, Ontario, Canada N6A 5L3. (519) 673-5050.

Laidlaw Transportation Ltd. A major waste management and trucking operation based in Canada. Has had excellent earnings and stock price growth over the past ten years. Operates throughout the U.S. and Canada. Revenues: $1.2 billion. 3221 North Service Road, Burlington, Ontario, Canada L7N 3G2. (416) 336-1800.

Lomas & Nettleton Mortgage Investors. Underwrites mortgages for apartments, office buildings, shopping centers, single-family residences and condominiums in 34 states. Interest on mortgage loans: $78 million. 2001 Bryan Tower, P.O. Box 655644, Dallas, TX 75265-5644. (214) 746-7111.

Loral Corp. Aerospace and defense contractor (airborne and shipborne self-protection, antisubmarine warfare, guidance and smart munitions, reconnaissance, surveillance, simulation and training). Sixteen consecutive years of earnings growth. Revenues: $1.4 billion. 600 Third Ave., New York, NY 10016. 697-1105.

Manor Care, Inc. Provides long-term health care services, operating nursing centers nationwide. It also operates an acute care hospital, assisted living units and pharmacy retail outlets. Owns Quality Inns, which owns leases and operates hotels and resorts in 48 states and several foreign countries. Revenues: $502 million. 10750 Columbia Pike, Silver Spring, MD 20901. (301) 681-9400.

Marsh & McLennan Companies, Inc. The world's leading insurance and reinsurance broker. Also involved in employee benefits and compensation consulting and insurance program administration. It manages a family of mutual funds and provides investment management services. Revenues: $2.1 billion. 1221 Avenue of the Americas, New York, NY 10020. (212) 997-2000.

Medtronic, Inc. World's leading manufacturer of cardiac pacemakers. Also manufactures such cardiovascular products as heart valves, therapeutic catheters and synthetic arterial grafts. Revenues: $502 million. 7000 Central Ave. NE, Minneapolis, MN 55432. (612) 574-4000.

Herman Miller, Inc. Manufactures office furniture and related products. Has worldwide distribution. Revenues: $714 million. 8500 Byron Road, Zeeland, MI 49464. (616) 772-3300.

Minnesota Mining and Manufacturing (3M). Manufactures a variety of consumer products, including Scotch tapes and video cartridges, Thinsulate insulating material, Scotchgard fabric protector, Post-it note pads, cables, connectors, reflective markers, sponges, scouring pads and thousands of other products. Has an outstanding shareholder perks program. Revenues: $9.4 billion. 3M Center, St. Paul, MN 55144-1000. (612) 733-1110.

Mobil Corp. Large international oil and petrochemical company. Excellent dividends. Revenues: $51 billion. 150 E. 42nd St., New York, NY 10017. (212) 883-4242.

Molex, Inc. Manufacturer of electronic interconnection systems, planar cable, control panels and application tooling. Produces more than 25,000 products at 37 manufacturing plants on six continents. Revenues: $387 million. 2222 Wellington Court, Lisle, IL 60532. (312) 969-4550.

Mortgage and Realty Trust. As a real estate investment trust, it has interests in a number of residential and commercial developments. Pays outstanding dividends—10 percent average the past few years. Revenues: $42 million. 8360 Old York Road, Elkins Park, PA 19117. (215) 881-1525.

NCR Corp. (formerly National Cash Register). Manufactures business information processing systems (computers) for a worldwide market. Revenues: $5.6 billion. 1700 South Patterson Blvd., Dayton, OH 45479. (513) 445-5000.

Newell Company. Manufactures housewares and hardware. Recently acquired Anchor Hocking. Revenues: $720 million. 29 E. Stephenson St., Freeport, IL 61032. (815) 235-4171.

Norfolk Southern Corp. Through its two railroad companies, Norfolk and Western Railway Co. and Southern Railway Co. operates more than 17,000 miles of railway in 20 states and Ontario. Also owns North American Van Lines. Revenues: $4.1 billion. One Commercial Place, Norfolk, VA 23510-2191. (804) 629-2680.

Ohio Mattress Co. The world's largest bedding manufacturer. Makes Sealy mattresses and box springs, Stearns & Foster beds and Advanced, Monterey, Wavecrest and Woodstuff water beds. Revenues: $598 million. 1501 Bond Court Building, 1300 E. 9th St., Cleveland, OH 44114. (216) 522-1310.

Olsten Corp. One of North America's leading temporary service companies, with two subsidiaries: Olsten Services and Olsten Health Care Services. Employs 275,000 temporary workers through 428 owned, franchised and licensed offices throughout all 50 states and Canada. Revenues: $566 million. One Merrick Ave., Westbury, NY 11590. (516) 832-8200.

The Pep Boys—Manny, Moe & Jack. Sells automotive parts and accessories and provides automotive maintenance and service through its chain of 207 Pep Boys stores in 12 states in the Mid-Atlantic, Southeast and Southwest. Twelve consecutive years of earnings growth. Revenues: $554 million. 3111 W. Allegheny Ave., Philadelphia, PA 19132. (215) 229-9000.

Premier Industrial Corp. Manufactures industrial maintenance products such as coatings, auto parts, lubricants and cleaning chemicals. Also makes fire-fighting equipment and distributes 100,000 electrical and electronic components to the maintenance and repair markets. Has had outstanding stock price and earnings growth over the past decade. Revenues: $525 million (fiscal 1988, ended 5/31/88). 4500 Euclid Ave., Cleveland, OH 44103. (216) 391-8300.

Progressive Corp. As an insurance holding company, owns 35 subsidiaries and two mutual insurance company affiliates. Specializes in property-casualty and automotive insurance. Revenues: $1 billion. 600 Parkland Blvd., Mayfield Heights, OH 44124. (216) 464-8000.

Property Capital Trust. As an unincorporated trust, invests in a variety of income-producing properties (office buildings, apartments, shopping centers, hotels) throughout the U.S. Pays high dividends. Revenues: $25 million. 200 Clarendon St., Hancock Tower, Boston, MA 02116. (617) 536-8600.

Provigo, Inc. Distributes food, drugs and other consumer goods to more than 2,000 stores throughout North America. Outstanding earnings and stock price growth in recent years. Revenues: $7.4 billion. 800 Rene-Levesque Blvd. West, Montreal, Quebec, Canada H3B 1Y2. (514) 878-8300.

Raytheon Company. Builds missiles and other aerospace and defense systems, and Amana, Speed Queen and Caloric appliances. Revenues: $7.7 billion. 141 Spring St., Lexington, MA 02173. (617) 862-6600.

Rohm and Haas. Manufactures chemicals used in house paints, household products, shampoos, plastics, siding, computer chips, herbicides and other applications. Revenues: $2.2 billion. Independence Mall West, Philadelphia, PA 19105. (215) 592-3000.

Ryland Group, Inc. Constructs and sells single-family "attached and detached" homes. Revenues: $847 million. 10221 Wincopin Circle, P.O. Box 4000, Columbia, MD 21044. (301) 730-7222.

Seagram Company, Ltd. World's largest producer of wines and spirits. Has affiliates in 27 countries. Revenues: $3.8 billion. 1430 Peel St., Montreal, Quebec, Canada H3A 1S9. (514) 849-5271.

Shared Medical Systems. Provides computer-based software systems to hospitals, clinics and physicians' groups. Revenues: $391 million. 51 Valley Stream Pkwy., Malvern, PA 19355. (215) 296-6300.

Shoney's Inc. Operates and franchises a chain of 1,500 restaurants and 41 Shoney's Inns in 30 states. Revenues: $694 million. 1727 Elm Hill Pike, P.O. Box 1260, Nashville, TN 37202. (615) 391-5201.

Smithfield Foods, Inc. The largest pork packer in the eastern U.S. Outstanding earnings and stock price growth over the past ten years. No dividend. Revenues: $916 million (fiscal 1988, ended 5/1/88). 501 N. Church St., Smithfield, VA 23430. (804) 357-4321.

SmithKline Beckman. Produces prescription and proprietary products for human and animal health care. Also manufactures diagnostic and analytical medical equipment. Revenues: $4.3 billion. One Franklin Plaza, P.O. Box 7929, Philadelphia, PA 19101. (215) 751-4000.

Snap-on Tools Corp. World's largest independent manufacturer and distributor of hand tools and equipment for the professional mechanic. Revenues: $754 million. 2801 80th St., Kenosha, WI 53141-1410. (414) 656-5200.

Standard Register Co. Makes a broad line of business forms and labels, as well as data systems and forms handling equipment. Has sales offices in

50 states and a strong international presence. Revenues: $666 million. 626 Albany St., Dayton, OH 45401. (513) 443-1506.

Stone Container Corp. Manufactures containerboard, unbleached kraft paper, newsprint, market pulp, corrugated containers, bags and sacks. Revenues: $3.2 billion. 150 N. Michigan Ave., Chicago, IL 60601-7568. (312) 346-6600.

Sysco Corp. The largest marketer and distributor of food service products in America. Caters to 150,000 restaurants, schools, hotels, hospitals and other institutions. Has grown from revenues of $200 million in 1969 to $3.7 billion in 1987. 1390 Enclave Pkwy., Houston, TX 77077. (713) 877-1122.

Teledyne, Inc. Builds unmanned airplanes for the military and aircraft engines, airframe structures and aviation electronic systems. Revenues: $3.2 billion. 1901 Avenue of the Stars, Los Angeles, CA 90067. (213) 277-3311.

Teleflex, Inc. Provides products and services for the aerospace, defense, medical and turbine engine repair markets. Revenues: $271 million. 155 S. Limerick Rd., Limerick, PA 19468. (215) 948-5100.

Times-Mirror Publishes the *Los Angeles Times, Newsday,* the *Denver Post,* the *Baltimore Sun,* the *Hartford Courant* and other papers. Also publishes books, magazines, maps, flight information directories and telephone directories. Owns television stations and cable systems. Revenues: $3.2 billion. Times-Mirror Square, Los Angeles, CA 90053. (213) 237-3700.

TransTechnology Corp. Manufactures aerospace and defense products, including helicopter rescue hoists and external hook systems, winches and hoists for aircraft and weapon systems. Also manufactures computer-aided design (CAD) and drafting display work stations, bank automation equipment and other industrial products. Revenues: $212 million. 15303 Ventura Blvd., Sherman Oaks, CA 91403. (818) 990-5920.

Tyco Laboratories, Inc. Manufacturer of fire protection and flow control systems, packaging materials and electronic components. Revenues: $1.1 billion. One Tyco Park, Exeter, NH 03833. (603) 778-9700.

Upjohn Co. Manufactures pharmaceuticals, health service products, seeds, agricultural specialties and chemicals. Founded in 1886. Revenues: $2.5 billion. 7000 Portage Rd., Kalamazoo, MI 49001. (616) 323-4000.

Wallace Computer Services, Inc. Offers a full line of computer-related products and services, including computer forms, commercial printing, computer labels, printer ribbons, computer hardware and software, computer accessories and other office products. Has posted 26 consecutive years of earnings and sales growth. Revenues: $340 million. 4600 W. Roosevelt Road, Hillside, IL 60162. (312) 626-2000.

Washington Post Co. Publishes the *Washington Post* daily newspaper (circulation: 770,000) and *Newsweek* magazine. Also owns several television stations and cable TV systems. Revenues: $1.3 billion. 1150 15th St., N.W., Washington, D.C. 20071. (202) 334-6000.

George Weston, Ltd. Large Canadian food processor and distributor. Revenues: $11 billion. 22 St. Clair Ave. East, Toronto, Ontario, Canada M4T 2S7. (416) 922-4395.

Worthington Industries, Inc. Steel processing company that also produces pressure cylinders, pipe fittings, cast steel, custom products and suspension ceilings. Revenues: $819 million. 1205 Dearborn Drive, Columbus, OH 43085. (614) 438-3203.

THE BEST 100 BY STATE

Alabama

Torchmark (Birmingham)

Arkansas

Tyson Foods (Springdale)
Wal-Mart Stores (Bentonville)

California

Walt Disney (Burbank)
Hewlett-Packard (Palo Alto)
Lockheed (Calabasas)
National Medical Enterprises (Los
  Angeles)
Rockwell International (El Segundo)

Connecticut

American Brands (Old Greenwich)
Kaman (Bloomfield)
Pitney Bowes (Stamford)
UST (Greenwich)

District of Columbia (Washington)

Marriott

Georgia

Genuine Parts (Atlanta)
Fuqua Industries (Atlanta)
John H. Harland (Decatur)
National Service Industries (Atlanta)
Shaw Industries (Dalton)

Hawaii

Alexander & Baldwin (Honolulu)

Idaho

Albertson's (Boise)

Illinois

Abbott Laboratories (Abbott Park)
Brunswick (Skokie)
Comdisco (Rosemont)
Dean Foods (Franklin Park)
R.R. Donnelley & Sons (Chicago)
McDonald's (Oak Brook)
Quaker Oats (Chicago)
Safety-Kleen (Elgin)
Sara Lee (Chicago)
Walgreen (Deerfield)
Waste Management (Oak Brook)
Wm. Wrigley Jr. (Chicago)

Indiana

Eli Lilly (Indianapolis)
Ball (Muncie)

Kentucky

Brown-Forman (Louisville)

Maryland

Giant Food (Landover)
Martin Marietta (Bethesda)
MNC Financial (Baltimore)
Noxell (Hunt Valley)

Massachusetts

Stanhome (Westfield)

Michigan

Kelly Services (Troy)
Kellogg (Battle Creek)
Ford Motor (Dearborn)
Masco (Taylor)

Minnesota

Bemis (Minneapolis)
Deluxe (St. Paul)
Jostens (Minneapolis)
Super Valu Stores (Eden Prairie)
Valspar (Minneapolis)

Missouri

Anheuser-Busch (St. Louis)
Marion Labs (Kansas City)
Ralston Purina (St. Louis)

Nebraska

ConAgra (Omaha)

New Jersey

Automatic Data Processing (Roseland)
C.R. Bard (Murray Hill)
Merck (Rahway)
Prime Motor Inns (Fairfield)

New York

American Home Products (New York)
Borden (New York)
Bristol-Myers (New York)
Carter-Wallace (New York)
Consolidated Edison (New York)
Dow Jones (New York)
Dreyfus (New York)
Dun & Bradstreet (New York)
Exxon (New York)
Gulf+Western (New York)
Loews (New York)
McGraw-Hill (New York)
Melville (Harrison)
New York Times (New York)
Pall (East Hills)
PepsiCo (Purchase)
Philip Morris (New York)

North Carolina

Food Lion (Salisbury)

Ohio

Banc One (Columbus)
Fifth Third Bancorp (Cincinnati)
The Limited (Columbus)
Philips Industries (Dayton)
RPM (Medina)
Rubbermaid (Wooster)
A. Schulman (Akron)
Sherwin-Williams (Cleveland)
Standard Products (Cleveland)

Oregon

Precision Castparts (Portland)

Pennsylvania

CoreStates Financial (Philadelphia)
Heinz (Pittsburgh)
Hershey (Hershey)
PNC Financial (Pittsburgh)
PPG Industries (Pittsburgh)
Rite Aid (Harrisburg)
Scott Paper (Philadelphia)
VF (Wyomissing)
Westinghouse (Pittsburgh)

South Carolina

Sonoco Products (Hartsville)

Texas

Browning-Ferris Industries (Houston)
Kimberly-Clark (Dallas)

Virginia

Gannett (Arlington)
James River (Richmond)

Washington

Nordstrom (Seattle)

THE BEST 100 BY INDUSTRY GROUP

Aerospace and Defense

Precision Castparts (41)
Rockwell International (60)
Kaman (62)
Lockheed (63)
Martin Marietta (96)

Alcoholic Beverages

Anheuser-Busch (1)
Brown-Forman (37)

Apparel

The Limited (12)
VF (13)
Melville (90)

Automotive

Standard Products (2)
Ford Motor (32)
Genuine Parts (93)

Chemicals, Coatings and Plastics

Sherwin-Williams (20)
A. Schulman (44)
PPG Industries (55)
Valspar (65)
RPM (80)

Computers and Office Equipment

Pitney Bowes (53)
Comdisco (66)
Hewlett-Packard (100)

Corporate Services

Kelly Services (46)
Dun & Bradstreet (70)
Automatic Data Processing (92)

Electronics

National Services Industries (56)
Westinghouse Electric (95)

Entertainment and Accommodations

Marriott (19)
Prime Motor Inns (43)
Walt Disney (75)

Financial and Insurance

Fifth Third Bancorp (17)
Torchmark (23)
MNC Financial (59)
Dreyfus (64)
CoreStates Financial (69)
Banc One (71)
PNC Financial (85)

Food and Beverage Production

Wm. Wrigley Jr. (8)
H.J. Heinz (9)
ConAgra (14)
Quaker Oats (18)
Dean Foods (51)
Kellogg (22)
Sara Lee (28)
Hershey Foods (30)
Ralston Purina (31)
Tyson Foods (40)
Borden (54)
PepsiCo (97)

Food and Drug Retail

Giant Food (5)
Walgreen (26)
Rite Aid (35)
Food Lion (42)

Food and Drug Retail *(continued)*

Albertson's (52)
McDonald's (81)
Super Valu Stores (86)

Health Care and Medical

Abbott Laboratories (4)
Marion Laboratories (6)
C.R. Bard (21)
Noxell (34)
Bristol-Myers (38)
Carter-Wallace (50)
National Medical Enterprises (61)
Merck (74)
American Home Products (88)
Eli Lilly (98)

Household and Commercial Furnishings

Shaw Industries (27)
Stanhome (29)
Philips Industries (45)
Rubbermaid (72)
Masco (99)

Industrial Equipment

Pall (36)

Jewelry

Jostens (91)

Leisure, Sports and Recreation

Brunswick (7)
Fuqua Industries (89)

Metal products

Ball (77)

Paper Products and Packaging

Sonoco Products (49)
Bemis (67)
Kimberly-Clark (73)
Scott Paper (78)
James River (83)

Petroleum

Exxon (94)

Printers

Deluxe (33)
John H. Harland (48)
R. R. Donnelley & Sons (79)

Publishers

New York Times (57)
McGraw-Hill (58)
Gulf+Western (68)
Dow Jones (76)
Gannett (87)

Retail Department Stores

Wal-Mart Stores (39)
Nordstrom (47)

Tobacco

Philip Morris (3)
UST (10)
Loews (15)
American Brands (82)

Transportation and Shipping

Alexander & Baldwin (24)

Utilities

Consolidated Edison (84)

Waste Handling

Waste Management (11)
Browning-Ferris Industries (16)
Safety-Kleen (25)

INDEX